THE DISPUTED TEACH

The Disputed Teachings of Vatican II

Continuity and Reversal in Catholic Doctrine

Thomas G. Guarino

WILLIAM B. EERDMANS PUBLISHING COMPANY
GRAND RAPIDS, MICHIGAN

Wm. B. Eerdmans Publishing Co. Grand
Rapids, Michigan
www.eerdmans.com

ISBN 978-0-8028-7438-2

Library of Congress Cataloging-in-Publication Data

Names: Guarino, Thomas G., author.
Title: The disputed teachings of Vatican II : continuity and reversal in Catholic doctrine /
    Thomas G. Guarino.
Description: Grand Rapids : Eerdmans Publishing Co., 2018. |
    Includes bibliographical references and index.
Identifiers: LCCN 2018035456 | ISBN 9780802874382 (pbk. : alk. paper)
Subjects: LCSH: Vatican Council (2nd : 1962-1965 : Basilica di San Pietro in Vaticano) |
    Catholic Church—Doctrines.—History—20th century.
Classification: LCC BX830 1962 .G77 2018 | DDC 262/.52—dc23
    LC record available at https://lccn.loc.gov/2018035456

Contents

Acknowledgments

I would like to express my gratitude, even if briefly and incompletely, to the many people who have aided the research for this book. These include the Rev. Dr. Joseph Reilly, dean of the school of theology of Seton Hall University, for his kind support of this work; Dr. John Buschman, dean of Seton Hall University libraries, for generously providing a suitable space for research and writing; the Rev. Dr. Lawrence Porter, director of Turro library, for his assistance in obtaining the necessary research materials; the faculty and staff of Seton Hall libraries, especially Anthony Lee, Stella Wilkins, Andrew Brenycz, Tiffany Burns, Mabel Wong, Stephania Bennett, Priscilla Tejada, and Damien Kelly, for their competent and friendly assistance; the Dominican friars of St. Vincent Ferrer Priory in New York City for their generous hospitality; and finally, Theresa Miller and Cathy Xavier for their kind help with many book-related tasks.

I am indebted to all of them for their benevolence.

Abbreviations

AG	*Ad gentes*: On the Mission Activity of the Church
AS	*Acta synodalia sacrosancti concilii oecumenici Vaticani II*
Carnets-AMC	André-Marie Charue. *Carnets conciliaires de l'évêque de Namur A.-M. Charue.* Edited by L. Declerck and Cl. Soetens. Louvain-la-Neuve: Faculté de Théologie, 2000.
Carnets-GP	Gérard Philips. *Carnets conciliaires de Mgr Gérard Philips, secrétaire adjoint de la commission doctrinale: Texte néerlandais avec traduction française et commentaires.* Edited by K. Schelkens. Leuven: Peeters, 2006.
Comm.	Vincent of Lérins. *Commonitorium.* Corpus Christianorum: Series Latina 64, edited by Roland Demeulenaere. Turnhout: Brepols, 1985.
DH	*Dignitatis humanae*: Declaration on Religious Freedom. Also referred to as *De libertate religiosa*.
DV	*Dei verbum*: Dogmatic Constitution on Divine Revelation. Also referred to as *De revelatione*.
LG	*Lumen gentium*: Dogmatic Constitution on the Church. Also referred to as *De ecclesia*.
NA	*Nostra aetate*: Declaration on the Relation of the Church with Non-Christian Religions. Also referred to as *De Judaeis*.
SCU	Secretariat for Promoting Christian Unity
UR	*Unitatis redintegratio*: Decree on Ecumenism. Also referred to as *De oecumenismo*.

Introduction

The Second Vatican Council was the cataclysmic Christian event of the twentieth century, changing the face of Catholicism and launching it into a new relationship with other Christians, with adherents of other religions, and with the modern world. Numerous questions about the council and its implications are still being disputed today: Was the council a legitimate development of the prior Christian tradition? Or was it, in fact, a naked reversal of significant dimensions of Catholic teaching? Didn't the council's liberalizing tendencies lead to a decline in religious practice? And aren't the rancid fruits of Vatican II traceable to its shameless kowtowing to the world, to its failure to insist on biblical truth?

These questions have been on the minds of many people, including faithful Catholics.[1] To answer them, this book will examine some of the

---

1. Benedict XVI, describing the tumultuous aftermath of Vatican II, invoked the fourth-century theologian Basil, who compared the church's agitated state after the Council of Nicaea to a raucous naval battle on a stormy night: "No one can deny that in vast areas of the Church the implementation of the Council has been somewhat difficult, even without wishing to apply to what occurred in these years the description that St. Basil . . . made of the Church's situation after the Council of Nicaea: he compares her situation to a naval battle in the darkness of the storm, saying among other things: 'The raucous shouting of those who through disagreement rise up against one another, the incomprehensible chatter, the confused din of uninterrupted clamoring, has now filled almost the whole of the Church, falsifying through excess or failure the right doctrine of the faith . . .' (*De Spiritu Sancto*, XXX, 77; PG 32, 213 A . . .)." "Address of His Holiness Benedict XVI to the Roman Curia Offering Them His Christmas Greetings," December 22, 2005, http://w2.vatican.va/content/benedict-xvi/en/speeches/2005/december/documents/hf_ben_xvi_spe_20051222_roman-curia.html.

most controversial teachings of Vatican II, making judgments as to their continuity or discontinuity with the prior Catholic tradition. The fundamental question at stake is this: Was the council an authentic development and extension of the prior doctrinal tradition, or was it in fact—at least in certain instances—an unabashed corruption of it?

I will proceed in three main steps. I will outline the crucial issue at stake in understanding Vatican II, namely, the material continuity or discontinuity of the council's teaching with the prior tradition (chapter 1). I will then examine the central theological principles necessary for interpreting the council properly (chapters 2 and 3). Finally, I will analyze and make judgments about the disputed issues themselves (chapters 4 and 5). Thus, this book will be primarily a theological rather than a historical account of Vatican II, even though the documents (and their successive drafts) will always undergird the theological judgments.

At several points in this book I will invoke the work of an early Christian writer, Vincent of Lérins. Vincent is in a unique position to help us with the continuity/corruption question because he himself thought deeply about this issue in the early days of the church. Writing in the fifth century, Vincent was embroiled in controversies about the proper understanding of Christ's person (as both human and divine), about Mary's role in salvation history (as the mother of God), and about grace and human freedom (and how they are related). Vincent was well aware that, over time, change inexorably occurred in Christ's church. Indeed, the Lerinian had an acute sense of history and its effects, rare for his epoch. He acknowledged that terms such as "consubstantial" (*homoousios*) and "God-bearer" (*Theotokos*)—terms that had been consecrated by early ecumenical councils—were not to be found in the New Testament. And yet he thought these words were legitimate representations of biblical teaching, fully congruous with scriptural witness. Vincent used a host of terms to show that development and growth—properly understood— were appropriate for the Christian church. But he also recognized that some changes could be injurious to the church's faith, betraying both Scripture and the solemn teachings of the first councils.

Indeed, a significant part of Vincent's work seeks to respond to those who believed that the Creed of Nicaea could be rewritten with rather less emphasis on the one divine nature (consubstantiality) shared by the Father and Jesus Christ, his Son. To combat the kind of change that distorted and corrupted Christian truth, the theologian of Lérins insightfully distinguished between two kinds of change, *profectus* and *permutatio*. The former, meaning "advance," refers to the harmonious progress that protects earlier teachings even while organically and homogeneously extending and expanding them. The latter refers to reversals that seek to overthrow and corrupt earlier church teachings by betraying or contradicting their fundamental meaning. For Vincent, a *profectus* is entirely legitimate and warranted. A *permutatio* leads inevitably to heresy and must at all costs be avoided.

We shall discuss Vincent's work, and in particular how this early Christian writer can help us understand the changes that took place at Vatican II, a bit more fully in chapter 1.[2] But even at this point, mentioning Vincent's thought alerts us to the fact that the issue of continuity/rupture is not a contemporary problem arising from the historical-critical study of Christian doctrine. Already in the early fifth century, theologians were examining how change, both proper and improper, occurs in the life of the church.

Vatican II initiated within Catholicism—and to some extent within Christianity at large—a period of intense reflection and examination that continues over fifty years later. Pope John XXIII, who convoked the council, clearly wanted the Catholic Church to face the challenges posed by both the Reformation and the Enlightenment: the relationship of Catholicism to other Christian churches, to other religions (particularly Judaism), to the modern liberal state, and to a world that often repudiated Christian beliefs. Did the responses that Vatican II gave to these issues constitute a collective *profectus fidei*? Or did the council endorse serious deviations from the prior tradition—Vincent's dreaded *permutatio fidei*? Given that Vatican II exhibited clear elements of discontinuity—as Benedict XVI himself candidly admitted—are such reversals necessarily *permutationes fidei*? Do they indicate that the Christian faith is as subject to the tides of contingency and provisionality as any other reality? Or are reversals, too, in some sense, consonant with the notion of continuity over time—and this without engaging in theological legerdemain? Can reversals be theologically assimilated without calling into question the continuity and perpetuity of divine revelation?

The genesis of this book is to be found in the various seminars I have taught on Vatican II over the past several years. In preparation for these courses, I have read scores of books on the council but found few entirely satisfying. One problem I consistently noticed was that theological principles and distinctions were often quickly and unsystematically invoked. At times

---

2. For an extended explanation of Vincent's key concepts, see Thomas G. Guarino, *Vincent of Lérins and the Development of Christian Doctrine* (Grand Rapids: Baker Academic, 2013).

they were subsumed into larger narratives, often with political overtones. But this led to the principles themselves being obscured.

For this reason I decided to offer in this book a close reading of the council, with the intention of shedding light on the crucial continuity/ discontinuity question. Obviously, the council taught much that is uncontroversial and in clear continuity with the prior Christian tradition. These statements will not occupy us in detail. But certain teachings—on religious freedom, for example—have aroused a good deal of controversy, with some seeing in these positions critical and inexplicable ruptures with the past. It is precisely these issues that will command our attention.

Outline of the Book

The book will proceed as follows. In chapter 1, I will examine the foremost problem connected with debates about Vatican II: the council's congruency, or lack of it, with the antecedent Christian tradition. Here I will sketch the strong Catholic accent on the material continuity of doctrinal teaching over time, with words such as *identity*, *perpetuity*, and *irreversibility* characterizing the theological tradition. Does Vatican II still allow these words to be used?

In chapter 2, I will discuss several foundational principles essential for understanding how the council handled continuity and rupture. This is a crucial chapter because one cannot simply approach Vatican II's texts cold. Although the conciliar documents are written in a highly accessible style, behind this style lies a world of theological learning and sophistication. Properly understanding the documents requires familiarity with distinct principles.

In the third chapter, I offer a more concentrated discussion of the all-important "change" words of Vatican II: *development*, *ressourcement*, and *aggiornamento*. These words are endlessly cited in relation to the council, but what, precisely, do they mean? Can we identify proper and improper understandings of these terms?

Finally, in chapters 4 and 5, I examine the disputed issues themselves, with an emphasis, once again, on how the council was congruent or incongruent with the prior Christian tradition. Which kind of change actually occurred at Vatican II?

While Catholic doctrine emphasizes the material continuity of its teachings over time, this does not mean that theology is immobile. Christian theology is always both preservative and creative. In every epoch it must face new crises, meet new challenges, and offer answers to new questions. As a living enterprise, it must remain intelligible to the men and women of the day. These themes were central to the programmatic allocution of John XXIII when he opened Vatican II on October 11, 1962. Pope John called for a new outpouring of the Holy Spirit, with the Catholic Church forging strong links with other Christians, with adherents of other religions (particularly Judaism), and with all men and women seeking the truth. The church needed to be rejuvenated so that the gospel of Jesus Christ could be heard with new urgency and appropriated with new vitality. Precisely in service to this quest, John made a crucial distinction between the *depositum fidei* (deposit of faith; 2 Tim. 1:14) and the *modus quo veritates enuntiantur* (the manner in which such truths are spoken). He also insisted, quoting Vincent, that new formulations must nonetheless retain the meaning of prior dogmatic teachings *eodem tamen sensu eademque sententia* (according to the same meaning and the same judgment). The conciliar task, as John saw it, was to maintain the substance of Catholic truth even while presenting it in a way that was biblical, ecumenical, pastoral, and intelligible, thereby helping the church forge links with all people.

In summary, this book will argue that Vatican II purveys neither flaccid relativism nor stolid archaism. For the most part, one sees cumulative development in its teaching, meaning by this organic, homogeneous, architectonic growth. But one may also discern significant moments of discontinuity. I will argue that these moments of discontinuity can, nevertheless, be incorporated into a proper understanding of development. Thus, they do not jeopardize the material identity of divine revelation over time.

Some Further Considerations

This volume is intended primarily for theology students, although certainly not for them alone. Many people are interested in the Second Vatican Council—its meaning, reception, and proper interpretation. I have sought, therefore, to make this material accessible to all interested readers. My intention is to help students and others understand how Vatican II is properly integrated into the theological tradition of the Catholic Church even as it significantly reorients Catholicism in some crucial areas.

While this book clearly has a Roman Catholic theme, I have written it with an ecumenical audience in mind. There are several reasons for this approach. One is that Vatican II itself was a council with profound ecumenical interests. From the very outset, John XXIII insisted that the unity of all Christians should constitute a significant part of the conciliar agenda—a point strongly reaffirmed by Paul VI when he was elected pope in 1963. The council made clear that Catholicism is fully committed to the ecumenical enterprise and, indeed, to the full, visible union of the Christian churches. How this will happen, of course, is known to God alone, but Vatican II committed the Catholic Church and its theology to this course of action.

A second reason is that the council was concerned with ecumenical issues at every stage of its deliberations—not simply when discussing ecumenism directly, but also when discussing the church, divine revelation, the Blessed Virgin Mary, and so on. The prominent place in St. Peter's Basilica given to the Protestant and Orthodox observers meant that ecumenism would necessarily loom large at the council. And the Secretariat for Christian Unity, one of the conciliar commissions, relentlessly ensured that ecumenical issues would never be placed on the back burner.

A third and final reason is that I have been fortunate to be involved in ecumenical endeavors for over twenty years as a member of Evangelicals and Catholics Together (ECT), serving as co-chairman of this dialogue since 2009. ECT was founded in 1994 by Chuck Colson and Richard John Neuhaus, two extraordinary witnesses to Jesus Christ. In my years of involvement with the dialogue, I have been able to study firsthand—and to appreciate and admire—the careful work of evangelical theologians. I have seen the advances that can occur when Christians meet in good faith to discuss foundational theological topics.[3] Concern for Christian unity therefore informs the content and style of this book, just as it informs the content and style of Vatican II. I hope that other Christians reading this volume will learn a good deal about how Catholic theology evaluates the achievements of the council. One of the arguments of this book is that much of the council rests on the principle of analogy—that is, a searching out of the similarities that exist between Catholicism and other points of view. This book is written in the same spirit.

---

3. The fruits of ECT may be found in a recent volume, *Evangelicals and Catholics Together at Twenty: Vital Statements on Contested Topics*, ed. Timothy George and Thomas G. Guarino (Grand Rapids: Brazos, 2015).

Translations

Many of the translations of the Vatican II documents found in this volume are my own. I have compared them to the translations found in other editions, particularly in the Abbott and Tanner translations as well as the multilingual translations found on the Vatican website.[4] As regards biblical translations, I have most often translated the texts cited by Vatican II directly from the Latin of the documents, comparing these with the Revised Standard Version, the New American Bible, and other translations.

---

4. Walter M. Abbott, ed., *The Documents of Vatican II* (New York: Herder and Herder, 1966); Norman P. Tanner, ed., *Decrees of the Ecumenical Councils* (London: Sheed and Ward, 1990). I have utilized the Latin text reprinted in Tanner: *Conciliorum Oecumenicorum Decreta*, 3rd ed. (Bologna: Istituto per le Scienze Religiose, 1973).

CHAPTER 1

The Central Problem of Vatican II

Why does Vatican II remain a contentious council more than fifty years after its conclusion? Why is it seen by many as having countenanced a revolution in Catholic thought? One significant reason is that Christianity has staked a great deal on the notion of the *material continuity of the faith* through generations and cultures. Authoritative Christian teachings—dogmas of the faith—are reflective of Sacred Scripture and apostolic tradition. What is believed today has been believed in substance—even if only embryonically—from the beginning.

Vatican II captures this idea when it says that "God has seen to it that what He revealed for the salvation of all nations would abide *perpetually in its full integrity and be handed on to all generations*" (*DV* §7; emphasis added). In other words, God's truth, the truth of divine revelation, is indelibly marked by the ideas of identity, perpetuity, and universality. The Christian narrative is not simply a matter of fascinating stories; its teachings are reflective of states of affairs. Absent the characteristics of continuity and objectivity, Christian doctrine is reduced to nothing more than a prudential, pragmatic, and ultimately dispensable guide to life. Citations attesting to the objectivity and perpetuity of divine revelation are easily adducible from Catholic and Protestant theologians alike.[1] As the International Theological

1. For these characteristics of Christian doctrine, as found in both theologians and church documents, see Thomas G. Guarino, *Foundations of Systematic Theology* (New York: T&T Clark, 2005), 1–31. The Methodist theologian Geoffrey Wainwright refers to the "irreversible deliverances" of the early creeds that have always been affirmed by classical Protestants. *Is the Reformation Over?* (Milwaukee: Marquette University Press, 2000), 39.

Commission, a body of Catholic theologians from around the globe, has stated in one of its most insightful documents, "The truth of revelation . . . is universally valid and unchangeable in substance."[2] But people often express uneasiness with Vatican II—at least in certain quarters of the church—because of the sense that the council "changed" Catholicism in significant ways. Identifying precisely *what* changed is often difficult. An obvious variation, of course, is the liturgy that is now celebrated in the vernacular and *versus populum*, whereas it was once offered in Latin and *ad orientem*. But there is also a deeper sense, vaguely articulated, that Vatican II somehow changed Catholicism itself—that the Catholic Church went from being the "one true Church" to simply one Christian denomination among many, and that it now holds positions (about religious freedom, ecumenism, interreligious dialogue, and church-state relations) that it formerly abhorred.

The customary self-understanding of Catholics was thrown into confusion by a council allegedly willing to modify fundamental teachings: Is explicit belief in Jesus Christ and the church still vital to salvation? Is evangelization still important? Is access to the sacraments, particularly the Eucharist, integral to a vibrant Christian life? Rather than the self-confident institution that it once was, the Catholic Church is now anxious and unsure about its identity, about its place in society, and about its future in general. Isn't this uncertainty the sad harvest of Vatican II?

Yves Congar, one of the principal theologians at the council, relates a story that sums up the sentiment of many. Toward the end of 1964, the French minister of education, Christian Fouchet, said to Bishop Elchinger of Strasbourg, "You are doing a bad job at the Council. You are calling everything into question. What was true yesterday is no longer true today."[3] Congar remarks, somewhat dismissively, that this idea that everything was changing was driven by the French press in hopes of creating sensational headlines. But Fouchet's comment is neither idiosyncratic nor geographically limited. It sums up the way many view Vatican II: what was true yesterday is no longer true today.

This concern is not without foundation. In the fifth century, the Christian theologian Vincent of Lérins saw changeability as a mark of heresy. Heretics are the ones who tell us to "condemn what you used to hold and hold what

2. International Theological Commission, "On the Interpretation of Dogmas," *Origins* 20 (May 17, 1990): 9. See also the commission's more recent statement, *Theology Today: Perspectives, Principles and Criteria* (Washington, DC: Catholic University of America Press, 2012), §§28–29.

3. Yves Congar, *My Journal of the Council*, trans. Mary John Ronayne and Mary Cecily Boulding (Collegeville, MN: Liturgical Press, 2012), 700 (December 25, 1964).

you used to condemn" (*Comm.* 9.8). In the seventeenth century, the Catholic apologist Jacques Bossuet argued that Catholicism is marked by immutability whereas Protestantism is subject to change. While Bossuet's description is contestable, his allegation is revealing: Protestantism changes—and therefore errs.[4]

One might argue that, for Catholicism, material continuity over time is the *articulus stantis et cadentis ecclesiae*—the article on which the church stands or falls. Why? Because if divine revelation is truly God's self-manifestation—his personal unveiledness to humanity—then God's own truthfulness demands that revelation be identical and continuous, the same yesterday, today, and tomorrow. If the church's teachings are *not* universally valid and materially identical over time, then one is driven to conclude that Christian doctrines are themselves fallible and changeable, able to be remade with time and tide, possessing little intrinsic stability. In that case, Christian teachings would be nothing more than historically conditioned attempts at self-transcendence, offering little insight into the life of God. Historical mutability and provisionality—not bedrock truth—would be the horizons within which all Christian teaching should be understood. It is precisely for this reason that the debate over continuity and discontinuity in Catholicism is so crucial and vigorous today. If the council simply "remade" the church in the image of the contemporary world—ecclesiogenesis in the proper sense of the term—then the church can ever and always be remade to correspond to the whims and tastes of the day.

These, then, are the central questions for the interpretation of Vatican II and are therefore pivotal for this book: Given that the council has significant elements of discontinuity—as Benedict XVI himself conceded—did Vatican II betray fundamental Catholic teachings? If not, then how should we understand the council's discontinuous moments?

I will argue that, for the most part, Vatican II is in clear congruence with the prior Catholic tradition—even while homogeneously developing it on certain points. (The precise meaning of "development" will be more carefully examined in chapter 3.) But one may also identify several important reversals at the council, even though such reversals were generally "masked." In the desire to give the impression that all conciliar change was smoothly continuous with the prior tradition—and to ensure that the documents themselves did not become distinction-laden textbooks—Vatican II glided over those points where it was reversing the immediately prior tradition. And there is no doubt that some earlier teaching was indeed reversed by the council. This, I believe, has been the source of much confusion and conster-

---

4. See Jacques Bossuet, *Histoire des variations des Églises Protestantes* (Paris, 1688).

nation, giving rise to the claim that Vatican II constituted a significant and substantial rupture with the antecedent tradition. Once again, I will argue that the discontinuity in conciliar teaching undermines neither the stability nor the solidity of the truth of revelation. But these discontinuous moments need to be identified and clearly understood.

Historical Responses to the Issue of Continuity

Let us now briefly discuss two theologians who directly treated the issue of change and development in Christian doctrine over time: Vincent of Lérins and John Henry Newman.

Vincent of Lérins

I have already mentioned the thought of the early Christian writer Vincent of Lérins. Here I intend to offer a somewhat fuller treatment of his theological insights. Can Vincent help us to interpret Vatican II properly? Can this fifth-century theologian still teach us about the difference between *change that is organic development and change that is corruption*? I believe that he can. Indeed, Vincent is important to this book because he is the first Christian writer to deal at length with the thorny issue of mutability and continuity.

In his most famous work, the *Commonitorium*, Vincent wrestled with several foundational questions roiling the early church: How could the recrudescence of Arianism, condemned at the Council of Nicaea (325) but remaining vibrant nonetheless, finally be overcome? Why were the clear errors of Bishop Nestorius, condemned by the Council of Ephesus (431), continually attractive to some theologians? And how should Christians understand the precise relationship between divine grace and human freedom? In response to these persistent theological problems, Vincent went to the root of the matter, posing his own questions: How can we distinguish between Christian truth and pernicious heresy? By which criteria do we make this all-important distinction? And does the preservation and conservation of the Christian faith mean that further development is impossible?

Vincent's answers are subtle and creative.[5] To distinguish truth from

---

5. For an extended treatment of Vincent's theology, see Thomas G. Guarino, *Vincent of Lérins and the Development of Christian Doctrine* (Grand Rapids: Baker Academic, 2013).

heresy, Vincent places a marked accent on the triple criteria of antiquity, universality, and ubiquity. These criteria are summarized in his famous "canon" or "first rule," which states that "in the catholic church, all care must be taken so we hold that which has been believed everywhere, always and by everyone" (2.5).[6] Vincent's famous words "everywhere, always and by everyone" (*ubique, semper et ab omnibus*) have been endlessly invoked by historians and theologians, although usually just as quickly dismissed. Many have argued that Vincent's canon represents an interesting attempt to separate truth from heresy but his rule is naive because, in fact, no Christian doctrine has *ever* been believed always, everywhere, and by everyone.

But this evaluation of Vincent's famous rule badly misses his point.[7] Moreover, it is transparently clear that the theologian of Lérins never meant his threefold canon to forestall continuing development in the life of the church. Vincent was convinced that *change inevitably occurs over time*—and with change, growth and development. He was well aware, for example, that neither the word *homoousios* of the Council of Nicaea (325) nor the word *Theotokos* of the Council of Ephesus (431) was to be found in Scripture. Nonetheless, he saw these signature words as legitimately and homogeneously developing the contents of the Bible.

Crucially important for our discussion is Vincent's careful distinction alluded to earlier: two kinds of change can occur in the church, *profectus* and *permutatio*. The former represents a legitimate advance, an organic extension, an architectonic development of prior teachings. The latter term, on the contrary, represents the reversal of some antecedent principle; as such it constitutes a corruption of the Christian faith. For Vincent, continuity in church teaching is essential but does not exclude authentic growth.

Illustrating this point is the famous chapter 23 of the *Commonitorium*, where the theologian of Lérins reconciles his first rule—that which is true is that which has been acknowledged *semper, ubique, et ab omnibus*—with his second rule, namely, that there exists authentic development in the church of Christ. Just here we see why Vincent is so important for understanding

6. Vincent of Lérins, *Commonitorium*, Corpus Christianorum: Series Latina 64, ed. Rolandus Demeulenaere (Turnhout: Brepols, 1985), 177–78. References to the *Commonitorium* will be to this now-standard edition, by chapter and line. An English translation may be found in *A Select Library of the Nicene and Post-Nicene Fathers of the Christian Church*, ed. Philip Schaff and Henry Wace, 14 vols. (Grand Rapids: Eerdmans, 1969–76), 11:131–56.

7. With these words—*semper, ubique, et ab omnibus*—Vincent is referring to the teachings embodied in ecumenical councils, Nicaea in particular. Unfortunately, Vincent's theological intentions have often been poorly understood. See Guarino, *Vincent of Lérins*, 2–3, 81–82.

Vatican II. He argues that preservation and development are entirely accordant realities.

> But someone will perhaps say: is there no progress of religion in the church of Christ? Certainly there is progress, even exceedingly great progress [*plane et maximus*]. For who is so envious of others and so hateful toward God as to try to prohibit it? Yet, it must be an advance [*profectus*] in the proper sense of the word and not an alteration [*permutatio*] in faith. For progress means that each thing is enlarged within itself [*res amplificetur*], while alteration implies that one thing is transformed into something else [*aliquid ex alio in aliud*]. It is necessary, therefore, that understanding, knowledge, and wisdom should grow [*crescat*] and advance [*proficiat*] vigorously in individuals as well as in the community, in a single person as well as in the whole church and this gradually in the course of ages and centuries. But the progress made must be according to its own type, that is, in accord with the same doctrine, the same meaning, and the same judgment [*eodem sensu eademque sententia*]. (23.1–3)

This famous passage indicates that Vincent, while deeply concerned with the preservation of Christian truth, insists that such preservation is fully consonant with development over time. As he says: Who is so "envious of others and so hateful toward God" as to try to prohibit progress? Examples of the distinction between authentic development and illegitimate corruption are obvious in Vincent's work. Proper development is exemplified in the Councils of Nicaea and Ephesus (with their insistence on the divinity of Jesus and on his divine-human unity).[8]

Where does one find deformations and corruptions, Vincent's dreaded *permutationes fidei*? One such place is in the various fourth-century imperial attempts to reverse the Council of Nicaea by reformulating the creed without the word *homoousios*. Such attempts also represent "changes"—but changes that are now *alterations* of the Christian faith, pernicious corruptions that transgress the bedrock doctrinal truth found in the Bible and formulated by an ecumenical council.

Again and again Vincent polemicizes against the Synod of Ariminum (Rimini, 359) because it is clearly discontinuous with the Council of Ni-

---

8. In chapter 13 of his *Commonitorium*, Vincent offers several christological affirmations that also display the kind of development he believes is fully warranted. See Guarino, *Vincent of Lérins*, 23–25.

caea—not homogeneously developing it, but nakedly reversing its affirmations. Against such attempts, Vincent ardently declaims, "Transgress not the landmarks inherited from the fathers!" (Prov. 22:28). Solemnly defined teachings, such as the Council of Nicaea's on the identity of Jesus Christ, represent doctrinal milestones that cannot be transgressed or traduced. Ecumenical councils represent the agreement of teachers/bishops from every part of Christendom (*ubique, omnes*) handing on biblical and apostolic truth (*semper*) and thereby establishing irreversible landmarks. Any attempt to reverse them is to introduce not a *profectus* but a *permutatio* into the life of the church. On heretical attempts such as these, Vincent invokes a biblical punishment: "Who should break through a wall, the serpent will bite!" (Eccles. 10:8).

The Lerinian's entire work is devoted to the preservation of the faith found in Scripture, the faith once and for all delivered to the saints. Substantial continuity of belief is a sign of truth; reversals are a sign of error. This is why Vincent endlessly cites St. Paul's letter to Timothy, "O Timothy, guard the deposit that has been entrusted to you!" (1 Tim. 6:20). Without such material identity over time—without such vigilant guarding of the deposit—we mock the faith of those who preceded us. Just here Vincent invokes the witness of the entire church against heterogeneous innovation:

> [Such novelties], were they accepted, would necessarily defile the faith of the blessed fathers. . . . If they were accepted, then it must be stated that the faithful of all ages, all the saints, all the chaste, continent virgins, all the clerical levites and priests, so many thousands of confessors, so great an army of martyrs . . . almost the entire world incorporated in Christ the Head through the catholic faith for so many centuries, would have erred, would have blasphemed, would not have known what to believe. (24.5)

We observe in this passage not only Vincent's strong accent on the continuity of the faith but also his equally firm insistence against reversals. If reversals occur in the church, then deleterious consequences inexorably follow. *If novelties are accepted, then the entire past of the church is called into question*—precisely because martyrs and saints witnessed to, and shed blood for, beliefs that may have been entirely false. Novelties inevitably lead to serious mutations that "change one thing into something else entirely" (*aliquid ex alio in aliud transvertatur*; 23.2).

Despite these strong preservative instincts, Vincent nonetheless fosters authentic development. A legitimate advance (*profectus*) is a matter of *organic, homogeneous progress*—that is, growth that builds on, but does not reverse or substantially alter, the church's prior doctrinal achievements. For insight into Vincent's concept of *proper* development, we do well to attend to his vocabulary and images. He tells us that authentic development means that something "is enlarged within itself" (*res amplificetur in se*; 23.2). That is to say, in the process of evolution and supplementation, a teaching does not lose its identity; rather, it expands it, even while remaining substantially the same. To illustrate this point, Vincent tells us that the growth of religion is parallel to the growth of bodies, which develop over time and yet remain essentially the same (23.4). While human beings change and develop from childhood to maturity, "their nature and personhood remain one and the same" (*eademque natura, una eademque persona sit*; 23.5). Christian doctrine, Vincent concludes, follows this same law of progress: "It is consolidated by years, developed over time (*dilatetur tempore*), rendered more sublime by age, but it remains without corruption or adulteration so that it is always complete and perfect in all its dimensions and parts . . . admitting no change, no debasement of its unique characteristics, no variation within its defined limits" (23.9).

In these two phrases, *res amplificetur* and *dilatetur tempore*, one sees that Vincent is not only unafraid of growth; he actively encourages it. Growth and change inevitably occur over time, as nature itself testifies. But this growth must, once again, be of a certain kind and shape, indicating organic and harmonious progress. Vincent offers another image to make his point, arguing that what is sown as wheat must be harvested as wheat:

> Original doctrine sown as wheat, when developed over the course of time and properly cultivated, must retain the property of the grain and should undergo no change in its character; there may be added change in shape, form, clarity [*species, forma, distinctio*], but there must remain the same nature [*eadem natura*] according to its fundamental character. (23.11)

Like wheat, Christian doctrine cannot be transformed into something essentially different. There will certainly be expansion and growth, since both wheat and doctrine flourish under cultivation. But there can be no change in their fundamental and substantial nature.

Both Vincent's vocabulary and his images attest to his insistence on development over time—but development that preserves the fundamental teachings of the past. While growth is both possible and desirable, *it can only be growth that is preservative of prior landmarks.* All later theological developments must vigilantly preserve the decisions of the Council of Nicaea, with its insistence on the divinity of Jesus Christ and thus on the doctrine of the Holy Trinity. Future growth must preserve as well the Council of Ephesus's teaching, which, with its bestowal of the title *Theotokos* on Mary, protected the unity of Christ's divinity and humanity.

In the following chapters, we will see how Vincent's thought on preservation and proper growth may be applied to the Second Vatican Council. Let us first, however, briefly review the thought of another artisan of doctrinal development.

John Henry Newman

Also helping us interpret the disputed teachings of Vatican II, at least to some extent, will be the work of John Henry Newman, a kind of nineteenth-century *Vincentius redivivus.* Several books have linked the council's work, particularly its evolution in Catholic teaching, to Newman's seminal 1845 volume, *An Essay on the Development of Christian Doctrine.*[9] Pope Paul VI even spoke of Vatican II as "Newman's hour":

> Many of the problems which he [Newman] treated with wisdom . . . were the subjects of the discussion and study of the Fathers of the Second Vatican Council, as for example the question of ecumenism, the relationship between Christianity and the world, the emphasis on the role of the laity in the Church and the relationship of the Church to non-Christian religions. *Not only this Council but also the present time can be considered in a special way as Newman's hour,* in which, with confidence in divine providence, he placed his great hopes and expectations. . . . And it is precisely the present moment that suggests, in a particularly pressing and persuasive way, the study and diffusion of Newman's thought.[10]

But Newman's thought on development did not come to fruition in isolation. Nor did he naively think he was the first one to acknowledge the impor-

9. See Avery Dulles, *Newman* (New York: Continuum, 2002), 150–64; and Ian Ker, *Newman on Vatican II* (Oxford: Oxford University Press, 2016).

10. See *L'Osservatore Romano* (English edition), April 17, 1975, 368; emphasis added. See also Dulles, *Newman*, 165n4.

tance of organic growth over time. As the Victorian says in his *Apologia pro vita sua*, "[The principle of development] is certainly recognized in the Treatise of Vincent of Lerins, which has so often been taken as the basis of Anglicanism."[11]

In fact, Newman was deeply influenced by Vincent and the latter's notion of authentic development. While still a young man, he translated significant portions of the *Commonitorium* into English, titling his annotated work "Vincentius of Lerins on the Tests of Heresy and Error" (1834).[12] The very title indicates that even at this early stage of his career Newman was concerned with the distinction between a proper *profectus* and a destructive *permutatio*. This distinction would preoccupy him for the rest of his life.

In his early (Anglican) period, Newman uses Vincent's work to argue that the Lerinian's "first rule" (*semper, ubique, et ab omnibus*) stands as a monument against later innovations to the tradition (such as Mariology and purgatory) by Roman Catholicism and against amputations of the tradition (on issues such as infant baptism and episcopal succession) by various Protestant churches. At this point in his life, Newman consistently invokes Vincent as a staunch bulwark for the Anglo-Catholic via media between Rome and the Reformation.

In his *Essay*, however (and throughout his Roman Catholic period), Newman again takes up Vincent's mantle, but now placing a much greater accent on his "second rule"—that there is growth over time, *eodem sensu eademque sententia*. For example, in his 1837 book, *The Via Media of the Anglican Church*, Newman insists that, for Vincent, the rule of faith is "unalterable, unreformable" with the church having no power over it. But in an 1877 footnote to this passage, the Roman Catholic Newman adds, "But Vincent . . . says that, though unalterable, it [the Rule of Faith] admits of growth."[13]

Newman did not hesitate to cite Vincent's distinction between the two kinds of change, *profectus* and *permutatio*: "Vincentius of Lerins . . . speaks of

---

11. *Apologia pro vita sua* (1864; repr., London: Longmans, Green, 1895), 197. Newman would never say, as John Noonan does, that "the inventor of the idea that Christian doctrine develops is John Henry Newman." See *A Church That Can and Cannot Change* (Notre Dame, IN: University of Notre Dame Press, 2005), 3.

12. Newman's (partial) translation of Vincent's *Commonitorium* may be found in *Tracts for the Times*, vol. 2, *Records of the Church* (1839; facsimile repr., New York: AMS Press, 1969), §§19–25.

13. See *The Via Media of the Anglican Church* (London: Longmans, Green, 1901), 1:224 and 224n6.

the development of Christian doctrine, as *profectus fidei, non permutatio.*"[14] But how can one distinguish between an authentic advance of the faith on one hand and an insidious corruption of it on the other? To answer this question Newman develops his seven "notes." The Victorian's first note—the criterion on which he spends the greatest amount of time by far—is *preservation of type*. With this term Newman is arguing that material continuity over time is a significant characteristic of faithful development.

The marked relationship between Newman's "identity of type" and Vincent's "*idem sensus*" is difficult to miss. Like Vincent, Newman speaks of doctrinal growth as equivalent to organic, homogeneous development. Authentic change must be *in eodem sensu* with that which preceded it. It is unsurprising, then, that Newman invokes the Gallic theologian's "law of the body" when explaining growth over time: Christian doctrine develops in a manner analogous to the human body, which grows from youth to maturity yet remains the same.[15] Invoking Vincent directly, Newman states, "Manhood is the perfection of boyhood, adding something of its own, yet keeping what it finds."[16] From the beginning to the end of his famous essay, the note "preservation of type" dominates Newman's thought, indicating his profound reliance on the theologian of Lérins for explaining the nature of doctrinal development.

It is not my intention to examine all the similarities between Vincent and Newman. My point is simply that Newman was deeply reliant on the Lerinian in developing his theory of doctrinal development. So how can Vincent and Newman help us in our examination of the continuity and discontinuity of Vatican II with the prior tradition?

Vatican II and Doctrinal Development

Just prior to the council (in the 1940s) a major theological controversy erupted around the issue of continuity and change, a controversy that foreshadowed the events at Vatican II. I am referring to the publication of—and subsequent polemics surrounding—the work of the French Jesuit Henri Bouillard, whose doctoral dissertation was concerned with grace and con-

---

14. John Henry Newman, *An Essay on the Development of Christian Doctrine* (London: Longmans, Green, 1894), 201.

15. Newman, *Essay*, 172.

16. Newman, *Essay*, 419–20.

version in the work of Aquinas.[17] Bouillard's conclusions about truth and history (and so about continuity and change) set the Catholic theological world ablaze, for Bouillard argued that doctrinal formulations are always products of their time, deeply conditioned by the historical circumstances in which they emerge. At the same time, he insisted, history and truth are not at antipodes; history does not inexorably lead to relativism.

Making a distinction between *affirmations* and *representations*, Bouillard argued that although theological vocabulary and concepts (representations) change with the times, these concepts mediate fundamental affirmations of divine revelation. For example, Christianity teaches that grace is a free gift of God that renders men righteous and empowers them to live holy lives. But this affirmation has been expressed differently by St. John's Gospel, by Augustine, by Aquinas, and so on. Similarly, since the twelfth century, Catholicism has commonly used the word *transubstantiation* to express its faith in the real presence of Christ in the Eucharist. But the language of *substance* and *accident* is only one way of expressing this mystery of faith. Other terms have been used in the past—and new ones may be used today—which also protect the church's faith in Christ's eucharistic presence. Bouillard's point, of course, was that there could be a plurality of conceptual formulations over time, all of which protected some fundamental Christian belief.

Christian truth, therefore, *is* deeply linked to temporality, but the recognition of history's effects does *not* inevitably lead to relativism. Bouillard concluded, "Ideas, methods, systems change with the times, but the affirmations which they contain remain, although expressed in other categories."[18] In arguing thus, Bouillard hoped to show that history witnessed to the material continuity of the truth of revelation, but it so witnessed with an accent on authentic plurality as well.

There is no need to recount the Bouillard controversy and its aftermath. It is a story that has been told several times before.[19] The critical point is that the relationship between continuity and change, between historicity and truth, had been robustly and polemically discussed several years before Vatican II opened. To what extent was Christian doctrine mutable? And if mutability was indeed possible, how much was legitimate? Further, how did one maintain the *idem sensus* in and through conceptual change? All

---

17. Henri Bouillard, *Conversion et grâce chez S. Thomas d'Aquin: Étude historique* (Paris: Aubier, 1944).

18. Bouillard, *Conversion et grâce*, 220.

19. See Guarino, *Foundations of Systematic Theology*, 146–48.

the issues Bouillard raised were to be part of Vatican II—and still continue in its aftermath.

Although Bouillard was disciplined (forbidden to teach) in 1950, it would not be long before Pope John XXIII, in his speech opening Vatican II (October 11, 1962), made points very similar to those Bouillard had put forth in his 1944 thesis. In his opening allocution, titled *Gaudet mater ecclesia*, John XXIII made clear that he wished to move beyond a recondite neo-scholastic theology so that the Catholic Church could speak the truth of the gospel in terms that were accessible and intelligible to men and women of the twentieth century. In a famous sentence, the pope says, "The *depositum fidei* or truths which are found in our venerable doctrine is one thing while the way [*modus*] in which these truths are expressed is another, always with the same meaning and the same judgment."[20] Much like Bouillard, the pope is making the point that the content of Christian doctrine can be expressed in a variety of ways, but always *in eodem sensu*, that is, with material continuity preserved over time.

Yves Congar argues that the distinction John makes—between the "deposit of faith" (2 Tim. 1:14) and "the way in which it is expressed"—summarizes the meaning of the entire council.[21] Congar asserts that with this distinction the council simultaneously sought to protect the material identity of the Christian faith and to encourage the church to express that faith in language and lexica appropriate for the times.[22] This point is supported by John XXIII's citation of Vincent's famous phrase at the end of the sentence. The truths of the faith may be expressed in a plurality of ways—but always protecting the same meaning and judgment (*eodem sensu eademque sententia*). In other words, any reformulation must protect the material continuity and universality of Christian teaching even while allowing for homogeneous development and growth.[23]

20. See *Acta apostolicae sedis* 54 (1962): 786–96, at 792. Also *AS* I/1, 166–75.

21. Yves Congar, *A History of Theology*, trans. Hunter Guthrie (Garden City, NY: Doubleday, 1968), 18–19. Giuseppe Alberigo has called the distinction between the *depositum* and its formulation one of the decisive motifs of the council. See "Facteurs de 'Laïcité' au Concile Vatican II," *Revue des sciences religieuses* 74 (2000): 211–25.

22. G. C. Berkouwer, a prominent Reformed observer at Vatican II, also saw this distinction as a significant ecumenical advance precisely because no one formulation could exhaust the mysteries of faith. See *The Second Vatican Council and the New Catholicism*, trans. Lewis B. Smedes (Grand Rapids: Eerdmans, 1965), 63–65. Berkouwer's theological evaluation of Vatican II is outlined at length in Eduardo Echeverria, *Berkouwer and Catholicism* (Leiden: Brill, 2013).

23. On John XXIII's opening allocution and his invocation of Vincent of Lérins, see

The Second Vatican Council's dual goal of protecting and preserving the Christian tradition while fostering its proper development is precisely the issue in dispute today. Was Vatican II faithful to Vincent's instruction that any development must be homogeneous in kind, congruent with antecedent Christian teachings? Or, in its eagerness for dialogue with the Reformation and the Enlightenment, did it "tip over" into a *permutatio fidei*, betraying landmarks that had been previously established? Did the council teach that Christian doctrine itself is deeply provisional and conditioned? In sum, did Vatican II speak in continuity with the prior tradition (*in eodem sensu*), or did it, as some charge, teach foreign doctrine (*in alieno sensu*)?

The argument of this book is that Vatican II was, in the main, a homogeneous *profectus* of the earlier tradition, adhering to Vincent's dictum about proper development. The council advances and expands the Catholic doctrinal tradition even while observing the fundamental landmarks established by biblical and conciliar teaching. In this sense, then, Vatican II is entirely legitimate according to the theological criteria established by the Lerinian. To support this assertion, I will, in the following chapters, examine some of the most disputed teachings of the council. At the same time, this clear accent on homogeneous development did not preclude moments of discontinuity. Reversals of antecedent Catholic teaching certainly took place at Vatican II. And, as noted, these reversals tended to be masked since the council never openly adverts to any break with prior magisterial statements. How these discontinuities may be integrated into an authentic notion of development will presently come into view.

Pope Benedict XVI, in his famous Christmas speech of 2005, pointedly referred to both continuity and discontinuity at Vatican II. The pope, himself a participant at the council, memorably contrasted a "hermeneutic of rupture" with a "hermeneutic of reform." Benedict offered no simplistic insistence on continuity, acknowledging that the council was a "combination of continuity and discontinuity at different levels."[24] Even before Benedict, John Paul II spoke about continuity and change in light of the postconciliar schism initiated by Archbishop Marcel Lefebvre. Lefebvre argued that, on crucial teachings, Vatican II initiated a violent rupture with the prior Cath-

---

Giuseppe Alberigo and Alberto Melloni, "L'allocuzione *Gaudet Mater Ecclesia* di Giovanni XXIII," in *Fede tradizione profezia: Studi su Giovanni XXIII e sul Vaticano II*, ed. Giuseppe Alberigo et al. (Brescia: Paideia, 1984), 187–283.

24. "Address of His Holiness Benedict XVI to the Roman Curia Offering Them His Christmas Greetings," December 22, 2005, http://w2.vatican.va/content/benedict-xvi/en /speeches/2005/december/documents/hf_ben_xvi_spe_20051222_roman-curia.html.

olic tradition. Responding to Lefebvre, John Paul stated, "The extent and depth of the teaching of the Second Vatican Council calls for a renewed commitment to deeper study in order to reveal clearly the Council's continuity with Tradition, especially in points of doctrine which, perhaps because they are new, have not yet been well understood by some sections of the Church."[25] In this sentence, one may see the entire theological problem of Vatican II. John Paul II wishes to accent the council's continuity with the great tradition of the church, but at the same time he acknowledges (somewhat hesitantly) that there are new points of doctrine. This is the heart of the matter: How are tradition and novelty, continuity and discontinuity, theologically reconciled?

Much of the discussion, of course, revolves around a proper understanding of development. As John Courtney Murray, an American expert at the council, rightly said, "It [the Declaration on Religious Freedom] was, of course, the most controversial document of the whole Council, largely because it raised with sharp emphasis *the issue that lay continually below the surface of all the conciliar debates—the issue of the development of doctrine.*"[26] Murray is entirely correct in identifying development—shorthand for continuity and discontinuity—as the crucial conciliar issue. Any change envisioned by Vatican II raised the question of material identity over time, and this inevitably entails the veracity and reliability of divine revelation itself.

Conclusion

The point of this chapter has been to discuss the central problem emanating from Vatican II: whether its principal teachings are in continuity or discontinuity with the antecedent Catholic tradition. As I have noted, Christianity, both historically and currently, places a high value on the perpetuity, universality, and material identity of doctrinal teaching over time. It places a similarly high premium on the objective truth of its foundational beliefs. As Tertullian famously said, "Our Lord Christ called himself truth not custom."[27]

It is precisely because of Catholicism's accent on these characteristics that Vatican II remains controversial. Many see the council as having initiated a significant rupture with the prior doctrinal tradition. Recall once

25. John Paul II, "Ecclesia Dei," July 2, 1988, http://w2.vatican.va/content/john-paul-ii/en/motu_proprio/documents/hf_jp-ii_motu-proprio_02071988_ecclesia-dei.html.

26. John Courtney Murray, "Religious Freedom," in *The Documents of Vatican II*, ed. Walter M. Abbott (New York: Herder and Herder, 1966), 673; emphasis added.

27. Tertullian, *De virginibus velandis* ("On the Veiling of Virgins") 1.1.

again the 1964 comment of the French minister of education to Bishop Elchinger: "You are doing a bad job at the Council. You are calling everything into question. What was true yesterday is no longer true today." It is just this sentiment that animates many people today—what was once Catholic truth is no longer the case. And if this sentiment is accurate, then what the church teaches today cannot be trusted.

Do the teachings of Vatican II represent a collective *profectus* or *permutatio fidei*? To answer that question more completely, I now proceed to outline the theological principles essential to interpreting the council. Although the documents of Vatican II are written in a highly accessible style, lurking behind that accessibility is a world of theological sophistication. The experts who composed the documents were, in the main, first-rank theologians who had wide familiarity with the principles of theological interpretation. Only some acquaintance with these fundamental tenets will allow for an informed and judicious judgment as to the council's continuity or discontinuity with the prior Christian tradition.

CHAPTER 2

Theological Principles for Understanding Vatican II

We have examined the fundamental problem concerning the teaching and reception of the Second Vatican Council: the sense, sometimes vague and ambiguous, that the council engaged in a significant rupture with the prior doctrinal tradition, even to the extent of redefining Catholicism itself. For some, this has led to a deep disquiet about Vatican II, with the thought that, perhaps unwittingly, it purveyed grave error. As we have seen, Catholic tradition emphasizes the continuity, perpetuity, material identity, and objective truth of its fundamental beliefs. Did Vatican II cast doubt on these characteristics, at least with regard to certain disputed topics? To answer that question properly, we need to examine several fundamental principles, themes that infuse the conciliar documents but are usually not visible on the surface of the texts.

Interpreting ecumenical councils—just like interpreting the Bible—is not always an easy task. What theological "moves" were made at the council? Gathered at Vatican II were many of the world's most distinguished Catholic theologians, and a review of their diaries and commentaries reveals their careful and judicious way of proceeding. But therein lies the problem. The conciliar documents mask a series of theological assumptions that the nonexpert can easily overlook. Vatican II's accessible, smooth, even conversational prose offers few clues to the premises undergirding the texts themselves. And yet these unnamed principles guided conciliar development, evolution, and reversal. Our discussion of these axial themes will help resolve the question of whether the council was an authentic development or a pernicious corruption of the antecedent tradition. Needless to say, a separate monograph could be written on each of the ideas discussed below. I will recount only the central dimensions of these foundational principles.

Analogy and Participatory Thinking

It is my contention that analogical and participatory thinking are crucial, though generally overlooked, themes at Vatican II. Indeed, one argument of this book is that analogy is a fundamental category for the council. It is not my intention to offer here a full examination of the massive theme of analogical denomination. I am interested, rather, in these questions: What part did analogical thinking play at Vatican II? How did it affect the council on the issue of continuity and discontinuity?[1]

I will argue that the conciliar employment of participation and analogy—two of Aquinas's most important theological tools—changed the optic by which the council evaluated other Christian churches, other religions, and other people sincerely seeking the truth. This accent on analogical reasoning helps to explain the remark of Yves Congar, one of the principal architects of Vatican II, soon after the council ended: while the council's explicit references to Aquinas are not numerous, "it could be shown . . . that St. Thomas, the *Doctor communis*, furnished the writers of the dogmatic texts of Vatican II with the bases and structure [*les assises et la structure*] of their thought. We do not doubt that they themselves would make this confession."[2] While Congar does not substantiate this assertion, I think he is referring to the analogical thinking that has been so central to the Catholic tradition and that is found, as we shall see, in several of the conciliar documents.

Illustrative of the claim that analogy is central to Vatican II is the work of the historian John O'Malley. In an influential book (and a variety of articles), O'Malley has persuasively argued that Vatican II adopted a new rhetorical style. Rather than speaking in the sharp, juridical tones of scholastic thought, the council adopted the language of persuasion and invitation. This shift leads O'Malley to conclude that the council

---

1. For a fuller discussion of the role of analogical thinking in theology, and the critiques that have been made of it, see Thomas G. Guarino, *Foundations of Systematic Theology* (New York: T&T Clark, 2005), 239–67.

2. Yves Congar, "La théologie au Concile: Le 'théologiser' du Concile," in *Situation et tâches présentes de la théologie* (Paris: Cerf, 1967), 53.

moved from the dialectic of winning an argument to the dialogue of finding common ground. It moved from abstract metaphysics to interpersonal "how to be." It moved from grand conceptual schemas or summae with hundreds of logically interconnected parts to the humble acceptance of mystery. In so doing it largely abandoned the Scholastic framework that had dominated Catholic theology since the thirteenth century.[3]

Vatican II, O'Malley points out, uses such words as *mutuality, friendship, partnership*, and *cooperation*. The council freely speaks of dialogue, collegiality, and freedom, thereby accenting not the church's adversarial alienation from but its sincere communion with the world.[4] One decisive speech at Vatican II, helping to orient both the council's goals and rhetorical style, was that of Cardinal Suenens of Belgium. Early in 1962, Suenens had argued that in tense times the council should accent "what unites Catholics with others, not what separates them."[5] In December of that same year, he developed this theme on the floor of St. Peter's, advising that the council should open a triple dialogue: with Catholics themselves, with those brothers and sisters who are not in visible unity, and with the world as it exists today.[6]

This conciliatory approach—emphasizing unity with, rather than difference from, all others—was indeed a shift for Catholicism. But it should be further asked: Which kind of thinking undergirds this change in tone and rhetorical style? Which mode of reasoning allows for the establishment of identity despite differences? Which theological construct sanctions *partial unity*, which is neither congruent identity nor utter dissimilarity? The answer to these questions involves analogical thinking. For the council, analogy became the crucial key for stressing the unity of Catholics with other men and women. How is this the case?

At the most basic level, all human beings participate in the same cre-

3. John O'Malley, *What Happened at Vatican II* (Cambridge, MA: Belknap Press of Harvard University Press, 2006), 46.

4. O'Malley, *What Happened*, 267, 306, 309. See also his article "Trent and Vatican II: Two Styles of Church," in *From Trent to Vatican II: Historical and Theological Investigations*, ed. Frederick J. Parrella and Raymond F. Bulman (Oxford: Oxford University Press, 2006), 301–20.

5. O'Malley, *What Happened*, 157.

6. *AS* I/4, 224 (December 4, 1962). John XXIII had seen a draft of Suenens's speech and had made some complementary suggestions. See Léon-Josef Suenens, "Aux origines du Concile Vatican II," *Nouvelle revue théologique* 107 (1985): 3–21.

ated human nature, the ultimate ground of similarity among people. As Genesis affirms, all people are made in the image and likeness of God. But participation goes much further than that: with other Christians, Catholics participate in a common faith in Jesus Christ; with the Jewish people, Catholics share a common belief in the one God of Abraham; with all seekers after wisdom, Catholics share a desire for truth and justice. Although there are differences among these groups, there is also *partial identity* based on participation in a determinate "perfection" (whether Jesus Christ, the God of Abraham, or human nature itself). Indeed, Catholicism's analogical similarity with others became a central conciliar theme. I think it can even be said that *analogy is the philosophical style undergirding Vatican II's rhetorical style.*

The critical role of analogy at Vatican II is overlooked for an easily identifiable reason: John XXIII ardently wished for a *pastoral* council, one that presented Catholic beliefs in an ecumenically sensitive way and in a language intelligible to the contemporary world. The pope recognized that Catholic theology, long reliant on the technical and abstruse language of neo-scholasticism, was experiencing a crisis of form. If the gospel of Jesus Christ were to be vigorously announced to the world, then the church needed to do this without the abstract conceptual arsenal of the thirteenth century.[7] But these pastoral and ecumenical intentions, which provided the rationale for circumventing the scholastic lexicon, have led many commentators to overlook the analogical reasoning deeply inscribed within the conciliar texts.

The same is true of traditional terms such as *primary and secondary analogates* and *intrinsic and extrinsic attribution.* These phrases were scrupulously avoided at Vatican II, precisely to adhere to Pope John's goals. Nonetheless, while the *terms* are absent, the *ideas* are clearly found in the conciliar texts. Gérard Philips, a Louvain theologian who occupied an influential position at Vatican II, says that unlike earlier councils (which condemned errors), this council—conforming itself to the will of the pope—expressed itself by means of a "positive doctrinal exposé."[8] The theologians

---

7. This crisis of form was emphasized by Bishop De Smedt of Bruges on November 19, 1962, during the debate on *De fontibus* (the sources of revelation). He insisted that the scholastic style and method of Catholic theology constituted a major stumbling block for non-Catholics. See *AS* I/3, 184–87, at 185. See also Joseph A. Komonchak, "The Conciliar Discussion on the Sources of Revelation," available at https://jakomonchak.files.wordpress.com/2012/10/debate-on-de-fontibus.pdf.

8. Gérard Philips, *L'Église et son mystère au IIe Concile du Vatican: Histoire, texte et commentaire de la Constitution "Lumen Gentium,"* 2 vols. (Paris: Desclée, 1967–68), 1:269. As the man who steered the Theological Commission, Philips played an extraordinary role at the

at the council chose to do this, often enough, by employing analogical reasoning.[9]

Vatican II wrestled with significant theological themes: identity and difference, continuity and change, unity and plurality. If the council brought an end to both the Counter-Reformation (through its Decree on Ecumenism) and the church's opposition to the secular state (through its Declaration on Religious Freedom), then it did so by rethinking the relationship of Catholicism to other Christian churches, to the modern state, and to the world at large. In all cases, the council insists, "others" formally participate in the unique attributes of Catholicism and are therefore intensively related to it. This is why Philips, the adjunct secretary of the Theological Commission (also referred to as the *Commissio de Fide* or simply *De Fide*) and the draughtsman of *Lumen gentium*, stated that "the [conciliar] accent is continually placed on the positive aspect of this [the relationship of Catholicism to others] problem."[10] In other words, partial unity—and so analogical similarity—was sought at every turn.

The phrase used by Philips to describe the council's work, "the positive aspect of this problem," should not be construed as a shallow, Pollyannaish slogan. The theological insight here is that similarities always exist among entities despite significant differences. In the attributes and "perfections" that the Catholic Church possesses (creeds, doctrines, sacraments, biblical text), there is real participation by others. Others do not participate in these attributes metaphorically, but actually and intensively, formally and substantially. Indeed, it is precisely this participation that allows for a positive evaluation of them.

Unlike other councils in the church's history, Vatican II was not called

---

council, perhaps not fully recognized even today. Jan Grootaers calls Philips the "*cheville ouvrière*" (the backbone or linchpin) of the most important conciliar texts. As regards *Lumen gentium*, Grootaers adds that Philips gave himself "body and soul to the success of this schema." See "Le rôle de Mgr. G. Philips a Vatican II," in *Ecclesia a Spiritu Sancto edocta* (Gembloux: J. Duculot, 1970), 343–80, at 353 and 344.

9. Of course, virtually all the theologians at the council had been educated in Thomist philosophy and theology, which had been de rigueur at Catholic universities and seminaries since Leo XIII's encyclical *Aeterni Patris* in 1879. For a bibliography, see Thomas G. Guarino, "Analogy and Vatican II," *Josephinum Journal of Theology* 22 (2015): 44–58.

10. See Gérard Philips, "La Constitution 'Lumen Gentium' au Concile Vatican II," in *Primauté et collégialité: Le dossier de Gérard Philips sur la Nota explicativa praevia*, ed. Jan Grootaers (Leuven: Leuven University Press, 1986), 190. This article by Philips is a French translation of an essay that appeared in the Dutch journal *De Maand* in February 1965, just three months after *Lumen gentium* was formally promulgated by Paul VI.

at a time of obvious crisis. There was no need for a Barmen-like declaration, a unique *status confessionis*. Because of this historical context, the council did not need to stress Catholicism's difference from and discontinuity with other churches, other religious faiths, or other points of view. That kind of dialectical approach was foreign to it, having been discouraged by John XXIII from the outset. At every turn, Vatican II sought to emphasize the significant points of contact between Catholicism and others. Analogical reasoning was crucial to this task.

Those who emphasize the semantic shift that took place at the council are entirely right. Vatican II did not use words of exclusion and alienation; unlike every other ecumenical council from Nicaea onward, it offered no condemnatory anathemas. However, this linguistic shift must be understood within the *theological and philosophical horizon* that undergirds the new lexicon. The accent on participation and analogy gave birth to the language of reconciliation. Without losing Catholic exceptionalism—which was vigorously expressed throughout the council—the conciliar accent was placed on Catholicism's *similarity* with other Christian faiths, with other religions, and with all men and women seeking truth and justice. It would have been easy for the council simply to condemn everything outside Catholicism as tainted by error. Vatican II took the more difficult but far more fruitful path of insisting on Catholicism's uniqueness even while acknowledging the strong links of truth and faith that bind Catholics to all others. In this sense, Vatican II is rightly called, to invoke Thomas Kuhn's famous phrase, a "paradigm change."

To what extent the council reoriented the Catholic Church—and to what extent this caused discontinuity with the prior tradition—will be the subject of the following chapters.

Doctrinal Statements

In this brief section, I wish to say something about formal church teaching that will illustrate how "change" can indicate either continuity or discontinuity, *profectus* or *permutatio*.

In the first place, it is important to recognize that all doctrinal statements are, by necessity, one-sided formulations. When an ecumenical council teaches about an issue, it normally addresses only one aspect of the faith, often an aspect that has been misunderstood. Consequently, conciliar statements should not be expected to be fully rounded expositions of Christian truth. In fact, the church's *reaction* to an error may be so defensive and polemical that the rebuttal itself becomes one-sided and unilateral. Further, the "error" may be exaggerated, simply to show where a mistaken tendency might ultimately lead. These considerations are integral to understanding Vatican II, a council that consciously attempts to redress earlier imbalances in Catholic doctrinal teaching.

This "partiality" of ecumenical councils is the basis for Karl Rahner's well-known claim that conciliar formulations are not the *end* of thinking about a theological topic but the *beginning*, since particular formulations will inexorably open up new avenues of thought: "The clearest formulations, the most sanctified formulas, the classic condensations of the centuries-long work of the church in prayer, reflection and struggle concerning God's mysteries: all these derive their life from the fact that they are not end but beginning."[11] Indeed, it is the common teaching of theologians that the Council of Constantinople (381) completed the insights into the Holy Trinity first established by the Council of Nicaea (325), while the Council of Chalcedon (451) plumbed the depths of Christ's person opened by that first ecumenical council. In each case, it was not a matter of contradiction but a matter of further precision, balancing, and supplemental development.

Gérard Philips expressed just this sentiment in an article written at the end of Vatican II's first session in which he reflected on two theological tendencies visible at the council. Describing a theologian of the more moderate type, he states, "[While this theologian] considers all the definitions sanctioned by the church as irreformable, he believes them nonetheless to be capable of a more profound clarity and a more lucid formulation. A new council is able to perfect the definition of a preceding council by, for example, showing how a solemn but partial teaching is integrated into the ensemble of a complex doctrine. History demonstrates this point."[12] Toward the end of the council, Philips was of the exact same mind: "Councils are not able to contradict each other. But every council is able to complete the preceding one and, by the precisions that it [a new council] brings, it is able to contribute to a more balanced exposition."[13]

Philips's and Rahner's assertions are echoed by Congar, who claims that although no council is authorized to relativize the truth, a later council

11. Rahner's original essay, "Chalkedon—Ende oder Anfang?," was redacted as "Current Problems in Christology," in *God, Christ, Mary, and Grace*, vol. 1 of *Theological Investigations*, trans. Cornelius Ernst (Baltimore: Helicon, 1969), 149–200, at 149.

12. Gérard Philips, "Deux tendances dans la théologie contemporaine," *Nouvelle revue théologique* 85 (March 1963): 229.

13. Philips, "La Constitution," 191.

can always perfect and redress the teaching of an earlier one.[14] This point was recently reiterated by still another Vatican II *peritus* (expert), Benedict XVI, who stated that the First Vatican Council (1869–70) "remained somewhat one-sided [and] incomplete"; the church was "left with a fragment" that needed to be brought to fulfillment.[15] These comments—from four theologians who served as *periti* at Vatican II (and all on the pivotal Theological Commission)—help us understand that no ecumenical council lies beyond further development.

Second, even though conciliar statements can be one-sided and unilateral, such statements truly mediate states of affairs. In other words, Christian doctrine, with all the necessary qualifications, is representational and ostensive in kind, telling us something about God's own life. Foundational ecclesial doctrines are not provisional and contingent statements whose fundamental meanings are malleable and reversible. If such provisionality and contingency were attributable to the dogmatic landmarks of the Christian tradition, then Vincent's pernicious *permutatio fidei* would be unavoidable.

To illustrate this point, let us briefly recall Karl Rahner's decisive and crucial debate with Hans Küng in the 1970s. In that controversial exchange, Rahner argued that solemn conciliar and papal definitions are often one-sided and subject to further correction and balancing. But he could not accept Küng's position that such solemn judgments could also be fundamentally erroneous. For Rahner (and, in fact, for the entire Christian tradition), foundational ecclesial teaching—while often in need of corrective balance—necessarily mediates states of affairs, allowing for cognitive penetration into God's own life.[16] For insisting on the enduring truthfulness of these teachings, Rahner was labeled "the last great (and stimulating) Neo-scholastic."[17] But there is nothing particularly scholastic in Rahner's position. It is simply the common faith of Catholicism (and much of Protestantism) that solemnly taught doctrinal statements mediate the truth about God. If Küng's position were correct—with all doctrinal formulas essentially provisional and pragmatic in nature—then Christianity itself would become deeply historicized.

---

14. Congar, "La théologie au Concile," 43.

15. Benedict XVI, speech of February 14, 2013, http://w2.vatican.va/content/benedict -xvi/en/speeches/2013/february/documents/hf_ben-xvi_spe_20130214_clero-roma.html.

16. For a useful summary of this debate, see Carl Peter, "A Rahner-Küng Debate and Ecumenical Possibilities," in *Teaching Authority and Infallibility in the Church*, ed. Paul C. Empie, T. Austin Murphy, and Joseph A. Burgess (Minneapolis: Augsburg, 1978), 159–68.

17. Hans Küng, *Theology for the Third Millennium* (New York: Doubleday, 1988), 188.

But would such a relativized faith be able to defend and sustain Christ's claim that he is the way, the truth, and the life?[18]

For Catholicism, as we shall see below, contingent church teaching does exist—and there are times when reversals of it may indeed be sanctioned. But such teaching must be carefully distinguished from the solemn landmarks that perdure in their essential meaning both transtemporally and transculturally. One cannot, under the guise of reinterpretation, empty a formal teaching of its meaning. Such an action would necessarily call into question the cognitive yield of Christian doctrine and, in turn, the reliability of divine revelation itself.

Finally, it should be noted that all doctrinal statements are inevitably encased in concepts marked by sociocultural specificity. Christian truth does not exist in an ahistorical bubble, entirely removed from the palpable effects of history, society, and culture. One never "has" the truth apart from the conceptual conventions of a given age. This means that doctrine is always subject—to some extent—to historical and cultural limitations. As we saw in the previous chapter, much Catholic theology since the mid-twentieth century has sought to give due consideration to the contingent dimensions of doctrinal formulations, even while defending the truth that is actually mediated by them.

As we have already seen, the term *transubstantiation* is not essential when discussing Christ's eucharistic presence. Other terms, not reliant on a philosophy of substance and accident, can equally mediate divine revelation. Rahner offers another example: For a long time in Catholicism the doctrine of original sin was linked with monogenism. Although monogenism has now been surpassed as an explanatory model, the church's teaching on original sin remains. We may conclude that an element of provisionality may be attached to the *formulation* even of landmark Christian doctrines. However, as Rahner insists, "this is not, of course, to maintain that the assertion does not remain the same."[19] He later adds that one "must . . . make simultaneously clear that the sameness of the dogma in the old sense is assured and the effort to do this must not be regarded in principle as dubious, as a feeble and

18. I have argued at length for the claim that, despite the overarching horizon of historicity, "states of affairs" are properly and actually mediated by doctrinal statements. History and Christian doctrine cannot be placed at antipodes. See Guarino, *Foundations of Systematic Theology*, 107–39.

19. Karl Rahner, "Considerations on the Development of Doctrine," in *Theological Investigations*, vol. 4, trans. Kevin Smyth (Baltimore: Helicon, 1966), 55. For more on Rahner's understanding of the "amalgam," see Guarino, *Foundations of Systematic Theology*, 192–93.

cowardly compromise."[20] What is emphasized here, of course, is the material continuity and identity of Christian truth even through changes in forms and conceptual models. The sociocultural specificity of a formulation does not vitiate the truth of the doctrinal statement. But it does call for sophistication in discerning precisely what that truth is.[21]

Content and Context

Let us return to the major question animating this study: Was Vatican II a proper development or a pernicious corruption of the prior doctrinal tradition? We remember that Vincent of Lérins was convinced that change inevitably occurs in the church of Jesus Christ. Crucially important is Vincent's distinction, discussed earlier, between two kinds of change, *profectus* and *permutatio*. The former represents legitimate growth, the homogeneous extension of the prior tradition. The latter, on the contrary, represents the reversal of some fundamental teaching, a reversal that constitutes a distortion of the Christian faith. One of Vincent's concerns is that in any *legitimate* change, fundamental identity must be retained. Thus, he says that although growth certainly occurs over time, this expansion must preserve earlier teaching *eodem sensu eademque sententia*.

One way that Vincent allows for authentic change is through a distinction between context and content. In a famous passage in the *Commonitorium*, the theologian of Lérins states, "The same things you were taught, teach, so that when you speak newly you do not say new things" (*dicas nove non dicas nova*; 22.7). Vincent is thinking of the signature terms *homoousios* and *Theotokos*. With these nonbiblical words, the church indeed spoke newly, but traditional affirmations were retained. This is why Vincent is wedded to biological images when he speaks of proper development: a child becoming an adult and a seed becoming a plant. In both instances growth clearly occurs, but it is expansion that is creative *and* preservative, maintaining the type or essence of the original.

Vincent's distinction received new life in a controversy that occurred

20. Karl Rahner, "Yesterday's History of Dogma and Theology for Tomorrow," in *Theological Investigations*, vol. 18, trans. Edward Quinn (New York: Crossroad, 1983), 13.

21. For an extended analysis of Rahner's (and other theologians') attempt to balance historicity and doctrine, see Thomas G. Guarino, *Revelation and Truth* (Scranton, PA: University of Scranton Press, 1993), 38–56. Along very similar lines, see Francis A. Sullivan, *Creative Fidelity* (New York: Paulist Press, 1996), 134–35.

not long before Vatican II began. In the previous chapter, we discussed the thought of Henri Bouillard, who distinguished between doctrinal *affirmations* and the conceptual *representations* in which they are expressed. For example, Christianity teaches that grace is a free gift of God that renders men and women righteous and empowers them to live holy lives. But this crucial affirmation has been expressed differently by John's Gospel, by Augustine, by Aquinas, and so on. With this distinction, Bouillard was trying to reconcile the immutable truth of divine revelation with historical change. He strongly defends the material continuity of the faith—there is substantial meaning-invariance through the centuries—while recognizing that the concepts (representations) used to express this meaning vary according to time, place, and circumstance. This very distinction—between the church's faith and its mode of expression—was appropriated by John XXIII in his famous address opening Vatican II on October 11, 1962. In this speech, the pope states that the *depositum fidei* (2 Tim. 1:14) is one thing and the *modus quo veritates enuntiantur* (the manner in which these truths are expressed) is another.[22] As previously mentioned, the decisive importance of the *depositum/ modus* distinction was noted by Congar, who stated that the entire meaning of Vatican II could be summed up in these few words.[23] John XXIII, recognizing that Catholicism was experiencing a crisis of form, wished to recast the Catholic faith in a language that would be understandable and appealing to men and women of the twentieth century and that would encourage the unity of all Christians.

Despite the importance of this crucial distinction, it is downplayed by some conciliar commentators. John O'Malley, for example, who carefully analyzes Vatican II's language, barely discusses it. Why is this the case? One reason, I suspect, is the fear that this distinction is a bit naive, failing to take account of the necessary intermingling of form and content. O'Malley insists that "style" cannot be understood as mere ornament: "The 'what' of speech and the 'how' of speech are inseparable."[24] And again: "The style of Vatican II . . . influenced content, just as the content . . . influenced the form. *Verba* and *res*—style and message—are inextri-

22. *Acta apostolicae sedis* 54 (1962): 786–96, at 792. This same distinction, along with the tagline *eodem sensu eademque sententia*, was repeated in the instructions for the revision of conciliar schemas distributed toward the end of the first session. This further indicates the importance attached to it. See *AS* I/1, 96–97 (December 6, 1962).

23. Yves Congar, *A History of Theology*, trans. Hunter Guthrie (Garden City, NY: Doubleday, 1968), 18–19. This distinction was also cited by the council itself in *Gaudium et spes* §62.

24. O'Malley, *What Happened*, 306.

cable in discourse."[25] Emphasizing the pope's critical distinction might weaken O'Malley's point about the inextricable relationship between form and content.

But even if one wishes, legitimately, to stress the interpenetration of content and context, surely it cannot be denied that such a distinction is possible, as has been consistently defended from Vincent's *noviter non nova* down through Pope John's (and *Gaudium et spes*'s) conciliar teaching. In fact, this distinction goes to the heart of Vatican II's intentions—to speak the ancient Christian faith in an intelligible, ecumenical, and pastoral way. It is precisely because of its importance that Congar singled out this distinction as a cornerstone of Vatican II's thought. Similarly crucial is the claim that the truths that are newly formulated must be expressed *eodem sensu eademque sententia*—according to the same meaning and the same judgment. With this phrase, Vincent (who coined it) and John XXIII and Vatican II (who adopted it) insisted that any growth or development must be in material continuity with the past.[26] Contemporary formulations, while always bringing new aspects of the Christian faith to light, cannot be excuses for distorting doctrine. Even within conceptual change, the stability of meaning persists. It is always a matter of homogeneous progress, *profectus non permutatio*.

One should be wary, then, of overemphasizing the interpenetration of context and content. To do so renders John XXIII's firm hope for the council—communicating the gospel of Jesus Christ in ways suitable for the times—illusory.[27] Several of the council fathers appealed to Pope John's crucial distinction in their speeches.[28] Many theologians, as well, recog-

---

25. O'Malley, "Trent and Vatican II," 310.

26. It has been noted that the Vincentian phrase *eodem sensu eademque sententia* was not in the original Italian but was in John XXIII's Latin text. For details, see Giuseppe Alberigo and Alberto Melloni, "L'allocuzione *Gaudet Mater Ecclesia* di Giovanni XXIII," in *Fede tradizione profezia: Studi su Giovanni XXIII e sul Vaticano II*, ed. Giuseppe Alberigo et al. (Brescia: Paideia, 1984), 187–283.

27. On the other hand, various theologians have expressed reservations about an *unsophisticated* invocation of the context/content distinction. Foremost among these is Karl Rahner, who himself utilizes the distinction, although with proper caution. I examine Rahner on this point in *Revelation and Truth*, 49–55. For my responses to other reservations, see *Revelation and Truth*, 34–37, and *Foundations of Systematic Theology*, 206n62. Sensible on this matter are the reflections of the Romanian Orthodox theologian Dumitru Stăniloae in "The Orthodox Concept of Tradition and the Development of Doctrine," *Sobernost* 5 (1969): 652–62.

28. For example, see Cardinal Alfrink, *AS* I/3, 44 (November 14, 1962); see also Cardinal Bea, *AS* I/3, 709–12 (November 14, 1962), and Archbishop Caggiano, *AS* I/3, 73 (November 16, 1962).

nized that to renew the Catholic Church, the council had to overcome the abstruse language of scholasticism while reemphasizing the Bible and the early Christian tradition. Gérard Philips, perhaps the most influential theologian at Vatican II because of his position on the Theological Commission, formulated one objection motivating John XXIII: scholasticism, with its reliance on Aristotle, "uses categories of thought and forms of language to which our contemporaries have lost the key. One may regret this loss of intelligibility . . . but it is a fact."[29] While scholastic categories are no longer helpful, the Christian truth can be expressed without that particular *Denkstil*. The contemporary theologian, Philips insists, "is far from wishing to relativize revealed truth, which he respects unconditionally. But he is convinced that his own view of the truth is not identified, in all its forms, with truth itself. He knows too well that our intellectual categories aim at this truth and really attain it, without empowering the theologian to give an adequate expression."[30]

In other words, the mysteries of faith may be expressed in new forms and concepts without emptying them of their fundamental meaning. Philips makes clear that what must be rejected at Vatican II is an arid and bloodless conceptualism. The council must adopt a way of speaking that is living and concrete, rooted in the Bible, even while clearly presenting Christian doctrine: "[One] cannot mindlessly sacrifice doctrinal food, but it must be rendered digestible and presented without diminution if one wishes that the present generation . . . will receive solid teaching which alone is capable of nourishing life—that is to say, nourishing the spirit and the heart and one's behavior."[31]

A final point on this topic: any novel "form" (concept or representation) will necessarily result in some new insight, even when it maintains material continuity with the past. Using a new form to express an aspect of the Christian faith will necessarily result in some further development, as it will cast fresh light on aspects of doctrine that may have become obscured over time. Bouillard made this point about the term *transubstantiation*. While this word throws into sharp relief the real presence of Christ in the Eucharist, it does not speak to the profound relationship between the Eucharist and the church. Speaking of the eucharistic presence of Jesus in terms other than transubstantiation (a word dating from the twelfth century)

---

29. Philips, "Deux tendances," 235.
30. Philips, "Deux tendances," 229.
31. Philips, "Deux tendances," 235.

might well throw youthful light on other dimensions of this sacramental mystery. John XXIII's distinction between *depositum* and *modus*, then, while protecting the material continuity of the faith, inevitably results in homogeneous development as well.

My intention is to put this Johannine distinction at the service of the larger questions of this volume: Did Vatican II maintain Vincent's *idem sensus*? Did it protect fundamental teachings with its new formulations? In this regard, we remember that Benedict XVI, in his crucial Christmas address of 2005, cited the *depositum/modus* distinction as well as the phrase *in eodem sensu*. But the pope also spoke of Vatican II's "continuity and discontinuity at different levels." How are these comments reconciled?

Pluralism

This distinction between content and context—with the perduring truth of the Christian faith now expressed in a variety of formulations—inexorably raises the issue of theological pluralism. And pluralism, in turn, raises the issue of continuity over time. The pertinent questions are these: When pluralism reigns, how is the material continuity of the faith preserved throughout generations and cultures? Are not identity and plurality at antipodes? Does not pluralism inevitably lead to developments that are distortive (*in alieno sensu*) of the prior tradition?

We have already discussed Bouillard's distinction between enduring affirmations and mutable representations. We have discussed as well John XXIII's contrast between the stable deposit of faith and changeable modes of expression. Both of these men sanctioned pluralism—but pluralism of a certain type and shape. The same is true for the council itself. On the one hand, the Dogmatic Constitution on Divine Revelation, *Dei verbum*, calls for the material continuity of Christian doctrine over time: "God has seen to it that what He revealed for the salvation of all nations would abide *perpetually* in its *full integrity* and be handed on to *all generations*" (*DV* §7; emphasis added). The stress here is clearly on the identity of the Christian faith through epochs and cultures. On the other hand, the council places a decided accent on legitimate pluralism, as evidenced by the discussions in St. Peter's itself. Early in the council, a document dealing with ecumenism, titled *Ut unum sint*, was proposed by the Commission for Eastern Churches. The document was quite advanced, arguing for *unitas in diversitate* (unity in diversity) and for distinguishing *catholica veritas a variis systematibus* (catholic truth from various systems of thought).[32] Although this schema was ultimately conflated with *De oecumenismo*—the Decree on Ecumenism prepared by the Secretariat for Christian Unity—it evoked several important speeches. Elias Zoghby, patriarchal vicar of the Egyptian Melchites, spoke of the substantially identical doctrine that exists in both East and West, although the same faith is differently expressed.[33] Cardinal Bea, president of the SCU, explicitly recalled John XXIII's opening speech, saying that the schema fulfilled the pope's wish for distinguishing between doctrine and the way of proposing it, *eodem tamen sensu atque eadem sententia.*[34] And Maximos IV Saigh, the Melchite patriarch of Antioch, insisted on the need to distinguish "apostolicity" from "Latinity."[35] In these episcopal speeches, one detects a call for authentic pluralism within an overarching unity.

As noted, *Ut unum sint* was ultimately conflated with the Decree on Ecumenism. In this latter document one reads, "But let all, according to the gifts they have received, enjoy a *proper freedom* (*debita libertas*) in their various forms of spiritual life and discipline, in their different liturgical rites, and *even in the theological elaborations of revealed truth.*"[36] The same decree says, "In the study of revelation, East and West have followed different methods, and have developed their understanding and confession of God's truth differently. It is hardly surprising, then, if from time to time one tradition has come nearer to a full appreciation of some aspects of a mystery of revelation than the other, or has expressed it to better advantage. In such cases, these various theological expressions are to be often considered as mutually complementary rather than contradictory" (§17).

Several other speeches ardently encouraged this conciliar accent on legitimate pluralism. On November 19, 1963, commenting on the draft of *De oecumenismo*, Leon Elchinger, coadjutor bishop of Strasbourg, deplored the emphasis on uniformity in the Catholic Church. He argued that the "separated brethren" have a right—not to differences in divine revelation—but to differences in theological expression and in all rites and prayers promoting

---

32. *AS* I/3, 528–45, nos. 8 and 21. This schema was discussed on the council floor on November 26–30, 1962.

33. *AS* I/3, 641.

34. *AS* I/3, 709–12.

35. *AS* I/3, 617.

36. *UR* §4; emphasis added. It is worth noting that one *modus* (or amendment) called for diversity "even in the theological elaborations of revealed truth" to be deleted from the decree. The SCU responded that the theological freedom affirmed is not unlimited but is a proper freedom (*debita libertas*). See *AS* III/7, 46.

the glory of God. Anticipating the charge that this will lead to relativism, Elchinger states that perhaps it will lead to a relativism of words, but not to a relativism regarding revelation itself.[37]

A few days later, Lorenz Jaeger, archbishop of Paderborn, argued that— in accord with John XXIII's *depositum/modus* distinction—the Decree on Ecumenism rightly avoids scholastic language since such terminology is inappropriate in ecumenical matters. As the pope himself affirmed, the *punctum saliens* (primary point) of the entire council involved retaining the substance of the faith (*substantia traditionalis doctrinae*) while finding ways of expressing it that are consonant with the times.[38] From the written comments on the draft, one may single out the observation of Archbishop Joseph Floribert Cornelis of Elisabethville (now Lubumbashi). Writing in the name of several Congolese bishops, he states that diversity is very important for the African church. The diversity that the new churches bring to the church universal is a sign of the richness of Jesus Christ.[39]

Clearly, many bishops hoped that the Catholic Church would move beyond the conceptual monism of neo-scholasticism so as to reinvigorate the church's preaching and to present the Catholic tradition in an ecumenically sensitive manner. An authentic pluralism could propel Catholicism to the forefront of the ecumenical movement. In fact, this conciliar accent on legitimate plurality allowed Catholics to recognize many of the formulations of Orthodox and Protestant Christians as authentic expressions of the Christian faith (and vice versa).[40]

The issue pluralism raises is always the same: How can there exist a variety of new expressions and formulations while maintaining the enduring truth (*idem sensus*) of divine revelation? One of the lasting fruits of Vatican II is its insistence that one need not be a scholastic—armed with a specific conceptual arsenal—in order to be a faithful Christian. The truth of revelation is dependent on neither conceptual nor cultural univocity. As the SCU stated in its *relatio* (explanation) when presenting the reworked draft of *De oecumenismo* in 1964: the decree sanctions legitimate diversity, but this pluralism is undertaken "*firma semper manente substantia ipsius*

---

37. *AS* II/5, 562–66.

38. *AS* II/5, 760.

39. *AS* II/6, 106.

40. One of the conciliar experts, Henri de Lubac, had long championed the ancient axiom *diversi sed non adversi*—that is, there can be diverse approaches to theological issues without thereby endorsing incommensurable conclusions. See "A propos de la formule: diversi sed non adversi," *Recherches de science religieuse* 40 (1952): 27–40.

veritatis revelatae" (always firmly maintaining the substance of revealed truth itself).[41]

In conclusion, pluralism is certainly sanctioned by Vatican II, but it is a diversity that does not jeopardize the unity of Christian faith and doctrine. This pluralism is always intended to be *in eodem sensu* with the foundational teachings of the prior tradition.

Reversals

If there is one topic that appears to militate against the very notion of the material identity of the Christian faith over time—and, consequently, to cast doubt on Vatican II's claim to be in continuity with the antecedent tradition—it is that of "theological reversals." But along with the topic of "theological notes" (below), the issue of reversals is crucial for understanding the council and the kind of continuity proper to it.

We recall the stinging critique of Vatican II made by the French minister of education, Christian Fouchet, in 1964: the conciliar bishops were "doing a bad job" and "calling everything into question." This critique still lies at the center of the debate. What was true yesterday in Catholicism is no longer true today. Congar brushes off the comment, saying that this reaction is caused by a headline-hungry press (mentioning Henri Fesquet of *Le Monde*). But Fouchet's criticism has lingered long beyond Fesquet's *Le Monde*. And blaming the press seems entirely too facile an answer.[42] Many people believe that the council engaged in significant reversals of the antecedent tradition—reversals so weighty as to call into question the authority of Vatican II itself.

Resistance to reversals is not a mark of retrogressive rigidity; it has a long tradition in the church. Vincent of Lérins, as we have seen, warns that a distinguishing mark of heretics is that they counsel doctrinal reversals: "Condemn what you used to hold and hold what you used to condemn"

41. *AS* III/2, 343. On the kind of pluralism sanctioned by Vatican II, which I have labeled "commensurable pluralism," see Thomas G. Guarino, "*Fides et Ratio*: Theology and Contemporary Pluralism," *Theological Studies* 62 (2001): 675–700.

42. On the other hand, it is instructive to read the comment of Bernard Pawley, the representative to Vatican II of the archbishop of Canterbury. At the outset of the council, Pawley stated, "There is no doubt that there are considerable sections of the press who are out to cause trouble, and if possible, even where no difficulties exist, to invent them maliciously." *Observing Vatican II*, ed. Andrew Chandler and Charlotte Hansen (Cambridge: Cambridge University Press, 2013), 137 (October 15, 1962).

(*Comm.* 9.8). Even more forcefully, Vincent argues that the acceptance of novelties—contrary to established teaching—mocks the faith of our predecessors: "[Novelties], were they accepted, would necessarily defile the faith of the blessed fathers. . . . If they were accepted, then it must be stated that the faithful of all ages, all the saints . . . so many thousands of confessors, so great an army of martyrs . . . almost the entire world incorporated in Christ the Head through the catholic faith for so many centuries, would have erred, would have blasphemed, would not have known what to believe" (24.5). These are forceful testimonies from an early Christian writer who, while warmly endorsing authentic growth, had grave reservations about the reversal of any landmarks of the Christian faith.

But if there were reversals at Vatican II (as indeed there were), these do not ipso facto indicate *permutationes fidei*, corruptions of the faith. Important to remember is that the term *church teaching* is *analogical rather than univocal*. Ecclesial teaching is proposed with varying levels of authority and certitude. Karl Rahner, for example, affirms that the Catholic Church may very well proclaim a dogma, a teaching that is irreformable and calls forth the definitive assent of faith. "But it [the Catholic Church] can also teach in such a way that a theological doctrine is put forward as 'authentic' . . . and yet not as ultimately binding, and thus the question remains open . . . as to whether this teaching may not turn out later to be in need of completion or even to be erroneous."[43] Rahner's point, of course, is that many church teachings are not proposed as definitive. They are proposed, rather, as authentic, "ordinary" teachings promulgated by magisterial authority to guide Christians in their understanding of the gospel. These doctrinal pronouncements should not be understood as irreversible, for they are not issued with the full weight of the church's authority. Catholics owe *obsequium religiosum* (religious assent) to ordinary ecclesial teachings, but, again, such pronouncements are not regarded as irreformable.

Rahner's further comment simply echoes the Catholic theological tradition: "It cannot be denied that such an authentic doctrinal pronouncement not only *can* in principle be erroneous, but in the course of history often *has been* actually erroneous; this is expressly admitted in a pastoral letter of the German episcopate on the magisterium."[44] The 1967 document of the Ger-

---

43. Karl Rahner, "Magisterium and Theology," in *Theological Investigations*, vol. 18, 56–57.

44. Rahner, "Magisterium and Theology," 57. Elsewhere, Rahner states that "the Church's magisterium can err and often has erred in its authentic declarations, and this is

man bishops to which Rahner refers states, "At this point we must soberly discuss a difficult question, which in the case of many Catholics today . . . either menaces their faith or their spontaneous confidence in the doctrinal authority of the Church. We are thinking of the fact that in the exercise of its office, the doctrinal authority of the Church can be subject to error and has in fact erred. The Church has always known that something of the sort was possible. It has stated it in its theology and developed rules for such situations."[45] Along the same lines, the theologian Piet Fransen has said, "The absence of any guarantee of infallibility does not signify that this act of the ordinary magisterium has no authority, but only that this act of authority is not final, it may be corrected or even, with certain limits, be called into question."[46] It is also worth listening to the aforementioned Gérard Philips, who argues that, when considering the teachings of popes, "one ought to keep what is positive and true in their declarations, that is to say, all that cannot be denied. *What is partial and narrow, or perhaps false, ought to be completed, rectified and corrected.*"[47] Philips's comment makes clear that ordinary papal teaching is, at times, in need of significant modification.

Given these considerations, it is reasonable to ask, Did Vatican II reverse earlier church teaching? And if so, how does this affect the claim that the council is Vincentian in kind, exemplifying homogeneous and architectonic progress *in eodem sensu*? Before answering these questions, I again wish to make clear that a reversal of church teaching is distinct from correcting one-sidedness or imbalance. For example, Vatican II placed a strong emphasis on episcopal collegiality, an emphasis that, because of historical and political considerations, was lacking at Vatican I. The more recent council left intact Vatican I's teaching on papal primacy even while supplementing and surrounding the primacy with the authority of the universal episcopacy. This was clearly a matter of "balancing" (and so a homogeneous *profectus fidei*).

But there were also instances of bare reversal at Vatican II. Do these undermine the claim that the council engaged in harmonious development?

obviously possible also in the future." See "Yesterday's History of Dogma and Theology for Tomorrow," 10.

45. See Karl Rahner et al., eds., *Sacramentum Mundi* (New York: Herder and Herder, 1968), 3:356–57. Ladislas Örsy points out that this statement of the German bishops, while never officially published, has been widely quoted. See *The Church: Learning and Teaching* (Wilmington, DE: Michael Glazier, 1987), 98n16.

46. Piet Fransen, "The Authority of the Councils," in *Problems of Authority*, ed. John Todd (Baltimore: Helicon, 1962), 61–62.

47. *Carnets-GP*, 125–26 (August 10, 1964); emphasis added.

Francis Sullivan is correct in stating that Vatican II acted freely with regard to the reformable teaching of the ordinary magisterium. He contrasts, for example, the conciliar Decree on Ecumenism with the encyclical of Pius XI, *Mortalium animos* (1928), and the Declaration on Religious Freedom with the authentic teaching of Leo XIII on the obligation of Catholic rulers to suppress Protestant evangelism.[48] Since we are here concentrating on general principles, comments about these and other reversals will be reserved for chapters 4 and 5.

Such reversals, however, should *not* be construed as betraying the material continuity of Vatican II with the antecedent tradition. Nor should they be thought of by Catholics as calling into question the authority of the church's magisterium. As the German bishops' conference noted, the possibility of reversals has long been accounted for in Catholic theology. At the council itself, the Theological Commission, responding to a question about dissent from magisterial teaching, urged the bishops to "consult the approved theological expositions."[49]

Nonetheless, reversals of authentic teaching were not initially expected at Vatican II. Henri de Lubac, for example, stated that some theologians had hoped that the council would simply repeat and intensify magisterial teaching of the last hundred years and "correct not even a word of this." Little desire to take account of new research, or to face contemporary problems head-on, was evident.[50] De Lubac's observation is confirmed by Joseph Komonchak, who states, "In general, that Commission's texts [those of the Preparatory Theological Commission] were intended to confirm, with the authority of an ecumenical council, the main emphases and condemnations of the ordinary teaching of the modern popes."[51] In fact, the council would turn out quite differently.

48. Francis A. Sullivan, *Magisterium* (New York: Paulist Press, 1983), 157, 209–10. See also Walter Principe, "When 'Authentic' Teachings Change," *Ecumenist* 25 (July/August 1987): 70–73.

49. *AS* III/8, 88, no. 159. Philips treats the case of individual Christians who dissent from the ordinary teaching of the church in *L'Église*, 1:323–24. He notes that the Theological Commission did not wish to enter into a detailed discussion of such cases.

50. Henri de Lubac, *Vatican Council Notebooks*, trans. Andrew Stefanelli and Anne Englund Nash (San Francisco: Ignatius, 2007), 1:93–94 (September 28–29, 1961). See also Jared Wicks, *Investigating Vatican II* (Washington, DC: Catholic University of America Press, 2018), 152.

51. See Joseph A. Komonchak, "Thomism and the Second Vatican Council," in *Continuity and Plurality in Catholic Theology*, ed. Anthony J. Cernera (Fairfield, CT: Sacred Heart University Press, 1998), 53–73, at 58.

The point of this section has been to emphasize that reversals of authentic magisterial teaching are possible *without betraying the material continuity of the faith.* This is, and has been, the settled teaching of the Catholic Church. If ordinary teaching were not reformable, then one would be obliged to hold that every teaching of the papal magisterium is, ipso facto, infallible—a position that has never been held by any theologian or by the magisterium itself. But the fact that there are any reversals at all—and that Vatican II reversed certain aspects of prior authentic teaching—has been, for some, a scandalous and worrisome aspect of the council. Such consternation is a testimony to how deeply ingrained in Catholic consciousness is the idea of the continuity, identity, universality, and perpetuity of doctrinal teaching.

As we shall see, the more conservative (minority) bishops at Vatican II often insisted that the council protect prior ordinary teaching. At times, their apprehensions forced clearer and more precise formulations (for example, on the role of tradition in *Dei verbum*).[52] But the danger, as de Lubac recognized, was that they understood the role of an ecumenical council as simply consecrating papal teaching rather than as reexamining the entire tradition of the church in order to address the dangerous crises confronting the Christian faith. De Lubac's hope was at least partially realized at Vatican II.

One may conclude that a reversal of ordinary magisterial teaching—as occurred in some instances at the council—does not, of itself, jeopardize the claim that Vatican II was in material continuity with the fundamental teachings of the antecedent tradition even while homogeneously developing them. To speak of a reversal of earlier teaching does not ipso facto constitute a *permutatio fidei.*

Masking

In his well-known work *The Structure of Scientific Revolutions*, Thomas Kuhn demonstrates that the textbook tradition in science, eager to establish the discipline's objectivity and credibility, sought to paper over the conceptual struggles (and reversals) that occurred in the history of scientific inquiry. This was done in the interest of showing that scientific discovery was a mat-

---

52. Congar himself acknowledged that the more conservative bishops and theologians on the Theological Commission forced sharper and more precise formulations. Indeed, he wished that such opposition had been stronger in the Secretariat for Christian Unity. See Yves Congar, *My Journal of the Council,* trans. Mary John Ronayne and Mary Cecily Boulding (Collegeville, MN: Liturgical Press, 2012), 727 (February 18, 1965).

ter of linear progress, of proceeding from strength to strength in expanding the boundaries of knowledge.

Kuhn notes that new textbooks are usually rewritten *after* revolutions have occurred. This leads them to disguise "the very existence of the revolutions that produced them." In fact, scientists tend to see their "discipline's past developing linearly toward its present vantage."[53] Kuhn adds that this desire to mute or mask the history of change and struggle within the scientific community results in "a persistent tendency to make the history of science look linear or cumulative," giving the impression that "one by one, in a process often compared to the addition of bricks to a building, scientists have added another fact, concept, law, or theory to the body of information." But, Kuhn states, "that is not the way a science develops."[54] The unhappy result of such "masking" is that the history of theory change is either ignored or glossed over. The impression is given that the "winning" theory or paradigm was the one visible all along to any objective observer of the obvious and "incontrovertible" facts.

The parallels here with the history of theology are clear. Theological manuals, while carefully illuminating the struggles between heresy and orthodoxy, rarely, if ever, show the struggles between different paradigms to succeed one other. As noted earlier, Henri Bouillard's work sought to unmask the history of conceptual change in Catholic theology,[55] arguing that the doctrine of grace as a free gift of God had been variously expressed throughout the ages. The reaction to Bouillard was intense and furious, largely because of a desire to prolong the fiction of conceptual immutability in Catholic thought. One theologian, Reginald Garrigou-Lagrange, claimed that Bouillard and his allies—in their desire for new formulations to express Christian truth—sought to relegate scholasticism to the ranks of a now surpassed Ptolemaic system.[56]

The most significant questions before us are these: Did Vatican II engage in "masking" so as to conceal the changes taking place at the council?

---

53. Thomas S. Kuhn, *The Structure of Scientific Revolutions*, 4th ed. (Chicago: University of Chicago Press, 2012), 137. First edition published 1962.

54. Kuhn, *Structure of Scientific Revolutions*, 138–40.

55. Henri Bouillard, *Conversion et grâce chez S. Thomas d'Aquin: Étude historique* (Paris: Aubier, 1944), 211–24. Among the many controversial points in Bouillard's conclusions was his assertion that "theology is linked to its times, linked to history—at the same time exposed to their risks and so capable of progress" (223).

56. R. Garrigou-Lagrange, "Vérité et immutabilité du dogme," *Angelicum* 24 (1947): 124–39, at 132.

Was it fearful that calling attention to these changes would jeopardize the Catholic emphasis on material continuity and doctrinal identity over time? Of course, the temptation to mask paradigm switches and theory changes is particularly intense in theology given that the content of the discipline is God's self-manifestation, which, ipso facto, is regarded as immutable and eternal (even, for some, in conceptual expression).

In fact, Vatican II did engage in masking. This was not the case, however, with changes in conceptual form and in conciliar style. John XXIII, in his opening speech of October 11, 1962, had laid his theological cards on the table. His distinction between *depositum* and *modus*—and his strong accent on ecumenism—signaled from the very outset of the council that he desired changes in genre and manner of expression. The conciliar documents themselves, however, offer few indications that the council is at times reversing prior *teachings* of the ordinary magisterium.[57] And yet *that* certain authentic teachings of the magisterium were reversed is surely the case. The conciliar hesitancy about such reversals is unsurprising. After all, proper development can only be *in eodem sensu* with the prior dogmatic tradition. Reversals of any kind have the whiff of a *permutatio fidei*, a corruption of the faith. Surely there was concern that openly adverting to changes might cause scandal, casting doubt on the authority, credibility, and reliability of the church's teaching—and even on divine revelation itself. We will have occasion to note several instances of masking in the following chapters.

But masking does not constitute a theological response to the challenge of change. There is no question but that Vatican II executed changes—in genre, in conceptual language, in philosophical approach (from dialectical to analogical), and, to some extent, even in the content of the church's teaching. Some have regarded *any* change in doctrinal content as indicting corruption. But, as I will argue, changes in style, conceptual lexica, and ordinary magisterial teaching do *not* constitute *permutationes fidei*, nor do they betray the material identity and continuity of the Christian faith in the sense defined by Vincent of Lérins and John Henry Newman. In fact, such changes, while not strictly developments, are themselves a legitimate part of the *process* of development.

---

57. For example, John O'Malley rightly states that Vatican II did not criticize earlier papal denunciations of modernity: "Its strategy was to reject them silently, as if they had never happened." "Trent and Vatican II," 312.

Spoils from Egypt

"Spoils from Egypt" is an unusual sounding—but decisive—theological idea. As with all the issues discussed in this chapter, I am not concerned with establishing a full-blown treatise on the subject but with showing the extent to which the topic of "spoils" is important for Vatican II and, particularly, for the question of continuity and discontinuity.[58]

The phrase itself comes from the book of Exodus, referring to the fact that the ancient Israelites carried gold and silver from their Egyptian neighbors as they began their journey to the promised land (Exod. 12:35–36). Several early Christian writers, Origen prominent among them, employed this image as a metaphor: just as the Israelites used gold and silver from the Egyptians to fashion vessels for the worship of God, so Christians could, analogically speaking, take philosophical gold and silver from thinkers like Plato and Plotinus, using these treasures for God's glory.[59] A host of prominent theologians, Basil and Augustine among them, duplicated Origen's employment of the spoils imagery.

Crucial to the idea of spoils is this corollary: while the church makes use of human wisdom, it always subordinates it to, and disciplines it by, the truth of divine revelation. Origen himself issued a strong caution about the taking of spoils: "Rare are those who have taken from Egypt only the useful, and used it for the service of God. There are those who have profited from their Greek studies in order to produce heretical notions and set them up, like the golden calf, in Bethel."[60] Basil similarly counsels that, with regard to pagan learning, Christians should learn from the bees: they extract only honey from the flower, leaving the rest behind.[61]

John Henry Newman reprised the notion of spoils in the nineteenth century, arguing that assimilating new perspectives is an essential part of theological reflection. The Christian "idea," Newman insists, must inevitably absorb other points of view. This is so because "whatever has life is characterized by growth." Indeed, "the idea never was that throve and lasted,

---

58. For a more complete analysis of "spoils," see Guarino, *Foundations of Systematic Theology*, 269–337, and Guarino, "*Philosophia Obscurans*? Six Theses on the Proper Relationship between Theology and Philosophy," *Nova et Vetera* 12 (Spring 2014): 349–94.

59. Origen, "Letter to Gregory," in *The Ante-Nicene Fathers*, vol. 4 (Grand Rapids: Eerdmans, 1956), 393–94.

60. Origen, "Letter to Gregory," 393–94.

61. Basil, "Address to Young People on Reading Greek Literature," in *The Letters*, vol. 4, trans. R. Deferrari and M. McGuire (Cambridge, MA: Harvard University Press, 1934), 365ff.

yet . . . incorporated nothing from external sources."[62] Assimilation is not without dangers, to be sure, but it must be undertaken: "Whatever be the risk of corruption from intercourse with the world around, such a risk must be encountered if a great idea is duly to be understood, and much more if it is to be fully exhibited."[63] To the counterargument that such assimilation could lead to substantial change, altering the nature of Christianity itself, Newman replied, "It is sometimes said that the stream is clearest near the spring." In fact, the stream (or idea) becomes "purer and stronger when its bed has become deep, and broad, and full."[64]

It is again worth mentioning the crucial point that "spoils" must always be disciplined by the gospel. History is instructive here: several early Christian writers assimilated Plato; Aquinas borrowed heavily from Aristotle; and Matteo Ricci took spoils from Confucius. In all of these thinkers, the biblical narrative was always primary. This same approach is found at Vatican II, which undoubtedly affirmed aspects of liberal modernity but without the least dissolution of Christian exceptionalism.

One example of Vatican II's absorption of spoils, discussed at greater length in chapter 5, is the declaration *Dignitatis humanae*, on religious freedom. As Benedict XVI stated in 2006, full and unencumbered religious freedom is one of the "conquests of the Enlightenment."[65] While the theme of religious freedom may be found in early Christian writers and in the subsequent history of Christianity, it was only formally and officially embraced by the Catholic Church at Vatican II. The council's ability to assimilate the authentic achievements of the Enlightenment—a movement that was, in several ways, a reaction *against* the Christian faith—indicated a rare courage and self-confidence. Just as the early church gradually absorbed the insights of the ancient world—a process that took centuries—so Vatican II began the lengthy process of integrating modernity into a more comprehensive Christian vision. Just here Ovid's comment is entirely appropriate: *Fas est doceri ab hoste*. It is right to learn, even from an enemy.

I should also point out that there is a relationship between spoils and

62. John Henry Newman, *An Essay on the Development of Christian Doctrine* (London: Longmans, Green, 1894), 186.

63. Newman, *Essay*, 39–40.

64. Newman, *Essay*, 40.

65. "Address of His Holiness Benedict XVI to the Members of the Roman Curia at the Traditional Exchange of Christmas Greetings," December 22, 2006, http://w2.vatican.va/con tent/benedict-xvi/en/speeches/2006/december/documents/hf_ben_xvi_spe_20061222_curia -romana.html.

ressourcement—an important conciliar theme that will be treated in the following chapter. Both are concerned with change over time. But whereas *ressourcement* is mostly concerned with development by employing resources *internal* to the Christian tradition—the Bible and the teachings of the ancient Christian writers—"spoils" is concerned with utilizing resources *external* to the Christian tradition but nonetheless congruent with it. Henri de Lubac, for example, insisted on utilizing both *ressourcement* and spoils in a proper theological methodology. On the one hand, he spent a good part of his life retrieving the tradition of the early church, particularly the writings of the church fathers. On the other, he claimed that insights could and should be absorbed even from the writings of Nietzsche and Marx: "In the church, the work of assimilation never ceases, and it is never too soon to undertake it!"[66]

Of course, the question remains: Did Vatican II use "spoils from Egypt" to glorify the God of Abraham? Did it uphold the unique person and work of Jesus Christ? Or did it bend its knee to the world, building the golden calf at Bethel? Did the council's change of rhetorical tone—from dialectical and condemnatory to analogical and conciliatory—lead to a certain flabbiness with regard to Christian faith and doctrine, an unhealthy desire to smooth over the sharp edges of Jesus Christ and the gospel so as to stress the fundamental similarity of all men and women? To what extent was Vatican II successful, given the employment of new spoils, in homogeneous development *in eodem sensu*?

Theological Notes

The topic of theological notes or qualifications is a massive one—and one on which reflection is much needed today.[67] As with the other sections in this chapter, we are primarily concerned with studying this issue in relation to Vatican II. How can the subject of theological notes help us to elucidate the

66. Henri de Lubac, *The Drama of Atheist Humanism*, trans. E. Riley (London: Sheed and Ward, 1949), vi. Like Origen, de Lubac thought spoils could be misused. He came to deplore the fact that, for some postconciliar theologians, the church "must no longer pretend to interpret the world to us in terms of the Christian faith." Henri de Lubac, *A Brief Catechesis on Nature and Grace*, trans. Richard Arnandez (San Francisco: Ignatius, 1984), 257.

67. Extended treatments of this topic may be found in the well-known books of Francis A. Sullivan, *Magisterium* and *Creative Fidelity*. A succinct summary of "qualifications" is provided by Gavin D'Costa, *Vatican II: Catholic Doctrines on Jews and Muslims* (Oxford: Oxford University Press, 2014), 12–15.

"moves" made within the conciliar documents? Important here is a point noted earlier: the term *church teaching* is analogical, not univocal. The theme of theological qualifications makes that point with crystal clarity.

One question often asked about the council is this: Are its teachings binding on all Catholics? The answer, of course, is yes. Even though Vatican II did not issue any dogmatic definitions, the council described its own teaching as authoritatively binding. On November 16, 1964, just prior to the final votes on *Lumen gentium*, the question arose as to the exact "note" to be assigned to the dogmatic constitution. This was a crucial question, for the gathered bishops wanted to know the precise weight of the document they would be voting on. Was it a dogmatic definition (as at Vatican I)? In response, the general secretary of the council, Pericle Felici, made this announcement:

> The Theological Commission has given the following response to the *modi* [comments and questions] that have been submitted with reference to chapter three of the schema *de Ecclesia*:
>
> > "As is self-evident, the council's text must always be interpreted in accordance with the general rules that are known to all."
>
> The Theological Commission then makes reference to its Declaration of March 6, 1964, the text of which we transcribe here:
> > "Taking conciliar custom into consideration and also the pastoral purpose of the present council, this sacred synod defines as binding on the Church in the matter of faith and morals only those things which are openly declared as binding. Other things which the sacred Synod proposes, inasmuch as they are the teaching of the supreme magisterium of the Church, ought to be accepted and embraced by each and every one of Christ's faithful according to the mind of this same sacred Synod—which mind is known either from the subject matter treated or from the manner of speaking, according to the norms of theological interpretation."[68]

In this simple statement, we see the centrality of theological notes in the life of both the church and the council. To the concerns submitted about the precise doctrinal weight of *De ecclesia*, the general secretary repeats the claim of the Commission: only those things are binding which are "openly declared

68. *AS* III/8, 10.

as binding." Nonetheless, as authentic documents of an ecumenical council, the teachings are from "the supreme magisterium of the church" and "ought to be accepted and embraced by each and every one of Christ's faithful."

Reflecting on the achievements of the council, Gérard Philips asked, To what extent did the conciliar decisions bind Catholics? He answers that already on March 6, 1964, the Theological Commission pronounced formally on this subject. After recounting the text above, he concludes, "To date, no point of doctrine has been characterized as infallible and irrevocable." Nevertheless, "all believers ought to accept and adhere to this doctrine according to the meaning which the Synod gives to it. . . . It is a matter, in effect, of the exercise of the most solemn magisterium of the Church by the entire episcopate under the direction of the Pope. *We have, therefore, the highest guarantee of certitude, after a declaration that is strictly infallible.*"[69] A couple of years after the conclusion of the council, Philips returned to the theological weight of the council's teachings: "None of the documents published by Vatican II contains a new 'definition of the faith.'" On the other hand, the council's teaching on the sacramentality and collegiality of the episcopate is taught with an insistence that cannot be considered simply a theological opinion. Indeed, Philips argues that in the conciliar documents Catholics possess the most solid certitude that ecclesial authority is able to furnish, "outside of an absolute and irreformable definition."[70] Attesting to the significance of theological notes, Philips avers, "The Church is able to prescribe different degrees of adhesion [to its teachings], determined according to norms that are known by all theologians."[71]

Paul VI himself, speaking at an audience just one month after Vatican II closed, still had the question of theological qualifications on his mind, again attesting to their importance in Catholic thought:

It is asked: what is the authority, the theological qualification, which the Council wished to attribute to its teaching, knowing that it has avoided giving solemn dogmatic definitions, employing the infallibility of the ecclesiastical magisterium. The response is noted in the conciliar declaration of March 6, 1964, repeated November 16, 1964: Given the pastoral

---

69. Philips, "La Constitution," 196; emphasis added.

70. Philips, *L'Église*, 1:268.

71. Philips, *L'Église*, 1:269. Nonetheless, at the outset of Vatican II, Philips complained about those theologians who "*do not always distinguish between the different levels of certitude* because they are preoccupied above all with placing the truth in a shelter from danger." "Deux tendances," 228; emphasis added.

character of the Council, it avoided any extraordinary statements of dogmas endowed with the note of infallibility, but *it still provided its teaching with the authority of the supreme Ordinary Magisterium which must be accepted with docility* according to the mind of the Council concerning the nature and aims of each document.[72]

By using different titles for its documents, Vatican II intended to indicate varying levels of authority. Certainly, the "constitutions" and particularly the two "dogmatic constitutions" are intended to evoke considerable theological gravity. More crucial is the distinction between the ordinary and the extraordinary teaching of the church. The latter represents those teachings that the church regards as irreversible and perpetual, either revealed or intrinsically connected to divine revelation. Precisely these are the "landmarks" to which Vincent of Lérins refers. On the other hand, the "ordinary" teaching of the church refers to the magisterium's attempt to guide the Christian faithful to a fuller appropriation of the gospel through encyclicals, apostolic letters, curial statements, and so on. To these documents the Catholic faithful owe "religious assent." It should be recognized, however—and certainly was recognized by the theologians at Vatican II—that not all ecclesial teaching is proposed with the same level of authority. While all formal teaching is "authentic," there exist diverse grades of weight and certitude.

Although invoked by Vatican II, theological qualifications died as a living force in Catholic theology immediately after the council. One reason for this was the sense that the notes were somewhat mechanical and artificial, especially since theological manuals were accustomed to assigning a precise qualification to every single doctrinal assertion. The living Christian faith could appear to be trapped in a kind of theological rationalism. Further, the very style of the council—warm, inviting, hortatory—did not seem to encourage these kinds of logic-chopping distinctions, even though the theologians writing the documents made frequent use of them.

In fact, theological qualifications help Catholicism to achieve clarity on the material continuity and perpetuity of Christian doctrine. Which elements of ecclesial teaching are truly landmarks, belonging to the deposit of faith or strictly related to it? Alternatively, which elements of church teaching, while authentic and authoritative, are not, strictly speaking, irreformable or irreversible? For foundational ecclesial teaching, any development

---

72. Paul VI, General Audience of January 12, 1966, http://w2.vatican.va/content/paul-vi /it/audiences/1966/documents/hf_p-vi_aud_19660112.html; emphasis added.

must be *in eodem sensu* with the prior tradition. Homogeneous and organic growth—a true *profectus*—is the only kind of legitimate change. A reversal of this kind of teaching would necessarily result in a distortive *permutatio fidei*.[73] But for ordinary magisterial teaching, this is not the case. Reversals are theoretically possible and were certainly enacted at the council.

Most ecclesial teachings are authentic and ordinary, not binding and irreformable. Soon after Vatican II ended, Philips observed that theologians sometimes subject the council's teachings to maximalist or minimalist interpretations. For the latter, the council did not define any new teaching, and so the bishops intended only some practical directives and disciplinary measures. Philips remarks, "But this is to deny the clarity of the sun." For at Vatican II we find ourselves before the authentic magisterium of the church, exercised by the entire body of bishops, including the supreme pastor. Further, the council clearly settled several disputed questions (e.g., collegiality).[74] On the other hand, Philips remarks that the council did not wish to pronounce the last word on matters since the council fathers were conscious of the progressive character of the knowledge acquired about revealed truth.

In sum, the entire subject of theological notes is crucial for understanding how Vatican II could reverse certain ecclesial teachings and yet remain in material continuity, *eodem sensu eademque sententia*, with the dogmatic tradition of the Catholic Church.

Conclusion

The principles outlined above form the basis for a careful reading of Vatican II and for determining whether the council was in continuity with the prior doctrinal tradition. Vincent of Lérins, in his desire to protect divine revelation, never tired of citing Paul's letter to Timothy, "Guard the deposit, Timothy!" (1 Tim. 6:20). With Vincent, Vatican II sees itself as guarding the fundamental landmarks of the Christian faith even while, in certain instances, developing them. Such development, as we have seen, was countenanced by the Lerinian, who insisted on organic growth over time, as a child becoming an adult and a seed becoming a plant. Even in the early

---

73. Even here, much is left to the free debates of theologians. See, for example, Sullivan's discussion of the differing lists of doctrines thought to have engaged the infallible magisterium of the pope. *Creative Fidelity*, 80–89.

74. Philips, *L'Église*, 2:307.

fifth century, Vincent argued that change inevitably occurs in the church of Christ. But there are two kinds of change, *profectus* (advance) and *permutatio* (corruption). While the latter is illegitimate, the former is entirely acceptable as long as it occurs *in eodem sensu* with the prior tradition.

But who determines which change is a *profectus* and which is a *permutatio*? It goes without saying—and was already obvious in Vincent's time— that one man's *profectus* is another's *permutatio*. One person's harmonious development of the gospel is another's distortive deformation of it. Who guards the gospel today? Who is "Timothy" today? Who today ensures that any development is congruent with the Sacred Scriptures and with apostolic tradition? Vincent, deeply versed in the teachings of Nicaea and Ephesus, answered that ecumenical councils are the primary source of such guarding. They can reliably orient the church toward the proper interpretation of the Word of God. Obviously, for Catholicism, Vatican II represents one of the highest and most authoritative "sources" for the correct interpretation of Scripture and for the organic development of church doctrine.[75]

Did the council engage in a true *profectus*, protecting the material continuity of the Christian faith? Or, with its reversals, did it transgress the landmarks of the prior tradition? To help answer these questions, we now proceed to an examination of the most significant "change" words of Vatican II: *development, ressourcement*, and *aggiornamento*. Each of these words is today freely invoked when explaining the changes introduced by the council. But how are these words properly understood?

75. While Vincent was deeply familiar with ecumenical councils, he would have found it difficult to understand an "ecumenical" council that did not involve all orthodox Christians, particularly those of the East. This, needless to add, is the crucial theological problem that Christianity faces today.

CHAPTER 3

Key Words for Change

As we have seen, Vatican II's sixteen documents are written in smooth, accessible prose, but behind each of these conciliar statements lies a world of theological learning. The men who composed the documents were, in the main, excellent theologians, deeply aware of the crucial nuances of the Catholic tradition. But the theological "moves" they make are usually not visible on the surface of the texts. Changes of course and reorientations are barely indicated, save for an occasional footnote. In the present chapter, we will concentrate on three words continually invoked in relation to Vatican II: *development, ressourcement*, and *aggiornamento*. Understanding these words more precisely will aid our examination of the disputed conciliar issues in the following chapters.

John O'Malley states that at Vatican II these three words were synonyms (and often euphemisms) for change.[1] Did the council need "soft" synonyms because of what O'Malley calls the "well-known Catholic allergy" to change?[2] Did these three words mask significant reversals and heterogeneous distortions? And to what extent is the term *development* a proper category for understanding Vatican II? Can this word be legitimately applied

---

1. John O'Malley, *What Happened at Vatican II* (Cambridge, MA: Belknap Press of Harvard University Press, 2006), 299.

2. John O'Malley, "Trent and Vatican II: Two Styles of Church," in *From Trent to Vatican II: Historical and Theological Investigations*, ed. Frederick J. Parrella and Raymond F. Bulman (Oxford: Oxford University Press, 2006), 316. O'Malley also refers to this "Catholic allergy" in "Vatican II: Did Anything Happen?," in *Vatican II: Did Anything Happen?*, ed. David G. Shultenover (New York: Continuum, 2007), 79.

when it is a matter of a bald reversal of prior teaching? Or does invoking development make reversals easier to swallow?

As we have already seen, change itself is not the crucial theological problem. As Vincent of Lérins pointed out in the fifth century, change always takes place in the church of Christ—just as it takes place in nature, with children growing to adults and seeds to full-blown plants. To recall his words from the *Commonitorium*: "But someone will perhaps say: is there no progress of religion in the church of Christ? Certainly there is progress, even exceedingly great progress [*plane et maximus*]. For who is so envious of others and so hateful toward God as to try to prohibit it? Yet, it must be an advance [*profectus*] in the proper sense of the word and not an alteration [*permutatio*] in faith" (23.1–2). The issue, then, is not change but the *kind* of change that occurs: *profectus non permutatio*. John Henry Newman, Vincent's translator into English, makes a similar point: "In a higher world it is otherwise, but here below to live is to change and to be perfect is to have changed often."[3] For Newman, any idea (including the Christian idea) must grow and develop over time in order to realize its potential. But, like Vincent, Newman sanctions only homogeneous, architectonic change (even making his own Vincent's biological examples), not distortive corruptions. In this chapter, I would like to examine the kind of change these three words—*development, ressourcement,* and *aggiornamento*—allow and endorse. Do they protect or betray the material continuity and identity of Christian doctrine over time?

Development

For both Vincent and Newman, development means a progressive and proportional expansion of an idea, with that idea's fundamental nature remaining intact. This is why Vincent was attracted to the aforementioned biological metaphors. The child and the adult, the seed and the plant, share the same foundational identity, although allowing for homogeneous expansion. In chapter 23 of his *Commonitorium*, Vincent uses phrases such as *res amplificetur* (the matter grows within itself) and *dilatetur tempore* (it is expanded with time), indicating the appropriate sense of doctrinal growth. Development, then, should not be taken as a synonym for change *tout court*. Harmonious and organic expansion is the authentic characteristic of any change labeled a "development."

---

3. John Henry Newman, *An Essay on the Development of Christian Doctrine* (London: Longmans, Green, 1894), 40.

Vincent adduces a host of verbs testifying to his notion of the proper development of Christian doctrine: *crescere, proficere, maturescere, florere,* and *enucleare.* But this growing, advancing, ripening, flourishing, and un-rolling must always preserve the fundamental landmarks—the foundational teachings—that the church has previously sanctioned. This is why Vincent, after acknowledging the inevitability of growth, concludes his crucial para-graph with a phrase clarifying authentic development: proper change must be *in eodem sensu eademque sententia* (in accordance with the same meaning and the same judgment) as the prior tradition. As we have seen, this was the very passage cited by John XXIII in his speech opening Vatican II.

O'Malley acknowledges that during the council, development meant, primarily, an unfolding of something already present implicitly or in germ. And both parties at the council (conservative minority and progressive ma-jority) recognized and embraced development as a legitimate and necessary category. The minority objected to development only when invoked, as in the Declaration on Religious Freedom, to justify a change that seemed to con-tradict the direction in which church teaching had been heading.[4] In other words, only when the Vincentian understanding of harmonious growth was jeopardized did the council become agitated and disputatious.

As we saw in chapter 1, John Courtney Murray, a significant theologian at Vatican II, speaks of development as *the* crucial issue for understanding the council correctly. As he says in his commentary on *Dignitatis humanae,* "It [the Declaration on Religious Freedom] was, of course, the most contro-versial document of the whole council, largely because it raised with sharp emphasis *the issue that lay continually below the surface of all the conciliar debates—the issue of the development of doctrine.*"[5] Murray's point is that the Second Vatican Council enacted changes, and each change called forth the same questions: Is this document homogeneous with the prior tradition? Is it a matter of organic development or of a transformation into something entirely different (*aliquid ex alio in aliud*)? Vatican II's controversial docu-ment on religious freedom will be examined in chapter 5. Here it is essential to recall two points. First, for Vincent as for Newman—and so for two major writers on doctrinal growth—the word *development* is legitimate only when it is a matter of advance and expansion *in eodem sensu.* For these theolo-gians, any "development" must retain earlier meanings while proportionally

4. O'Malley, *What Happened,* 300.

5. John Courtney Murray, "Religious Freedom," in *The Documents of Vatican II,* ed. Walter M. Abbott (New York: Herder and Herder, 1966), 673; emphasis added.

expanding them; the word cannot be used to describe a reversal of prior teaching. Second, reversals, although courting the danger of *permutationes fidei*, are theologically possible, but such reversals should be carefully distinguished from developments properly so called.

Vatican II's teachings include both developments and reversals. And the distinction between those two types of change remains foundational when evaluating the council's achievements. As will be argued in the following chapters, reversals of *ordinary ecclesial teaching*—which must be distinguished from reversals of fundamental landmarks—can be understood as part of the *process* of doctrinal development, even if these reversals cannot be called developments themselves. As noted in the previous chapter, not every teaching of the Catholic Church is regarded as irreformable—although, certainly, a transgression of a foundational Christian doctrine would constitute a *permutatio*, a corruption of the faith.

Even with this distinction between change as development and change as reversal, *change* itself was not always a welcome word at Vatican II. O'Malley says that the word was so distasteful that it "stuck in the throat of Paul VI."[6] But a study of the conciliar diaries shows that the pope was deeply involved in the redaction of Vatican II's documents and was well aware that changes were being introduced into church teaching. For example, Paul was deeply concerned about—but ultimately accepted and sanctioned—the strong conciliar accent on episcopal collegiality, a *novum* in the recent life of the Catholic Church.

It would be more accurate to say that Paul VI (with many of the conciliar bishops) was not afraid of change per se, but of changes that called into question the continuity of Christian doctrine. Changes needed to be harmonious advances and proportionate supplements, not distortions of prior teaching. The crucial questions, recognized by Paul himself, were: Which kind of change is being affirmed by Vatican II—development or reversal? And if a reversal, does it touch a doctrinal landmark? These are the questions that go to the core of Vatican II's theological concerns—then and still today.

Ressourcement

Ressourcement is a word consistently invoked in all discussions about Vatican II. It is a word with roots in the Renaissance, which itself counseled *ad*

---

6. O'Malley, *What Happened*, 300.

fontes—back to the sources.[7] At the council, the Christian "sources" from which the participants sought to draw nourishment were, primarily, the Sacred Scriptures and the writings of the church fathers. *Ressourcement* became conciliar shorthand for the desire to broaden Catholicism's reach beyond the scholastic formulations of Thomist inspiration—and to determine whether newer biblical and patristic research could reinvigorate theology, shedding fresh light on contemporary questions.

Gérard Philips, the adjunct secretary of the Theological Commission, offered one understanding of the term: "It would be mistaken to conceive of *'ressourcement'* as the return to a source which has been for a long time abandoned and now finally recovered."[8] Rather, it is a matter of looking at the divine Word of God as it was preached and committed to writing and as it was transmitted in the living tradition of the church from the apostles, through the fathers, the councils, the liturgy, the witness of the Christian people, and the acts of the magisterium. Surprisingly, Philips is insistent that *ressourcement* cannot mean circumventing scholasticism. Scholastic and post-Tridentine thinkers also transmit the Word of God; they extend the chain of theological reflection, and "we are not qualified to skip a single link."[9] Properly understood, *ressourcement* means, Philips argues, taking account of the entire theological tradition of the church.

That *ressourcement* occurred at the council is beyond doubt. But that simple statement misses the truly important question: In its use of the sources of theology—particularly Scripture and the fathers—did Vatican II still preserve the continuity of Christian doctrine? John O'Malley makes a provocative point: "Of the three categories [development, *aggiornamento*, and *ressourcement*], *ressourcement* was the most traditional yet potentially the most radical. It was also the most pervasive at the council."[10] But how was it "potentially the most radical"? To answer that question, let us look at the way some prominent conciliar theologians understood the idea of *ressourcement*.

---

7. Yves Congar cites some of the theological precedents for this word, singling out Erasmus: *"ex fontibus praedicare Christum."* See *True and False Reform in the Church*, trans. Paul Philibert (Collegeville, MN: Liturgical Press, 2011), 39n35.

8. Gérard Philips, *L'Église et son mystère au IIe Concile du Vatican: Histoire, texte et commentaire de la Constitution "Lumen Gentium,"* 2 vols. (Paris: Desclée, 1967–68), 2:324.

9. Philips, *L'Église*, 2:324.

10. O'Malley, *What Happened*, 301.

Theological Perspectives on *Ressourcement*

A good place to start is Henri de Lubac, who, with his penetrating research into the fathers of the church and the history of biblical interpretation, is often regarded as the *ressourcement* theologian par excellence. As noted in the previous chapter, de Lubac makes a distinction between two kinds of theologians. On the one hand are those who do not wish to "correct even a word" of papal teaching from the last century. Indeed, they wish to intensify it, consecrating these statements with the authority of an ecumenical council. To any new idea they quickly respond, "*Hoc non fundatur in documentis.*" In other words, recent ecclesial teaching is taken as the preeminent guide for all theological investigation. On the other hand are the *ressourcement* theologians (a word de Lubac does not use in this instance) who wish to reread Scripture and the fathers, the Eastern writers, and the entire living tradition of the church and bring these to bear on contemporary problems.[11] De Lubac's simple point is that the ordinary magisterium of the past hundred years cannot be equated with the great theological tradition of Christianity. It is the broader and deeper tradition that must be mined for resources as the church faces new challenges.

De Lubac's point is intensified by Philips, who was destined to play a major role in all the discussions of the Theological Commission. In an article examining the "two theological tendencies" visible at the council's initial session (September–December 1962), Philips states that for some theologians "tradition is confused with opinions current in the last centuries." Indeed, these theologians "consider as novelties ideas belonging to a tradition that is more authentic and more ancient [than the recent one], but which has become somewhat obscured. From there, they easily become suspicious and tutiorist, with their teaching taking on a polemical and negative cast."[12] On the other hand, the *ressourcement* theologian has a different point of view. He is far from wishing to relativize divine revelation, which he respects unconditionally, but he recognizes that no conceptual formulation exhausts divine truth.[13] While the Louvain theologian insists on the urgency of Catholic theology returning to the sources of revelation—the Bible and the church fathers—this cannot mean forgetting the achievements of scholasticism: "To

---

11. Henri de Lubac, *Vatican Council Notebooks*, vol. 1, trans. Andrew Stefanelli and Anne Englund Nash (San Francisco: Ignatius, 2007), 93–94.

12. Gérard Philips, "Deux tendances dans la théologie contemporaine," *Nouvelle revue théologique* 85 (March 1963): 228.

13. Philips, "Deux tendances," 229.

disown scholasticism purely and simply would not happen without loss."[14] Indeed, Philips insists that "*ressourcement* cannot neglect any of the historical configurations of Revelation achieved until today." He even encourages theologians "to study more attentively the brilliant apogee reached by the thirteenth century" and to drop their prejudices "against an important period in the history of dogma."[15] Throughout Philips's work, *ressourcement* has the strong sense of *supplementing*, rather than simply *supplanting*. For Catholicism to advance—to answer new challenges and face new questions— the legitimate insights of Aquinas must now be surrounded, enriched, and enhanced with theological wisdom from the entire Christian tradition.

To illustrate the breadth of sources adduced by the council, Philips cites some statistics. He points out that in the first (withdrawn) schema of *De ecclesia*, Eastern fathers are cited only five times, whereas in the final document (*Lumen gentium*) there are forty-two citations of Greek authors, with Ignatius of Antioch alone cited seventeen times. Among the Latin fathers, Cyprian is cited fourteen times and Augustine twenty-five times. The ancient creeds are cited seventeen times, and there are twenty-nine extracts from earlier ecumenical councils. A quick glance at chapter 8 (on Mary, the Mother of God) will show that the council warmly recommends careful study of the Bible, the fathers, the doctors of the church, and the liturgy. In all of this, Philips contends, one sees the profound conciliar accent on *ressourcement*.[16]

Finally, let us add the insights of Yves Congar, much of whose theological work was dedicated to a recovery of the Christian tradition beyond recent papal and magisterial teaching. Illustrating the "dangers" of *ressourcement*, Congar relates an encounter he had with the redoubtable Cardinal Ottaviani (president of Vatican II's Theological Commission) during the first session. Ottaviani rebuked Congar for his negative assessment of the original schemas. Reflecting on the incident, Congar concludes, "My work displeases them [the curia] because they realize very well that its whole aim is to bring back into circulation certain ideas, certain things, that they have been endeavoring to shut out for four hundred years."[17]

---

14. Philips, "Deux tendances," 235.

15. Philips, *L'Église*, 2:325. At just this point, while reading a theologian who shaped several of Vatican II's most significant documents, it is useful to recall Congar's remark that St. Thomas's thought structured the dogmatic texts at Vatican II.

16. Philips, *L'Église*, 2:327–28.

17. Yves Congar, *My Journal of the Council*, trans. Mary John Ronayne and Mary Cecily Boulding (Collegeville, MN: Liturgical Press, 2012), 222 (November 30, 1962).

Congar's marked accent on returning to the church's earlier tradition—on *ressourcement*—is at the center of his most influential volume, *Tradition and Traditions*. Always the ecumenist, Congar carefully examines the phrase *sola Scriptura*, uncovering its roots deep within the life of the church. And he goes to great lengths to show—following in the footsteps of Josef Geiselmann—that the language of "two sources" of revelation (Scripture and tradition) was not to be found in the decrees of the Council of Trent. Indeed, Congar demonstrates that changes to the text of the Tridentine decree allowed for the recovery of a Catholic understanding of "Scripture alone."[18]

Congar was convinced that serious historical research on the wellsprings of Christian doctrine could help Catholicism move forward in many areas, including evangelization: "Many would receive the faith fairly easily if it were offered to them in the form that it receives from its sources (the Bible and early tradition). But they have trouble recognizing the Gospel beneath the historical baggage that hides its living reality and that seems foreign to it."[19] Congar insists that in this return to biblical and patristic sources, "the movement of *ressourcement* has found its true character."[20] But this does not mean that the church should jettison later developments. Sounding much like Philips, Congar argues that *ressourcement* means returning to tradition in its authentic and integral unity. This includes the church's insights "in all the stages of its development," encompassing Scripture, the apostolic and patristic witness, the church's treasury of prayer, and the theological insights of the doctors and spiritual masters. He concludes that "'to go back to the sources' . . . means to rethink the situation in which we find ourselves in the light and in the spirit of everything that the integrity of the tradition teaches us about the meaning of the church."[21]

---

18. See Yves Congar, *Tradition and Traditions*, trans. Michael Naseby and Thomas Rainborough (New York: Macmillan, 1967). For more on Congar and the Catholic understanding of *sola Scriptura*, see Thomas G. Guarino, "Catholic Reflections on the Truth of Sacred Scripture," in *Your Word Is Truth*, ed. Charles Colson and Richard John Neuhaus (Grand Rapids: Eerdmans, 2002), 79-101.

19. Congar, *True and False Reform*, 50.

20. Congar, *True and False Reform*, 295.

21. Congar, *True and False Reform*, 295.

Two Conciliar Uses of *Ressourcement*

Having summarized some prominent conciliar theologians on the meaning of *ressourcement*, we may now ask, How was this idea actually implemented at the council? I think we can speak of two ways in which *ad fontes* was employed at Vatican II—as supplement and as reversal.

In the first place, the council uses "*ressourcement* thinking" to *supplement and enrich* prior Catholic teaching. This is the most extensive use of the idea and can be illustrated by a couple of examples. First, Vatican I had defined the infallibility of the papal magisterium under carefully restricted conditions. Vatican II left the prior council's teaching intact (and, in fact, repeated much of it) but explicitly added the authority of the universal episcopal college, which, together with the pope, may also teach with infallible authority. Thus, the primacy of the Petrine ministry is not called into question by Vatican II, but there is an addition, a supplement to papal authority—the teaching authority of the universal episcopacy when united with the bishop of Rome.

Philips, the draughtsman of *Lumen gentium*, thought that Paul VI had insisted too strenuously on additions to the document so as to confirm the uniqueness of the papal magisterium. The result, as the Louvain professor saw it, was that the dogmatic constitution's emphasis on synodality and collegiality was somewhat muted. Nonetheless, Philips concluded that "the idea of communion is one of the most beautiful restorations that *Lumen gentium* has made to Catholic ecclesiology, which has been for too long stiffened by the idea of law."[22] Collegiality was an ancient idea rooted in the life of the early church and diametrically opposed to the pontifical aloofness that characterized most of the nineteenth century. Precisely in this example one sees *ressourcement* as supplementation at work. The prior doctrinal landmark of Vatican I is maintained by Vatican II, and so its material continuity is never placed in jeopardy. But the later council enhances this doctrine with the restoration of the teaching authority of the universal episcopacy.

A second example of *ressourcement* as supplement may be found in the idea of the priesthood of all the baptized. Vatican II recovered this important scriptural and patristic theme, which itself had received new life and vigor at the hands of Martin Luther and the Reformation. But the council accomplished this recovery without calling into question the uniqueness of the

---

22. See Jan Grootaers, ed., *Primauté et collégialité: Le dossier de Gérard Philips sur la Nota explicativa praevia* (Leuven: Leuven University Press, 1986), 207.

ministerial priesthood, which, Vatican II affirmed, represented a sui generis participation in the one priesthood of Jesus Christ. We shall have more to say about this point in the following chapter. Important here is that, once again, an element of the earlier tradition was recovered by Vatican II—but it was retrieved as a *supplement* to earlier landmarks that were themselves still taught *in eodem sensu*. On this matter, too, there is no sense of reversing or supplanting earlier doctrinal teaching.

In both cases, *ressourcement* is used to develop, expand, and extend church teaching even while preserving earlier ecclesial affirmations. The material continuity of the Catholic doctrine is maintained along with its homogeneous growth and development. As Philips wrote soon after the promulgation of *Lumen gentium* in November 1964, "Each council is able to complete the preceding one, and by the precisions that it brings, contributes to a more balanced approach."[23]

Second, Vatican II occasionally uses "*ressourcement* thinking" to *reverse* the prior ordinary teaching of the church. This should remind us that not all ecclesial teaching rises to the level of dogmatic landmarks; it should remind us as well that "church teaching" is itself an analogical term. One need not find material continuity across generations and cultures on every single doctrinal matter. What are some examples of conciliar reversals attributable to *ressourcement*? One example, mentioned in the previous chapter, is Vatican II's Declaration on Religious Freedom, which, with its emphasis on the sovereign freedom of every person in religious matters, recovered the insights of the early church—and this in opposition to the authentic teaching of Leo XIII and other popes on the obligation of Catholic rulers to suppress Protestant evangelism.[24]

Perhaps a more striking instance of *ressourcement* that resulted in a reversal of ordinary teaching is the insistence of Vatican II that the three *munera* (powers or functions) of teaching, governing, and sanctifying are bestowed on bishops with episcopal ordination. Common teaching prior to the council was that although the power of sanctifying came with ordination, the task of governance was bestowed only by delegation of the Roman pontiff. *Mystici corporis*, for example, a 1943 encyclical of Pius XII, spoke of bishops receiving the ordinary power of jurisdiction "directly from the

---

23. Gérard Philips, "La Constitution 'Lumen Gentium' au Concile Vatican II," in Grootaers, *Primauté et collégialité*, 191.

24. As we shall discuss in chapter 5, *Dignitatis humanae* blends aspects of both *ressourcement* and *aggiornamento*, combining insights from both the early church and liberal modernity.

same Supreme Pontiff" (§42). Vatican II, on the contrary, teaches that such powers are bestowed through episcopal ordination. This is so clearly a reversal of prior teaching that the *Nota praevia explicativa* (an addendum to *Lumen gentium*) coyly adds, "The documents of recent Pontiffs regarding the jurisdiction of bishops must be interpreted in terms of this necessary determination of powers" (§2). On this point, Vatican II "abandons the position of Pius XII *in order to restore a more traditional position*: episcopal consecration confers not simply the power of sanctifying, but also the power of teaching and of governing."[25]

Just here we have a clear example of *ressourcement* leading to a reversal of prior papal teaching. As noted in the previous chapter, Catholic theology does not regard ordinary teaching as intrinsically irreformable or irreversible. Such teaching does not intend to establish incontrovertible dogmatic landmarks; consequently, material identity, continuity, and perpetuity are not characteristics that belong to it *necessarily and essentially*. Such authentic teaching, while received by Catholics with religious respect and submission, is not proferred with the church's full authority, and so a reversal does not constitute a *permutatio fidei* or distortive corruption.[26] If the magisterium of the Catholic Church could never be wrong, then its every utterance would need to be shrouded with the veil of infallibility—a theologically indefensible position. That is why it is important to see the two ways *ressourcement* was employed at Vatican II: as the supplementation and enrichment of prior ecclesial teaching and, at times, as the reversal of ordinary magisterial teaching.

Even though Catholic theology can account for reversals of authentic teaching, the *effect* of these reversals should not be underestimated. Vincent of Lérins tells us that it is heretics who cry out, "Condemn what you used to hold and hold what you used to condemn" (*Comm.* 9.8). And as we have seen, Bossuet's prosecutorial charge (unfair as it is) was that, unlike Catholicism, Protestantism changes and therefore errs. Continuity and material identity are inscribed in the Catholic soul, while change and discontinuity

---

25. Claude Troisfontaines, "À propos de quelques interventions de Paul VI dans l'élaboration de 'Lumen gentium,'" in *Paolo VI e I Problemi Ecclesiologici al Concilio* (Brescia: Istituto Paolo VI, 1989), 97–143, at 126n57; emphasis added. Philips, the principal author of the *Nota praevia*, treats of this reversal in *L'Église*, 1:274–75.

26. Precisely for this reason, Benedict XVI could logically state that Vatican II was not a "rupture" with the prior tradition but a "combination of continuity and discontinuity at different levels." "Address of His Holiness Benedict XVI to the Roman Curia Offering Them His Christmas Greetings," December 22, 2005, http://w2.vatican.va/content/benedict-xvi/en /speeches/2005/december/documents/hf_ben_xvi_spe_20051222_roman-curia.html.

are seen as distinguishing marks of error. It is unsurprising, then, that the council "masked" changes of direction—at least partially out of concern that discontinuities might call into question the reliability of magisterial teaching and, ultimately, the reliability of divine revelation itself.

Aggiornamento

Of the three words discussed in this chapter, *aggiornamento*, "bringing up to date," most clearly implies reform. Development can mean growth absent reform. *Ressourcement* can mean the addition of supplementary perspectives but with little else modified. But "updating," by its very nature, indicates some kind of reform, at the very least in the language of Christian doctrine.

How did Vatican II use the term *aggiornamento*? On November 18, 1965, in the penultimate general session of the council, Paul VI gave a speech about proper and improper ways of understanding *aggiornamento*, making clear that misconstruals of the word were unacceptable. He insisted that with this term John XXIII did not intend the "relativizing" of the Christian faith—understanding the church's dogmas, laws, structures, and traditions in accordance with the spirit of the world. This, the pope insisted, is precisely what *aggiornamento* does *not* mean. How could it be otherwise, he added, given that Christian doctrine was a cornerstone of his predecessor's thought? Properly understood, *aggiornamento* means "wise penetration into the spirit of the council and the faithful application of the conciliar norms."[27]

But let's back up for a moment. At the council's opening, on October 11, 1962, John XXIII delivered his programmatic speech in which, as earlier noted, he made a crucial distinction between the "deposit of faith" and the "way in which the truths [of the faith] are expressed." From this distinction we can conclude that the pope, at the very least, intended an "*aggiornamento* of form"—keeping the traditional content of the faith while expressing it in ways that are understandable to contemporary men and women. This kind of updating, John XXIII thought, was essential if the gospel was to flourish in the modern world. Theologians such as Gérard Philips endorsed John's point of view, insisting that while the church's faith must be presented without diminution, the pressing contemporary question is this: How can the

27. *AS* IV/6, 689–95, at 693.

council nourish contemporary Christians in their heart and their spirit?[28] Surely one task of Vatican II was to communicate the life-giving message of Jesus Christ in the concrete language of the Sacred Scriptures and of the early Christian writers.

But developing fresh "forms" is only one aspect of *aggiornamento*; another part of updating involves the appropriate use of "spoils." In the previous chapter, we discussed the ancient trope of spoils from Egypt, a metaphor with a pedigree extending from Origen through Clement, Basil, Augustine, and throughout the Christian tradition. Prior to Vatican II, Hans Urs von Balthasar pleaded for a renewal of the spoils typology within Catholicism, arguing that the church must imitate Aquinas, who employed wisdom and knowledge from every possible quarter.[29] De Lubac similarly contended that the early church was so confident of the gospel that it was able to use and transform deeply pagan ideas. This fortitude should inspire contemporary Christians as well. In some new theological synthesis, the church should absorb even ideas derived from Nietzsche and Marx, thereby taking every thought captive to Jesus Christ (2 Cor. 10:5).[30]

At Vatican II, *aggiornamento* meant that the church had to come to terms with modernity and the Enlightenment, entering into dialogue with them and taking "spoils" from them—but without, of course, betraying the gospel. In fact, the council's dialogue with modernity can be found throughout the conciliar documents.[31] Even a quick glance at the Declaration on Religious Freedom, for example, will show the profound influence of liberal modernity at Vatican II. But the crucial theological questions are these: *How* was modernity assimilated at the council? *How* did Vatican II establish strong and respectful links with the modern world but without abandoning the truth of the Christian faith? These are the neuralgic concerns that cluster around the word *aggiornamento*.

There are significant risks in taking spoils from the world, as Origen pointed out in the third century. But as Newman subsequently argued, only if the Christian "idea" enters into interchange with the world can the

28. Philips, "Deux tendances," 235.

29. Hans Urs von Balthasar, "On the Tasks of Catholic Philosophy in Our Time," *Communio* 20 (1993; orig., 1946), 147–89.

30. Henri de Lubac, *The Drama of Atheist Humanism*, trans. E. Riley (London: Sheed and Ward, 1949), vi.

31. The same could be said for ecumenism, which was central not simply to *De oecumenismo* but to all the conciliar documents. The Reformation and the Enlightenment were continually on the minds of the bishops and theologians at Vatican II.

idea itself thrive and flourish, breathe and grow. This reciprocity, however, is not an exchange between equals. The church must always *discipline* the world's wisdom with the gospel of Jesus Christ. While the church ingests ideas from every quarter, it must always purify them in the "refiner's fire," stamping on them "a deeper impress of her Master's image."[32] In other words, all spoils need to be measured by the truth found in Scripture and in Christian doctrine.

Improperly understood, then, *aggiornamento* means that the church bends the knee to the world, melting its "thick" faith, life, and doctrine into the claims of liberal modernity, with Christian truth either abandoned or deeply muted. Properly understood, the term describes the church's ongoing and productive assimilative imagination. Christianity absorbs and utilizes every form of thought no matter its provenance, judging each by the standard of the gospel.

So when John O'Malley says that "*aggiornamento* made clear that Catholicism was adaptive to 'the modern world' . . . by appropriating certain cultural assumptions and values,"[33] his statement needs to be carefully qualified. Catholicism did indeed appropriate certain cultural assumptions at Vatican II, but it was a matter of displaying the "common ground" that Catholicism genuinely shared with others. With all seekers after truth and justice, Christianity possesses an analogical similarity—of that there is no doubt. But the council's appropriation of these "assumptions and values" was, in accordance with the church's prior history, measured by the gospel.

We need to be similarly cautious when O'Malley says that *aggiornamento* is an "indicator of a more historical, and therefore more relativized and open-ended, approach to issues and problems."[34] *Relativize* is the very word that Paul VI rejected in his speech of November 18, 1965, when addressing improper understandings of *aggiornamento*. Nonetheless, the words *historical* and *open-ended*, properly understood, may be legitimately invoked. For example, by making a distinction between the *depositum fidei* and the *modus enuntiandi*, John XXIII allowed for the possibility of reconceptualization. A plurality of concepts or "representations" could authentically preserve the fundamental affirmations of the doctrinal tradition. Of course, the *process* of reconceptualization does not expire at a certain date; it represents

---

32. Newman, *Essay*, 382.
33. O'Malley, *What Happened*, 38.
34. O'Malley, "Trent and Vatican II," 316–17.

the church's continuing (and in this sense "open-ended") mission to transmit the Christian faith to every culture and in every epoch.

The issue, then, is not open-ended theological exploration. Such exploration belongs to the church's lifeblood and is essential for its vitality. The crucial point, rather, is that this ongoing process of assimilation, exploration, and reconceptualization must respect the material continuity and identity of the church's dogmatic landmarks. As John XXIII insisted in his opening allocution, change is possible and necessary. But only that change which is *in eodem sensu* with the antecedent tradition. The pope's citation of Vincent of Lérins's *Commonitorium* alludes directly to Vincent's crucial point: change always occurs in the church of Christ, even great change—but it must be *profectus non permutatio fidei.*[35]

O'Malley himself acknowledges the need for caution when he concedes that by saying Vatican II moved from "static to changing" and from "definitive to open-ended," there is need of "a thousand qualifications."[36] Such phrases do indeed require careful *theological* qualification, otherwise they can be badly misunderstood. All ecumenical councils—indeed, all church teaching—must respect the established landmarks of the faith, the fundamental Christian convictions that cannot be transgressed under the guise of some vague open-endedness to the future.

Conclusion

In this chapter we have examined three important "change" words unceasingly invoked in relation to Vatican II: *development, ressourcement*, and *aggiornamento.* These terms indicate modification, transition, and reform. But, properly understood, they do not call into question the material continuity of Christian faith or doctrine.

35. Also to be treated with theological caution is the statement of Roberto de Mattei, who implies that John XXIII's distinction between *depositum* and *modus* opened Pandora's box: "The idea that one could be liberated from traditional forms, without distorting the substance of doctrine, contains in embryo form the 'spirit' of Vatican II." See *Il Concilio Vaticano II: Una storia mai scritta* (Turin: Lindau, 2010), 118. De Mattei does not appear to realize that the distinction between context and content is deeply rooted in the Christian tradition. For several ancient theologians on this issue, see Thomas G. Guarino, *"Philosophia Obscurans?* Six Theses on the Proper Relationship between Theology and Philosophy," *Nova et Vetera* 12 (Spring 2014): 349–94, at 377–82.

36. O'Malley, "Trent and Vatican II," 318.

Vatican II rarely referred to the changes, reorientations, or at times reversals in Catholic teaching called for by the conciliar documents. But it is precisely these changes that continue to make the council a deeply disputed event, even at the distance of more than fifty years. Archbishop Marcel Lefebvre, for example, complained that he did and said exactly the same things before the council as after it. Prior to Vatican II he received plaudits, honors, and the friendship of popes, whereas in the postconciliar period he "finds himself suspended *a divinis*, almost considered a schismatic, almost excommunicated as an enemy of the Church."[37] How to explain Lefebvre's complaint?

One response is to invoke the famous work of Thomas Kuhn, who argued that when a scientific paradigm significantly changes, the scientist now works "in a different world."[38] After Vatican II, Lefebvre clearly felt that he was now "practicing his craft" in an alternative universe. Why? One reason, discussed briefly in the previous chapter, is that Vatican II moved away from a dialectical approach—toward other churches, other religions, and the world itself—to an analogical perspective. While previously Catholicism emphasized its *difference* from all other groups, the council now stressed the *profound similarity* between Catholicism and other entities. A crucial doctrinal principle did not change: before, during, and after Vatican II, there was a strong accent on the uniqueness of Catholic Christianity—in the Catholic Church one finds the fullness of God's revelation. But instead of seeing everything outside of Catholicism as thoroughly wounded and distorted by error, the council put a decided emphasis on the *substantial truth* that may be found elsewhere. This analogical approach deeply pervades the conciliar documents: significant dimensions of God's truth may be found in other Christian churches, in other religions (particularly Judaism), and in the world itself. In this sense, surely, the world changed—for Archbishop Lefebvre and for Catholics at large.

Paul VI, though cautious and moderate in his approach, clearly recognized that Vatican II was making significant changes. He was deeply involved with the final drafts of the conciliar documents, often insisting, to the consternation of others, on last-minute changes.[39] The decisive issue,

37. De Mattei, *Il Concilio Vaticano II*, 579.

38. Thomas S. Kuhn, *The Structure of Scientific Revolutions*, 4th ed. (Chicago: University of Chicago Press, 2012), 121.

39. Paul VI's interventions with the various commissions are amply documented in Jan Grootaers, "Le crayon rouge de Paul VI," in *Les Commissions Conciliaires à Vatican II*, ed.

once again, was, which *kind* of change was being sanctioned by Vatican II? The pope's speech closing the council's third session (November 21, 1964) is significant in this regard. He speaks of that which is immutable and certain (*immobile et certum*) and that which allows for legitimate development (*legitima progressione*), clearly indicating that authentic progress is also important for the church's life.[40]

More recently, the issue of conciliar continuity and change was brought to center stage by Benedict XVI in his Christmas address of 2005. In that crucial speech, the pope speaks of Vatican II as representing a "combination of continuity and discontinuity at different levels," and he makes a distinction between an illegitimate "hermeneutic of discontinuity and rupture" and an authentic "hermeneutic of reform." Benedict's rejection of "rupture" yet avowal of "discontinuity" (at certain levels) indicates an acknowledgment of reversals within a greater stream of material identity. By rejecting any interpretation sanctioning a "rupture" between the preconciliar and postconciliar church, Benedict is making the point that no fundamental dogmatic landmarks of the church were transgressed by Vatican II—and so the council is not subject to the charge of a *permutatio fidei*.[41]

At the same time, Benedict points to the *undeniable novelty* of Vatican II, even marshaling a drumbeat of affirmations about its innovations:

1. "The Council had to determine in a *new way* the relationship between the Church and the modern era."
2. "The relationship between faith and modern science had to be *redefined*."
3. It was necessary to give "a *new definition* to the relationship between the Church and the modern State."
4. There was required "a *new definition* of the relationship between the Christian faith and the world religions."
5. And "it was necessary to evaluate and *define in a new way* the relationship between the Church and the faith of Israel."

M. Lamberigts, Cl. Soetens, and J. Grootaers (Leuven: Bibliotheek van de Faculteit Godgeleerdheid, 1996), 317–52.

40. *AS* III/8, 909–18, at 911.

41. Benedict's rejection of a conciliar "rupture" is repeated in the strongest terms in an October 11, 2012, article in *L'Osservatore Romano* (on the fiftieth anniversary of the council's opening) calling the hermeneutic of rupture "absurd" and "contrary to the spirit and to the desire of the Council Fathers." See "It Was a Splendid Day," Vatican News, http://www.news .va/en/news/it-was-a-splendid-day-benedict-xvi-recalls.

In such statements the pope makes clear that change and novelty were significant and even essential parts of the council.[42] In the following two chapters, I will examine several of the issues Benedict mentions, arguing that analogical reasoning, extensively used in the documents, accounted for a new optic at Vatican II. This new point of view generally preserved the prior tradition—harmoniously developing it *in eodem sensu*—but with reversals of ordinary teaching as well.

Let us now proceed to some of the most disputed issues of Vatican II, examining the extent to which they are developments or reversals of the prior tradition.

---

42. Citations are taken from "Address of His Holiness Benedict XVI to the Roman Curia Offering Them His Christmas Greetings," December 22, 2005, http://w2.vatican.va/content /benedict-xvi/en/speeches/2005/december/documents/hf_ben_xvi_spe_20051222_roman -curia.html; emphasis added.

CHAPTER 4

Disputed Topics and Analogical Reasoning

In the present chapter and the next, we will examine various teachings of Vatican II that remain disputed even after more than fifty years. Were these teachings proper developments? Were they harmonious expansions of Christian doctrine? Or were they *in alieno sensu* with the antecedent tradition? In this chapter we will concentrate on those disputed teachings that utilize *analogical reasoning* as a significant structuring principle. Participation and analogy, two traditional Thomist themes, are invoked at significant moments in the conciliar texts. But these principles have been largely overlooked in subsequent analyses because of John XXIII's intention that Vatican II remain a *pastoral* council, avoiding technical and abstract terminology.

Before investigating individual issues, I would like to discuss once again, although more briefly than in chapter 2, the role of participatory and analogical reasoning at Vatican II. It is my contention that the use of analogy allowed the council to maintain Catholic uniqueness while insisting that much truth may be found in other Christian churches, in other religions (particularly Judaism), and in all well-intentioned seekers after wisdom. To achieve its objectives, the council relied heavily on analogical thought. Vatican II is unusual among ecumenical councils because it is the only universal synod that did not condemn errors and issue anathemas. As Pope John had indicated from the outset, the council was to utilize the "medicine of mercy." One dimension of that medicine was the conciliar insistence on the similarities between Catholicism and all others. Dialectical difference was not the style of Vatican II—analogical similarity was.

As we shall see, participation and analogy are the *structuring ideas* when Vatican II speaks about the priesthood, Mary, the church, ecumenism, and world religions. The use of these traditional ideas justifies the assertion of Yves Congar that, while citations of St. Thomas are not numerous, "it could be shown . . . that St. Thomas, the *Doctor communis*, furnished the writers of the dogmatic texts of Vatican II with the bases and structure [*les assises et la structure*] of their thought. We do not doubt that they themselves would make this confession."[1] Congar does not substantiate this assertion, but I think it is clear he is referring to the participatory and analogical forms of thinking that have been so central to the Catholic theological tradition and that are found at several critical junctures in the conciliar documents. As I hope to show in this chapter, analogical reasoning was so critical for the council that it can be called *the philosophical style beneath the rhetorical style* of Vatican II.

Congar's comment is itself an extraordinary statement because it is often intimated that Aquinas was an uninvited guest at the council. What was ardently desired was not Thomas's abstruse discourse with its precise, logic-chopping distinctions. What was needed, rather, was existential and personalist language—warm expressions inviting all men and women to enter into a relationship of mutual trust with Christ and his church.

But the conciliar decision to avoid the *language* of scholasticism did not mean that the council avoided scholastic *ideas*. These ideas were clearly employed, even if technical terms—primary and secondary analogates or intrinsic and extrinsic attribution—were submerged. And the use of such ideas should not be surprising. As we have seen, Gérard Philips noted that *ressourcement* cannot mean discarding the achievements of the Middle Ages. Indeed, he encouraged theologians "to study more attentively the brilliant apogee reached by the thirteenth century" and to drop their prejudices "against an important period in the history of dogma."[2] My point is simply that a highly influential conciliar theologian looked favorably on the contributions of scholasticism. *Ressourcement*, properly understood, involved a recovery of the *entire* theological tradition. Could not Thomist concepts, too, contribute to Vatican II?

Analogy was the perfect idea for a council that wished to stress the unity that existed among all peoples despite continuing differences. Let us

---

1. Yves Congar, "La théologie au Concile: Le 'théologiser' du Concile," in *Situation et tâches présentes de la théologie* (Paris: Cerf, 1967), 53.

2. Gérard Philips, *L'Église et son mystère au IIe Concile du Vatican: Histoire, texte et commentaire de la Constitution "Lumen Gentium,"* 2 vols. (Paris: Desclée, 1967-68), 2:325.

recall the comments of Cardinal Suenens of Brussels, who argued early in 1962 that in difficult times Catholics should stress what unites them to others rather than what separates them. In his important conciliar intervention on December 4 of the same year, Suenens expanded on this idea, encouraging the council to open a triple dialogue: with the Catholic faithful, with those brothers and sisters not in visible unity, and with all men and women of the modern world.[3]

Theologically speaking, how is unity—particularly partial unity—best expressed? This has traditionally been accomplished by means of participation and analogy. To cite a common example: How is it possible that very different entities—humans, angels, camels, and rocks—are all properly called "beings"? All of these entities may be so called because they participate in the perfection of being, of *esse*, even though they share in this attribute in essentially different ways. Humans participate in being more intensively than do rocks; nonetheless, both humans and rocks formally, substantially, and intrinsically participate in the attribute of being. It is not as if this perfection of being exists truly in one entity and only metaphorically in another. Rather, the attribute of being subsists in both. As we shall see, this kind of reasoning is featured in several of the conciliar documents.

Those who point to Vatican II's rhetorical emphasis on mutuality and reciprocity are surely right to do so. André-Marie Charue, the bishop of Namur, Belgium, and a vice president of the Theological Commission, confirms their insight. Speaking of a draft of *Gaudium et spes*, Charue writes in his journal that the document seeks "an intelligible, dynamic and warm style for all."[4] But the crucial question is this: How does one theologically *express* mutuality, reciprocity, and conciliation while still insisting on important differences? How does one express partial similarity and partial divergence? Analogy allows for imperfect unity—absent perfect identity and utter incongruence.

A final point should be made before moving to particular issues. Analogical reasoning allowed Vatican II to overcome old theological antinomies, thereby recovering the traditionally Catholic "both/and" way of thinking. To cite a couple of examples: At the council, it is never a matter of *either* the ministerial priesthood *or* the universal priesthood of the baptized. The council seeks to preserve *both* priesthoods, upholding each one's unique participation in the one priesthood of Jesus Christ. Similarly, it is never a matter

3. *AS* I/4, 222–27.
4. *Carnets-AMC*, 233 (February 11, 1965).

of the one mediator Jesus Christ *as opposed to* any other kind of mediation. The council explains that the unique mediator between God and man, Jesus Christ, allows for the mediation of Mary and the saints, who participate in the unique source.

I would now like to turn to three themes in the Dogmatic Constitution on the Church, *Lumen gentium*, where participation and analogy are clearly the structuring principles. *Lumen gentium* is a good test case because, as O'Malley has argued, this document is the "centerpiece of the council," providing "the stylistic model for [the] subsequent documents."[5] The use of analogical reasoning in *Lumen gentium* allows the council to make theological advances over the prior tradition even while preserving the tradition's foundational teachings *in eodem sensu eademque sententia.*

The Priesthood

It is sometimes intimated that Vatican II, by accenting the importance of the priesthood of all the baptized, ignored or downplayed the unique role of the ministerial priest. But this complaint has little foundation in the documents of the council. On the contrary, *Lumen gentium*, which discusses both the ministerial priesthood and the universal priesthood, offers a good example of how the themes of participation and analogical reasoning were utilized at the service of divine revelation. At the outset, let it be noted that *Lumen gentium* is the first conciliar document in the church's history to speak of the common priesthood of the faithful. The Council of Trent, convened in the sixteenth century in response to the Reformation, was primarily concerned to defend the office of the ministerial priest. As such, Trent made no reference to the biblical texts of 1 Peter that clearly call all believers "priests." Vatican II sought to remedy that defect.[6]

---

5. John O'Malley, "Erasmus and Vatican II: Interpreting the Council," in *Cristianesimo nella storia: Saggi in onore di G. Alberigo*, ed. A. Melloni, D. Menozzi, G. Ruggieri, and M. Toschi (Bologna: Il Mulino, 1996), 195–211, at 197.

6. Philips remarks that an older theological method tended toward unilateralism since it wished only to rebuke the position of an "adversary." But this approach inexorably obscures some important aspect of Christian doctrine. Priesthood is an example, with post-Tridentine theology ignoring the *regale sacerdotium*. Such one-sidedness, Philips concludes, is not appropriate for Catholicism, which seeks to balance grace and human effort, faith and works, Scripture and tradition, primacy and collegiality, and so on. See Gérard Philips, "Deux tendances dans la théologie contemporaine," *Nouvelle revue théologique* 85 (March 1963): 233–34.

Our story begins with Pius XII, who, in his allocution *Magnificate Dominum*, delivered on November 2, 1954, acknowledges that Scripture refers to all the faithful as priests (citing 1 Pet. 2:5 and 2:9). While recognizing this fact, Pius nonetheless insists that the universal priesthood must be carefully distinguished from those called "priests" properly and truly (*proprie vereque*). Only the latter (ministerial priests) possess the *potestas sacrificandi* (the power of offering the sacrifice of the Mass). The pope's language found its way into the first draft of *De ecclesia*, which reached the council floor in December 1962 and which explicitly speaks of those who are priests properly so called: *sacerdotes proprii nominis*. To drive this point home, the theological commentary accompanying the draft says that the text was written in such a way as to "make clear both the metaphorical and analogical nature of the universal priesthood."[7] In other words, analogy is invoked here, but it is the analogy of *improper* proportion or extrinsic denomination, with baptized Christians called "priests" only in a metaphorical sense rather than properly and truly (*proprie vereque*) as are ordained priests.[8]

Several bishops reacted negatively to the attempt to limit the phrase "priests properly so called" to the ministerial priesthood.[9] Given the clear biblical texts from 1 Peter, is it not true that the priesthood of all the baptized is also a true priesthood, a *sacerdotium veri nominis*? Taking account of these criticisms, the Theological Commission significantly redacted *De ecclesia*, with the second draft appearing in the spring of 1963. The offending phrase, stating that only ministerial priests are *sacerdotes proprii nominis*, was dropped, as was the description of the universal priesthood being of only a metaphorical nature (*indoles metaphorica*).[10] The final document speaks of

---

7. *AS* I/4, 44, note B.

8. The analogy of improper proportion is at work, for example, when one calls God a rock or a mighty shield as in Psalm 18. These terms, obviously, are not attributed to God in a representational sense. The psalmist means, rather, that God possesses qualities that are rock-like or shield-like. Calling the baptized "priests" in this metaphorical sense means that the baptized have priestlike qualities but are not properly called priests. On the other hand, the analogy of intrinsic attribution or proper proportion means that an attribute *formally and substantially* exists in an entity. As earlier noted, rocks, camels, angels, and humans all participate in the perfection of *esse*. Even though these entities have essential differences, the perfection of "being" inheres in all of them actually and intensively, even if quite differently.

9. The episcopal speeches on this point are examined in Thomas G. Guarino, "The Priesthood and Analogy: A Note on the Formation and Redaction of *Lumen Gentium*, no. 10," *Angelicum* 67 (1990): 309–28.

10. For the various drafts of *De ecclesia*, see Giuseppe Alberigo and Franca Magistretti,

the ministerial priesthood and the universal priesthood of the faithful as each, in its own unique way, participating in the one priesthood of Jesus Christ (*suo peculiari modo de uno Christi sacerdotio participant*). This section of the dogmatic constitution reads, "Though they differ from one another in essence and not only in degree, the common priesthood of the faithful and the ministerial or hierarchical priesthood are nonetheless interrelated: each of them in its own special way is a participation in the one priesthood of Christ" (§10).

In the development from the initial schema to the final text, one may discern a gradual abandonment of the analogy of improper proportion in favor of the analogy of intrinsic attribution. In other words, in the first schema, the attribute of priesthood is predicated to the faithful in a metaphorical sense only: the universal priesthood is *priestlike* but is not a formal sharing in the priesthood of Jesus Christ. In later redactions, both Christ's faithful and his ministers truly, formally, and intrinsically participate in his priesthood, although this priesthood exists in essentially different ways in the two analogates.[11]

In the understanding of priesthood presented by *Lumen gentium*, then, Christ is the prime analogue, the one who possesses the priesthood in its fullness. As Aquinas says, Jesus is the true priest, the *verus sacerdos*.[12] But although Christ uniquely possesses the priesthood, his ministers and his faithful *participate* in this attribute, with *both* possessing it formally and substantially. To express it another way, the priesthood belongs *per se et per essentiam* (of its nature and essentially) to Christ, while his ministers and faithful possess the attribute *per participationem* (by participation). This point of view is buttressed by Philips, the primary spokesman for the document within the Theological Commission.[13] He states that in the New

---

eds., *Constitutionis Dogmaticae Lumen Gentium, Synopsis Historica* (Bologna: Istituto per le Scienze Religiose, 1975).

11. *Lumen gentium* states that the universal priesthood and the ministerial priesthood differ not only in degree but also in essence. The reasons for this are discussed in Thomas G. Guarino, "'*Essentia et non gradu tantum differant*': A Note on the Priesthood and Analogical Predication," *Thomist* 77 (October 2013): 559–76, at 567–73.

12. *Summa contra Gentiles*, book 4, chapter 36.

13. Gustave Thils, who also served as an expert on the *De Fide*, writes of Philips, "He was, in all truth, the chief draughtsman of the dogmatic constitution *Lumen gentium*. The text of this document was written and revised by him." As the council fathers presented suggestions and amendments, these were redacted or reviewed by him. Philips was so deeply involved in *Lumen gentium* (as well as other documents) that, as Thils states, "one is able to say that he was the *homo conciliaris* par excellence." Jan Grootaers, ed., *Primauté et collégialité: Le dossier de Gérard Philips sur la Nota explicativa praevia* (Leuven: Leuven University Press, 1986), 10.

Testament only Jesus "has by full right the name of priest," even though this name or attribute is extended to others.[14] By this he means that although Christ possesses the priesthood in its fullness (in traditional terminology, the prime analogue), Christ's priesthood is intensively shared by both his ministers and his faithful (the secondary analogates).

Philips was well aware of the need for precision on this issue. As he says in his commentary, "This paragraph [no. 10] is the first conciliar document in which the magisterium pronounces explicitly on the common priesthood of the faithful."[15] And in a 1965 article, written shortly after *Lumen gentium* was formally promulgated, Philips notes that the dogmatic constitution contains the church's "first official doctrinal declaration on the subject of the *universal priesthood* of the faithful."[16] A man with his sharply honed theological intelligence knew that this teaching, a *novum* in conciliar history, had to be expressed with exactness. The classical tools of participation and analogical attribution were critical to the task.[17]

In Vatican II's teaching on the priesthood, one clearly discerns material continuity—*eodem sensu eademque sententia*—with the antecedent tradition. The singularity of the ministerial priesthood is affirmed together with its unique participation in the one priesthood of Jesus Christ. Through the sacrament of holy orders, the priest liturgically actualizes the Lord's sacrifice at Golgotha. *Lumen gentium* affirms this when it states, "The priest alone can complete the building up of the Body in the Eucharistic sacrifice. Thus are fulfilled the words of God, spoken through his prophet: 'From the rising of the sun until its setting, my name is great among the gentiles, and in every place sacrifice and a pure oblation is offered to my name'" (§17, citing Mal. 1:11). A little later the dogmatic constitution says, "Acting *in persona Christi*, and proclaiming his mystery, priests join the offering of the faithful to the sacrifice of their Head. Until the coming of the Lord, priests re-present and apply in the sacrifice of the Mass the one sacrifice of the New Testament"

---

14. Philips, *L'Église*, 2:268.

15. Philips, *L'Église*, 1:138.

16. Gérard Philips, "La Constitution 'Lumen Gentium' au Concile Vatican II," in Grootaers, *Primauté et collégialité*, 190.

17. Significantly, when discussing the difference between the common and ministerial priesthoods, Philips says, "Once again, we refer to an explanation *on the basis of analogy*." *L'Église*, 1:143; emphasis added. While Philips does not often invoke analogy in his discussion, the idea is clearly on his mind. This can be confirmed by turning to his thoughtful comments on Augustine's use of the word *proprium* when attributing the term *sacerdos* to bishops and ministerial priests in the *City of God* 20.10. See *L'Église*, 1:146.

(§28). The ministerial priest, by a sovereign gift of God's unmerited grace, is enabled to re-present in the liturgy the mystery of Christ's own oblation. All the faithful join him in offering Christ to the Father, but they do so with and through the ministry of one who stands, by God's grace, *in persona Christi*. One may conclude that Christ's priesthood is such that both the laity and the clergy share in this perfection, but distinctly so. It is precisely this notion of *diversified participation in a perfection* that undergirds the analogical attribution of the word *priest* to both Christ's ministers and his faithful. Both *sacerdotia* (priesthoods) truly share, with proportional differences, in Jesus's unique priesthood.

While Vatican II's teaching on the ministerial priesthood stands in clear continuity with the Catholic doctrinal tradition, one also sees at the council a development (and, to some extent, reversal) of the church's earlier teaching on the universal priesthood. For the first time, as noted, an ecumenical council pronounced explicitly on the common priesthood, stating that both the ministerial priest and the baptismal priest formally and substantially participate in the one priesthood of Jesus Christ. The council's teaching on this point reversed aspects of Pius XII's *Magnificate Dominum*, which was very hesitant about ascribing the term *priest* to all the baptized for fear of obscuring the uniqueness of the ministerial priesthood.

In the development and (mild) reversal achieved by Vatican II, one sees the influence of *ressourcement* reasoning, with the council recovering biblical and patristic thinking on the universal priesthood of the faithful. We have already mentioned the important citations in 1 Peter. To this we should add the text of Augustine in the *City of God* (20.10). There the African doctor speaks of those presbyters "who are now properly [*proprie*] called priests [*sacerdotes*] in the church." The temptation, Philips says, is to use this citation of Augustine to speak of a real priesthood and a figurative one (the baptismal priesthood). But this would betray Augustine's intent since for the bishop of Hippo the universal priesthood, too, is a true gift from God.[18] This is why Philips can firmly state that Vatican II "does not teach that the common priesthood of the faithful ought to be interpreted in a figurative sense; it treats of this gift as a reality which is in no way identified with the ministerial priesthood, but which approaches it by way of a certain resemblance. *Still again we return to an explanation on the basis of analogy*."[19]

Philips resists calling the universal priesthood a "spiritual" priesthood

18. Philips, *L'Église*, 1:146.
19. Philips, *L'Église*, 1:143; emphasis added.

because "the priestly dignity of the [baptismal] community is equally 'real,' even if one ought to explain it in an *analogical manner* when comparing it with the work of the ministers." It is the participation of all Christians in the priesthood of Jesus Christ that is truly crucial. As Philips remarks, "The fullness of the priesthood *in which all others participate*, ministers included, is that of the one High Priest."[20] By means of analogical reasoning, then, the council preserved the uniqueness of the ministerial priesthood—an ancient Catholic theme—even while making clear that all the faithful participate formally and intrinsically in the priesthood of Jesus Christ. Precisely through the employment of participation and analogy we see confirmed (at least partially) Congar's 1967 comment that the thought of St. Thomas structured the dogmatic texts of the council.

Vatican II here offers a legitimate development that is nonetheless fully commensurate with the church's prior teaching on the ministerial priesthood. If the council had reversed that teaching—holding, for example, that the ministerial priesthood was simply an exercise of the baptismal priesthood, with particular persons pragmatically designated for leadership in the community—or if the council had argued that the difference between the two *sacerdotia* was only by degree (*secundum magis et minus*) and not by essence, then Vatican II could well have been accused of transgressing significant doctrinal landmarks. On the contrary, Vatican II's teaching on the priesthood was in material continuity with the prior tradition, a *profectus fidei, eodem sensu eademque sententia.*[21]

This point needs to be emphasized since some seem to think that the (biblical) affirmation that all the baptized share in the priesthood of Jesus Christ ipso facto detracts from the uniqueness of the ministerial priesthood.[22] And yet the council was very careful to preserve the apposite distinctions even while insisting that all Christians share in Christ's priesthood. Participation and the analogical reasoning were essential to achieving the proper theological balance.

---

20. Philips, *L'Église*, 1:147; emphasis added.

21. Needless to add, the council undoubtedly placed some new theological accents on the presbyteral office without denying older ones. For example, Joseph Ratzinger says that Vatican II wanted to overcome a "one-sided" link between *sacerdos* and *sacrificium*, placing greater emphasis on preaching the Word of God. See *Theological Highlights of Vatican II*, trans. Henry Traub, Gerard C. Thormann, and Werner Barzel (New York: Paulist Press, 2009), 249–50.

22. See Moyra Doorly and Aidan Nichols, *The Council in Question* (Charlotte, NC: Tan, 2011), 17–19.

Mary

Another important facet of the "centerpiece" document of Vatican II, *Lumen gentium*, is its teaching on Mary, the Mother of God. The question of whether to have a separate document on Mary or to include her in the Dogmatic Constitution on the Church—precisely as the preeminent disciple of Christ—resulted in a pitched conciliar battle. Indeed, the closest vote of the entire council was on just this issue. It will not be our concern, however, to relate the details of the debate, which are readily available in various conciliar histories.[23] I would like, rather, to concentrate on certain theological issues that cluster around the person of Mary (such as the disputed title of *mediatrix*), examining the crucial but largely overlooked role that analogical reasoning played in framing her precise place in salvation history.

Mary's Mediatorial Role

The theological significance of the Mother of God was a sensitive question at Vatican II, particularly given the polemics that had surrounded her since the time of the Reformation. Moreover, the Catholic Church had infallibly defined two dogmas about Mary: her immaculate conception (1854) and her bodily assumption into heaven (1950). These dogmas further divided Catholics from Protestant and Orthodox Christians. How could the council—which had deeply ecumenical intentions and was replete with Protestant and Orthodox observers—express Mary's role in salvation history in a biblically and ecumenically sensitive way, yet one that was fully appreciative of Catholic teaching on this matter? Just this was the task of the Theological Commission.

Gérard Philips played the principal role in drafting the entire schema *De ecclesia*, but particularly the chapter on Mary. As he says in his conciliar journal, "I have drafted a schema *De Beata* [On the Blessed Virgin] which more than the rest is my work."[24] At the beginning of June 1964, Philips's text on Mary was approved as the base text for discussion by the *Commissio de Fide*. But his schema was not accepted without controversy. Archbishop

---

23. See, e.g., Herbert Vorgrimler, ed., *Commentary on the Documents of Vatican II* (New York: Herder and Herder, 1967), 1:285–96. Also see Giuseppe Alberigo and Joseph A. Komonchak, eds., *History of Vatican II* (Maryknoll, NY: Orbis Books, 2000), 3:367–72.

24. *Carnets-GP*, 115 (November 15, 1963).

Parente, an official of the Holy Office and a conservative member of the Commission, expressed his grave disappointment that there was no mention in the schema of Mary as the *mediatrix* of God's graces. Parente's position was echoed by another expert, Charles Balić, a Franciscan theologian and an ardent Mariologist. Balić blamed Philips directly for failing to include Mary's mediatorial role in the text.[25] Philips defended his schema, responding that while he personally accepted the unique role of Mary in salvation history, he did not believe that the council had the authority to impose the title of *mediatrix*.[26]

Unsatisfied, Parente pressed his case, asking Philips to reconcile the two theological trajectories: Mary as Christ's exemplary disciple and Mary as *mediatrix*. Philips strongly resisted the suggestion, prompting André-Marie Charue, a vice president of the Commission, to express shock that Philips, a man who normally took pains to reconcile opposing points of view, now refused to speak of Mary's mediation.[27] Hoping to resolve the impasse, Cardinal Ottaviani, the president of the Theological Commission, established a subcommittee to deal with the question, naming Charue as chairman and including several experts, including Yves Congar, Karl Rahner, and Philips. At the meeting of June 3, 1964, Parente acknowledged that Christ should, of course, be given priority. Mary's mediation would only be mentioned after stressing Christ's unique mediatorial role. But other bishops and theologians opposed *any* use of the word *mediatrix* since it was bound to cause theological confusion and ecumenical offense. Parente conceded that not all would welcome the term, but he felt there should be a compromise. One may understand the mediatorial role of the Mother of God without in any way detracting from the unique mediation of Jesus Christ. Parente then offered a possible formula: "It is a fact that in the Catholic Church, the Blessed Virgin Mary, beyond other titles with which she has been adorned, has been

---

25. Congar evaluates Balić rather negatively, saying he "thinks of nothing except super-exalting Mary." See Yves Congar, *My Journal of the Council*, trans. Mary John Ronayne and Mary Cecily Boulding (Collegeville, MN: Liturgical Press, 2012), 14. Philips, too, expresses reservations about Balić's mariological maximalism, saying that the Franciscan continually refers to Mary as *Alma socia Christi* (beloved associate of Christ), as if this title were "almost an article of faith." See *Carnets-GP*, 116 (December 2, 1963).

26. *Carnets-AMC*, 194 (June 2, 1964).

27. *Carnets-AMC*, 194 (June 2, 1964). Charue surmised that Philips knew (through Bishop Colombo, a close confidant of Paul VI) that the pope did not want the term *mediatrix* to appear in *De ecclesia*. Charue reiterates the pope's opposition to the title on the following day (197).

called '*mediatrix.*' But this title has been understood so that it neither dero-gates from, nor adds to, the dignity and efficacy of the mediatorship of Jesus Christ."[28]

Among the experts on the subcommittee, Philips, Rahner, and Congar opposed Parente's formula, while Balić and others found it acceptable. The Franciscan, speaking with a rising tone of voice, declared that he would not yield on the title of *mediatrix*. Seeking compromise, Charue tweaked Parente's formula, placing even more emphasis on the uniqueness of Christ. It was to no avail; opposition to the term remained. How to resolve the impasse?

The subcommittee concluded that only the full Theological Commis-sion could decide whether the term *mediatrix* should be employed in the schema. Meeting on June 6, 1964, the *De Fide* voted 12–9 in favor of includ-ing the term in the schema.[29] Charue stated that he was opposed to citing the title for two reasons: (1) it would harm ecumenical relations with the separated Christian brethren, and (2) the last two popes, John XXIII and Paul VI, generally avoided this expression.[30] Nevertheless, together Philips and Parente hammered out the wording on Mary's mediation, language that is found today in *Lumen gentium* §62.

But vigorous disagreements about the Blessed Mother were not over. Cardinal Suenens was unquestionably the head of the Belgian delegation at Vatican II, and the Belgians, as Congar relates, were extraordinarily influ-ential at the council. Indeed, Congar goes so far as to claim that Vatican II could rightly be dubbed the first council of Louvain, *primum concilium Lo-vaniense.*[31] Despite this Belgian *esprit de corps*, there was not always perfect unity. On August 2, 1964, Philips wrote in his journal, "The cardinal [Suen-ens] generally makes good sense, but in what concerns Mariology he is pas-sionate and does not examine the issue in either a critical or an ecumenical manner. He presents me with a text which utilizes, on the subject of Mary and the apostolate, such 'shortcuts' that Mary herself almost appears as the

28. *Carnets-AMC*, 197 (June 3, 1964).

29. *Carnets-AMC*, 204 (June 6, 1964). Philips puts the vote at 13–9 in favor of *mediatrix*. See *Carnets-GP*, 120 (July 12, 1964).

30. *Carnets-AMC*, 207 (June 8, 1964).

31. Congar, *My Journal*, 508 (March 13, 1964). Congar adds that Philips, the Louvain theologian, is "the architect no. 1 of the theological work of the council" (510). On the role of the Belgians, and Philips in particular, see Jan Grootaers, "Le rôle de Mgr. Philips a Vatican II," in *Ecclesia a Spiritu Sancto edocta* (Gembloux: J. Duculot, 1970), 343–80; and D. Donnelly et al., eds., *The Belgian Contribution to the Second Vatican Council* (Leuven: Peeters, 2008).

source and basic principle [of the apostolate]. I will now have to attempt to write an acceptable version. This is a challenge."[32]

Suenens was not the only one causing theological problems for Philips. In mid-August 1964, Philips made a pilgrimage to the Marian shrine at Lourdes, where the local bishop threw cold water on *De beata*: "[I was] at table today with bishop Pierre-Marie Theas. He says to me very frankly that the schema *De beata* satisfies no one."[33] Despite this lack of enthusiasm, Philips was nonetheless hopeful that the Marian schema would ignite productive theological debate among the bishops in the basilica: "It is difficult to foresee what kind of turn this will take. It seems good that we find here [on the council floor] very spirited debate among Catholics on the subject of Our Lady—and in the presence of the Protestant observers. . . . In any event, I have tried honestly to write a true Mariology. Nonetheless, the whole affair is in the hands of God. If the schema is rejected, or if it must be profoundly changed (by me or by others) this would be equally good."[34]

At the council's third session, which opened in September 1964, the revised schema on Mary was discussed by the bishops. Philips remarks, "In what concerns *De beata*, the unfolding of the discussion passes with less pain than I had feared. There was a certain number of strong approbations [of the text], but also a number of 'defenses' of Our Lady and some dramatic propositions concerning the consecration of the world, etc."[35] Despite this positive report, there was a deeply critical speech and from a wholly unexpected source, Cardinal Suenens himself: "Today, September 17, 1964, there was an intervention by Cardinal Suenens who accuses the schema [*De beata*] of minimalism and of anti-Marian Christocentrism, without making any reference to precise texts." Philips found this intervention to be deeply regrettable, noting, "One has the impression that the cardinal has lost prestige with this speech."

Suenens was considered to be a progressive bishop. Accusing Philips's carefully wrought schema on Mary of purveying "anti-Marian Christocentrism"—on the floor of St. Peter's, no less—seemed an act of betrayal, both personal and theological. Philips continues, "The bishops, above all the Belgians, are very indignant. Several friends are concerned that I am deeply affected. But there is no reason for such concern. I am not at the service of

---

32. *Carnets-GP*, 124 (August 2, 1964).
33. *Carnets-GP*, 128 (August 14, 1964).
34. *Carnets-GP*, 128 (August 14, 1964).
35. *Carnets-GP*, 130 (September 17, 1964).

the cardinal, but at the service of the Church and of the truth. It appears now, even more clearly, that I am not 'his man.' In fact, I have never been that."[36] Suenens's unexpected attack on the schema *De beata* was criticized by other Belgian bishops such as Charue and Heuschen. Exasperated by the ill-advised speech, Charue confided to his journal, "[Cardinals] Bea and Alfrink will reply [to Suenens] tomorrow on the need to distinguish conciliar teaching from devotion. It's elementary!"[37]

Suenens was not the only critic of the chapter. Max Thurian, one of the distinguished Protestant observers from the Taizé community, asked Charue to remove the word *mediatrix* from the schema. Charue, in turn, told Bishop Colombo (Paul VI's theological advisor) that only an intervention of the pope would at this point be sufficient to withdraw it. Paul, however, did not act.[38]

Writing on October 11, 1964—with the final vote on the entire schema *De ecclesia* (including the chapter on Mary) just a few weeks away—Philips considered the theological possibilities before him as he revised *De beata*: (1) leaving the term *mediatrix* in the schema as is, (2) deleting it altogether, or (3) surrounding it with other devotional titles such as *advocata, adjutrix*, and so on, so that *mediatrix* would no longer possess an isolated, technical meaning to be developed in a systematic manner. As we know from the final text of *Lumen gentium* (§62), Philips chose the last option, which was approved by both the Theological Commission and the conciliar bishops.[39]

The conciliar vote on chapter 8 of *De ecclesia* took place on November 18, 1964. Philips was elated with the result: "As for the vote on *De beata*, only twenty-three Fathers vote against it. After all the noise, it is a success greater than one hoped. God be praised. *Laus Mariae, matri nostrae.*"[40] In the final solemn vote of November 21, 1964, the day of promulgation, only five negative votes were cast against the entire schema of *Lumen gentium*.

A couple of important points emerge from this discussion of *De beata*.

36. *Carnets-GP*, 130 (September 17, 1964).

37. *Carnets-AMC*, 215 (September 17–18, 1964). Heuschen strongly criticized the phrase "anti-Marian Christocentrism," an extraordinary expression omitted by Suenens in his text distributed to the press.

38. *Carnets-AMC*, 215 (September 17–18, 1964).

39. Philips deemed that the strategy of surrounding *mediatrix* with other titles had been successful: "The enumeration of the various titles, each of which is widespread, shelters the term '*mediatrix*' from abusive interpretations." Philips feared all attempts to "reify" Mary, developing a systematic Mariology apart from Christ. See *L'Église*, 2:265.

40. *Carnets-GP*, 140 (November 18, 1964).

First, one sees how close the infighting was on disputed theological issues, both in the *De Fide* and in the basilica of St. Peter's. Even individual words— such as *mediatrix*—were the source of fierce theological debate. This should lead us to conclude that there was no cavalier overturning of the prior tradition by the council. Most of the bishops and theologians knew the Catholic tradition well. The crucial issue was, How does one present a theologically and ecumenically responsible portrait of the Mother of God while transmitting the doctrinal tradition with integrity? Participants at the council could and did differ in their responses, but no one sought to destroy an authentic Mariology.

Second, one may see from the discussion of *De beata* the freedom exercised at Vatican II. While Paul VI did not always refrain from imposing his will on the documents (as we will see with the Decree on Ecumenism), he normally allowed the council free rein in its discussions. As Charue's diary makes lucidly clear, Paul would have preferred that the word *mediatrix* not be inserted into the chapter on Mary, recognizing that this title is difficult to explain and could easily infringe on ecumenical sensitivities. Yet he allowed the very close vote of the Theological Commission to stand, not seeking to overturn it.[41]

Having related some of the conciliar discussions on the Mother of God, I would now like to show how Philips sought to resolve theologically the disputed title of *mediatrix*.

Participation and Analogy in Mariology

As we have seen, the seemingly innocent word *mediatrix* launched a bitter conciliar discussion. To resolve the question satisfactorily, Philips again turned to participation and analogy, themes he had successfully employed when dealing with the "two priesthoods" in *Lumen gentium* §10. In this case, participation in the unique mediatorial work of Jesus Christ will ground the analogical naming of Mary as *mediatrix* and the saints as mediators in their own right.

As noted, several bishops and theologians argued that the title *mediatrix* was deeply injurious to the ecumenical cause. But other members of

---

41. Paul VI even hesitated about granting Philips an audience with him lest it appear to compromise the latter's independence on the Theological Commission. See *Carnets-GP*, 121 (July 12, 1964).

the *De Fide* insisted the title was essential to any truly Catholic Mariology. A glimpse into Philips's thinking on the matter is afforded by his reflections some six months after *Lumen gentium* had been formally promulgated in November 1964. Looking back on the chapter on Mary, Philips states, "In the *Communio Sanctorum* [communion of saints] all is referred to the Lord, and the cult of the saints is in this sense 'relative.' That is to say, we venerate the individual person, but this person is only venerable because he or she is referred to Christ as source and fulfillment. The dignity of Mary also comes from Christ. Naturally, no one denies this origin. But the method employed by many does not always take sufficient account of it."[42] In other words, the cult of Mary and of the saints must always be understood in reference to Jesus Christ as the source of all holiness. Christ is the *mediator per se et per essentiam* (1 Tim. 2:5), just as he is the holy one *per se et per essentiam*. The Blessed Mother and the saints, who truly *possess* holiness, can only be understood in reference to Christ, the *source* of holiness.

In more philosophical language, we can say that Christ is the prime analogue, the fullness of holiness and truth, while Mary and the saints are secondary analogates who *participate* in the holiness of Jesus. Precisely for this reason, Philips can say that the cult of Mary and the saints is "relative"— that is, their holiness is not absolute and foundational as is Christ's. Failing to understand the secondary character of the cult of the saints leads one to develop theologies that isolate and reify Mary, as if she could be treated theologically on her own apart from the Lord Jesus. Looking back to 1963, when his draft of *De ecclesia* was first discussed in the Theological Commission, Philips recalls, "During the first phase of the Council, many of the [council] Fathers had the impression that I wished to reduce the figure of Our Lady, precisely because I wished to see her *in* the Church. But if I place her outside the Church, she is no longer Our Lady, and no longer the first image and the beginning of the Church. The goal is therefore—finally—not the glorification of Our Lady, but the recognition of the fact that God communicates himself to men '*im-primis*' [in the first place] in her."[43]

In his journal, Philips rarely speaks directly of participation and analogy as structuring themes. But in his reflections on Christ as the unique source—of holiness, of mediatorship, and of priesthood—Philips makes

---

42. *Carnets-GP*, 147 (May 27, 1965).

43. *Carnets-GP*, 147–48 (May 27, 1965). Philips's approach with Mary parallels his approach with the pope. In *De ecclesia* he consistently used the term "head of the college" rather than "head of the church" precisely to keep the pope in—not above—the church of Christ.

clear that Jesus possesses these attributes *per se et per essentiam*, while others (Mary and the saints, in the case of holiness) share in them only secondarily, by participation (*per participationem*). This explains why Philips says of the liturgical expression *Mirabilis Deus in sanctis*, "Notice, we do not say that it is the saints who are marvelous, but rather that *God is marvelous in his saints*. And for this reason we thank God for his saints."[44] In other words, the saints participate in the holiness of God, who is himself the source of all holiness and goodness.

If we carefully examine *Lumen gentium* §62, we see that Philips clearly employed the themes of participation and analogy in order to preserve the uniqueness of Christ's mediation between God and man—but without excluding the intercession (and so mediation) of Mary and the saints. The apposite section of the dogmatic constitution reads:

> Therefore the Blessed Virgin is invoked by the Church under the titles of Advocate, Auxiliatrix, Adjutrix, and Mediatrix. This, however, is to be so understood that it neither takes away from nor adds anything to the dignity and efficaciousness of Christ the one Mediator.
>
> For no creature could ever be counted as equal with the Incarnate Word and Redeemer. Just as the priesthood of Christ is shared in various ways both by the ministers and by the faithful, and as the one goodness of God is really communicated in different ways to His creatures, so also the unique mediation of the Redeemer does not exclude but rather gives rise to a manifold cooperation which is but a sharing in this one source. (§62)

How was *mediatrix* to be understood so as to avoid any conflict with the clear biblical teaching that there is one mediator between God and man, Jesus Christ (1 Tim. 2:5)? Philips explicitly turns to what has already been said about the priesthood in *Lumen gentium*. There Jesus is presented as the "true priest," the priest *per se et per essentiam*, who offers himself to the Father. Both ministerial priests and the baptized Christian faithful participate in this one priesthood of Jesus. Insofar as they share in Christ's priesthood, all Christians are truly, intensively, formally, and substantially called "priests." But this attribute, once again, belongs preeminently and essentially to Jesus Christ and only secondarily to others.

Philips invokes precisely the same reasoning when explaining how

44. *Carnets-GP*, 148 (May 27, 1965); emphasis added.

Mary can be called *mediatrix*. Does this title infringe on Christ's unique-ness and so ignore biblical teaching? Philips and the council respond: "Just as the priesthood of Christ is shared in various ways by the ministers and by the faithful" (*sicut sacerdotium Christi variis modis . . . participatur*), so in the same way "the unique mediation of the Redeemer does not ex-clude but rather gives rise to a manifold cooperation which is but a *sharing in* this one source" (*participatam ex unico fonte*). In other words, just as Christ is the model and exemplar as priest, so also is Christ preeminently and essentially (*per se et per essentiam*) the one mediator between God and humanity. However, this unique status does not exclude "secondary analogates" who share in Christ's mediatorial work by participation—just as creaturely priests are not excluded from sharing in Christ's priesthood.

Philips later explained that the council tried to illustrate the proper meaning of the word *mediatrix* by analogy. In the New Testament, only Christ is called "priest" with full right—and yet Scripture calls the people of God "priests" and the Roman Catholic Church designates those engaged in ordained ministry as "priests." Similarly, the Bible attributes "goodness" to God alone (Mark 10:18). But no one concludes from this that no man can be good. Jesus wishes us to understand, rather, that the grandeur of God surpasses every creature. Further, no one would sensibly deduce from Mat-thew 23:9-10 that the words *father* and *mother* can no longer be attributed to human beings simply because Christ instructed his disciples to avoid titles that serve only flattery and pride. On the contrary, although Christ's priest-hood and God's goodness and paternity are unique, they are not exclusive.[45]

Ultimately, Philips is arguing—and Vatican II is teaching—that terms such as *priest* and *mediator* belong preeminently to Jesus Christ, the true priest and the one mediator between God and man. But this uniqueness is not jeopardized when others are called "priests" and "mediators" as long as it is clearly understood that such terms are applied secondarily and analog-ically to those who participate in Christ's unique offices.

From this discussion I would like to draw two conclusions. First, Philips and the council clearly avoided words associated with scholasticism. One does not find terms such as *prime analogue* and *secondary analogates* in the conciliar documents. Nonetheless, these *ideas* were clearly utilized to explain disputed themes such as the priesthood of the baptized and Mary as *mediatrix*. And these ideas serve, once again, to substantiate Congar's claim that the thought of "St. Thomas, the *Doctor communis*, furnished the

45. Philips, *L'Église*, 2:269.

writers of the dogmatic texts of Vatican II with the bases and structure of their thought. We do not doubt that they themselves would make this confession." Second, while Vatican II's Mariology is clearly in continuity with the prior tradition, the council ardently sought to develop a Mariology that was ecumenically sensitive, one that was determined to prune back Marian excesses so as to avoid theologies that developed Mary's place in the church without explicit reference to Jesus Christ.

Subsistit In

Having shown that the themes of participation and analogy were crucial at Vatican II for explaining both the priesthood and the role of the Mother of God, we now ask, Will these same ideas help us understand the most disputed term to emerge from Vatican II—namely, *subsistit in* of *Lumen gentium* §8? In this section I will argue that by employing the notions of participation and analogy, Vatican II was able to maintain the unique status of Catholicism while concomitantly affirming that other churches truly and actually, formally and substantially, participate in the church of Jesus Christ.

Let us first cite the passage with the much-disputed term:

> This is the one Church of Christ which in the Creed is professed as one, holy, catholic and apostolic, which our Savior, after His Resurrection, commissioned Peter to shepherd and . . . which He erected for all ages as "the pillar and mainstay of the truth" (1 Tim. 3:15). This Church, constituted and organized in the world as a society, subsists in [*subsistit in*] the Catholic Church, which is governed by the successor of Peter and by the Bishops in communion with him, although many elements of sanctification and of truth are found outside of its visible structure. These elements, as gifts belonging to the Church of Christ, are forces impelling toward catholic unity. (§8)

The original draft of *De ecclesia* had made a simple equivalence: "The Roman Catholic Church is [*est*] the Mystical Body of Christ."[46] But the Theological Commission first changed the word *est* to *adest* (is present in) and finally to *subsistit in* (subsists in).[47] We now know that this last term was suggested by

46. AS I/4, 15.
47. For the history and meaning of these changes, see Karl Becker, SJ, "The Church

Sebastian Tromp, the theologically conservative secretary of the Theological Commission.[48]

Before embarking on a more concentrated analysis, I would first like to mention a frequent misunderstanding of the phrase *subsistit in*. Brunero Gherardini, for example, a longtime theologian at the Lateran University in Rome, recently complained that inasmuch as Vatican II teaches that elements of sanctification and truth are present in non-Catholic churches and communities, this "confirms the impression that the Catholic Church and Christ's Church may not be one and the same reality."[49] Gherardini's comment reflects a common charge: it would have been better if *De ecclesia* had stayed with the simple equivalence found in the original text, "The Catholic Church *is* [*est*] the Mystical Body of Christ." But as I shall argue, this point of view fails to see that the council took a far more sophisticated and theologically fruitful path, using the ideas of primary and secondary analogates to explain the uniqueness of Catholicism *together with* the intensive participation of other Christian churches in the one church of Christ.

This conjunctive style of reasoning has deep roots in Catholic theology. As we have seen, for the Theological Commission and the council in general, it is a matter of the ministerial priesthood *united with* the baptismal priesthood of all Christians, it is a matter of Mary as exemplary disciple *together with* her role as *mediatrix*, and it is a matter of papal primacy *conjoined with* the universal episcopacy—not one over against the other. In the instance at hand, it is a matter of sanctioning *both* Catholic claims *and* the formal participation of Protestant churches in the one church of Jesus Christ.

This relationship between Protestant churches and the Catholic Church was clearly on Philips's mind in his aforementioned "Deux tendances" article of 1963. In that essay, written around the same time he was preparing a new draft of *De ecclesia*, Philips reflects on the ecumenical problem. He notes that among Catholics and other Christians "several links subsist (*subsistent*) in the sacramental and juridical orders and, even more, in the spiritual order. Protestant and Orthodox Christians are at the same time separated from

---

and Vatican II's *Subsistit In* Terminology," *Origins* 35 (January 9, 2006): 514–22; Francis A. Sullivan, "A Response to Karl Becker on the Meaning of *Subsistit In*," *Theological Studies* 67 (2006): 395–409. See also Alexandra von Teuffenbach, *Die Bedeutung des 'subsistit in' (LG 8): Zum Selbstverständnis der Katholischen Kirche* (Munich: Herbert Utz, 2002); and Christopher J. Malloy, "*Subsistit In*: Nonexclusive Identity or Full Identity?," *Thomist* 72 (2008): 1–44.

48. Becker, "Vatican II's *Subsistit In*," 517.

49. Brunero Gherardini, *The Ecumenical Vatican Council II: A Much Needed Discussion*, trans. Franciscans of the Immaculate (Frigento: Casa Mariana, 2009), 27.

us and united to us. This is, at base, the ecumenical problem. Theologically, how can one describe their complicated situation?"[50] Philips here frames the problem in terms that cry out for an analogical solution. There is partial similarity and partial difference between Catholics and other Christians. How to describe these degrees of unity? How to speak of a relationship that is neither absolute identity nor utter dissimilarity? Philips even speaks of those Christians whose membership in the church has an "analogical character." While Catholics and Protestant have a different conception of the true church, nonetheless "the elements of union . . . subsist (*subsistent*) even in the separation." After all, the adjunct secretary avers, *to belong to Christ means belonging, in some proportion, to his church*. Philips's comments here show that analogical reasoning was clearly on his mind.[51]

A very similar point of view is expressed by Philips in an article published shortly after the promulgation of *Lumen gentium*. He states that it was essential to determine with precision the relationship of Catholics "with separated Christians, with non-Christians and even with unbelievers." But how to uphold the positive links existing among all Christians without blurring differences?

Philips states that only Catholics are members of the church "in the full meaning [*sens plein*] of the term." Why is this so? Because, he responds, only Catholics profess the true faith, accept all the means of salvation, and remain united in the power established by Christ. Nevertheless, "the [Catholic] Church remains united in diverse ways—imperfect certainly—to other Christians."[52] Philips's remark takes us back to the issue of primary and secondary analogates. Only Catholics are members of the church "in the full meaning of the term." But other Christians are neither unrelated nor only metaphorically related to the people of God. After all, to belong to Christ, to be attached to him, to be baptized into him, means "to belong or to be attached in the same proportion to his Church."[53] In other words, other Christians formally and substantially—even if not fully—participate in the church of Jesus Christ.

---

50. Philips, "Deux tendances," 231.

51. Philips, "Deux tendances," 232. Grootaers says that one finds in the conciliar work of Philips "a certain aversion to the dilemma and to the alternative of 'either/or' and a marked preference for the middle way, 'this and that' (*ceci et cela*)." This judgment is correct but is surely reflective of Catholic theology in general. See Jan Grootaers, "Le role de Mgr. G. Philips a Vatican II," in *Ecclesia a Spiritu Sancto edocta* (Gembloux: J. Duculot, 1970), 376.

52. Philips, "La Constitution," 190.

53. Philips, "Deux tendances," 232.

Philips's comments about membership in the church help clarify the precise meaning of the disputed term *subsistit in*. He writes in his 1965 article:

> The one Church of Christ, the text [*Lumen gentium*] states, is constituted by the Catholic community which is directed by the successor of Peter and the bishops united with him. The term utilized is "*subsistit in*," which is rather difficult to translate. The expression means that the Church of Christ is fully present [*pleinement présente*], it is "*en vigueur*," in the ecclesial organization of which the supreme head is Rome. It is not stated that it "*est*" [is] the Roman Church, and nothing more because . . . there exist outside of this visible institution some elements of the Church of holiness and truth. This shows already the ecumenical consciousness that was attained by almost all the conciliar Fathers. For them, the divisions among Christians became a problem which they refused to avoid.[54]

In his commentary on *Lumen gentium* published just a couple of years later, Philips sounds a similar note: "It is there [in the Catholic Church] that we find the Church of Christ in all its plenitude and all its force, as St. Paul says of Christ risen that he has been established Son of God *en dynamei*, i.e., with power (Rom. 1.4)."[55]

If we consolidate Philips's comments, we see that by using the term *subsistit in*, *Lumen gentium* sought to accomplish two goals. On the one hand, the exceptionalism of the Catholic Church was affirmed since the Catholic Church "considers itself the true church of Christ" and the church of Christ is "fully present" in it.[56] On the other hand, by avoiding the term *est* the council affirmed that other Christian churches formally *participate* in Christ's church with different degrees of intensity depending on the *elementa ecclesiae* (creeds, sacraments, etc.) maintained within them. Catholicism, Philips insists, does not deny the salvific efficacy of the elements existing in other churches. Indeed, outside of Catholicism there exist elements of sanctification and truth that belong to the order of grace and salvation. The Catholic Church, Philips continues, is able to recognize these authentic values without renouncing the unicity that her Master impressed on her substance.

But how is Catholicism able to reconcile its self-understanding—as

54. Philips, "La Constitution," 189–90.

55. Philips, *L'Église*, 1:119.

56. For this entire paragraph, see Philips, *L'Église*, 1:119. See also *AS* III/7, 12, where it is affirmed that only the Catholic Church is the true church of Christ.

possessing the fullness of divine truth—with an acknowledgment of the grace and truth found in other churches? It does so by means of participation and analogy, which are of vital assistance in yielding the proper understanding of *subsistit in*. Let us recall for a moment our prior analyses: Christ is the prime analogue as priest, the *per se* realization of the priesthood, in whose unique priesthood the secondary analogates (his ministers and faithful) truly participate. Christ is also the prime analogue as mediator, in whose mediatorship the Blessed Mother and the saints participate—always secondarily—as they accompany Christians on their journey to eternal life.

One finds precisely the same logical structure with the assertion that the church of Christ "subsists in" the Catholic Church. The Catholic Church, to quote Philips again, is where one finds "the church of Christ in all its plenitude and all its force." Catholicism, then, is the *per se* and *per essentiam* realization of Christ's church. But—and this is the truly crucial and innovative work that *subsistit in* accomplishes at Vatican II—other Christian churches are not only metaphorically the church of Christ, nor are they the church of Christ by extrinsic denomination (with this perfection attributed merely as a courtesy title). Rather, other Christian churches *formaliter et substantialiter* participate in Christ's church with various levels of intensity. These churches clearly possess holiness, grace, and truth—and so share in the church of Christ even if, from the Catholic point of view, they lack certain objective means of salvation and the fullness of Christian doctrine.[57]

In Vatican II's understanding, there exists full but not exhaustive identity between the church of Christ and the Catholic Church. This point is crucial lest some think that Christ's church is a Platonic idea, not fully realized in any one denomination. But that is the thinking neither of Philips nor of Vatican II. As Philips plainly states, the church of Christ is "fully present" in the Catholic Church. Other churches participate—truly, intensively, and substantially—in Christ's church to a greater or lesser extent. To invoke again the traditional terms, the Catholic Church is the *per se* realization of Christ's church—but not exhaustively so. Other churches are the church of Christ by participation, *per participationem*.[58]

---

57. Adherents of other Christian churches may, understandably, regard it as a grudging concession that other communions formally and intensively participate in the church of Christ. It should be noted, however, that Vatican II is at a significant remove from the encyclical *Mortalium animos* of 1928, which came close to speaking of Protestant churches as purveying a "false Christianity, *ab una Christi Ecclesia admodum alienae*" (entirely alien from the Church of Christ).

58. Some theologians have noted that nineteen bishops called for the phrase "*subsistit*

With the term *subsistit in*, Vatican II wished to make clear that the identity between Catholicism and Christ's church is not an exhaustive identity, with Catholicism, so to speak, sucking all the oxygen out of the term. As we have already seen, no attribute is exhausted by its prime analogue. The unique priesthood of Jesus Christ does not exhaust the attribute of priesthood since it is also found, secondarily, in his ministers and his faithful. Similarly, the unique mediatorship of Christ does not exhaust that perfection since there are secondary mediators, Mary and the saints, who draw their power from the prime analogue. In the same way, the church of Christ is not exhausted by Catholicism but may be found in other churches and communions in different degrees of intensity. In all cases, the prime analogue is the model, the exemplary realization of the attribute or perfection, while others share in the attribute by participation.[59]

In the case of *subsistit in*, Vatican II relies, once again, on the analogy of attribution to explicate similarity in difference. While Catholicism is the full realization of the church of Christ, other Christian churches—Orthodoxy first and then the Reformation churches—participate in that church in varying degrees.[60] Christ's church, then, is not a zero-sum game any more than Christ's priesthood or Christ's mediatorial role are sole and exclusive, allowing no further participation. Vatican II's accent on the analogical similarity of other churches to Catholicism is one of the council's most significant theological fruits. It has given rise to a vibrant ecumenical spirit within the Catholic Church.[61]

---

integro modo *in Ecclesia catholica*" to be added to the text of *Lumen gentium* §8. In response to this emendation, the Theological Commission stated that, after a long discussion, *subsistit in* was the wording approved by all present. As regards the specific phrase *integro modo*, the Commission references *Lumen gentium* §14, which reads: those are fully incorporated into the Church "who, possessing the Spirit of Christ accept her entire system [*integram eius ordinationem*] and all the means of salvation given to her." See *AS* III/6, 81, and III/1, 188. The Theological Commission makes clear that to be *fully incorporated* as a member of the church of Christ requires not only the objective *means* of salvation and holiness but a *life* of holiness as well.

59. Christopher J. Malloy argues that the change in the conciliar drafts from *est* to *adest* to *subsistit in* does not imply a negation of the identity of the Catholic Church with the church of Christ. I agree. But I would add that while the Catholic Church is fully the church of Christ—and therefore the prime analogue—she does not exhaust that "perfection." There is a real, though qualified, participation in this attribute by other churches and communions. See Malloy, "*Subsistit In*," 26n95.

60. As for the uniqueness of Orthodoxy, one recalls Paul VI's statement to Athanagoras that between the Catholic and Orthodox churches "there already exists a communion which is almost complete—though still short of perfection." E. J. Stormon, ed., *Towards the Healing of Schism* (New York: Paulist Press, 1987), 232.

61. I have not seen the idea of analogy developed at length with regard to *subsistit*

In some sense, the term *subsistit in* embodies the entire problem and entire achievement of Vatican II. For in this simple term, the council sought to express the uniqueness of Catholicism while simultaneously insisting on the authentic ecclesial value of other Christian churches—a balancing act that required disciplined theological reasoning. But the question remains: By abandoning *"est"*—with its unequivocal identification between Catholicism and the church of Christ—did Vatican II betray the antecedent tradition, as is sometimes implied?

This would have been the case if the council had taught that Catholicism was one Christian denomination among many others, with none possessing revealed truth in its fullness. Then, indeed, one could draw the conclusion of a *permutatio fidei*, with a fundamental doctrinal landmark clearly transgressed. But this was hardly conciliar teaching. The use of *subsistit in* did not call into question the unique claims of the Catholic Church. The traditional teaching—that the Catholic Church is the fullness of Christ's church, its *per se* realization—was clearly maintained. However, this teaching was homogeneously supplemented and developed. The obvious links between Catholics and other Christians—baptism, the creeds, the written Word of God—were now integrated into an intelligible theological structure. With the term *subsistit in*, one finds material continuity with the prior tradition along with harmonious growth, *eodem sensu eademque sententia*.

*　　*　　*

We have now examined three disputed issues at Vatican II—the priesthood, Mary as *mediatrix*, and *subsistit in*—with the help of philosophical tools that belong squarely to the Thomist tradition: participation and analogical denomination. Some may legitimately protest that the language of analogy—of *per se, per essentiam*, and *per participationem*, of primary and secondary analogates, and of *analogatum princeps*—cannot be found in the conciliar documents. Of course, that is true. But to this I respond that John XXIII wanted an accessible, pastoral council that expressed the gospel in terms that were ecumenically sensitive and intelligible to contemporary men and

---

in. Certain theologians have adopted some form of it—e.g., Roch Kereszty, "The Unity of the Church," *Communio* 41 (2014): 694-720, at 708. Francis A. Sullivan has warned against interpreting *subsistit in* in a philosophical sense unless there are clear indications to the contrary. See *The Church We Believe In* (New York: Paulist Press, 1988), 26. But such indications are plainly found in *Lumen gentium* and in Philips's own writings. And recall again Congar's remark that the thought of St. Thomas structured the dogmatic texts of the council.

THE DISPUTED TEACHINGS OF VATICAN II

women. A repetition of the conceptual arsenal of thirteenth-century scholasticism was not appropriate for the renewal of the church that John had in mind. Further, a drumbeat of conciliar speeches appealed to the pope's allocution of October 11, 1962, with its distinction between the *depositum fidei* and the *modus* in which it was expressed. Scholasticism was not the appropriate vehicle for the goals that John XXIII intended.

For all these reasons, one does not detect the least hint of scholastic *language* in the documents of Vatican II. But this should not lead one to conclude that *ideas* carefully developed by scholastic doctors, such as participation and analogy, were absent from the council. How else does one make sense of Congar's comment that the thought of St. Thomas structured the dogmatic texts of Vatican II?[62] John O'Malley is certainly right when he insists that Vatican II placed its rhetorical accent on reciprocity, mutuality, dialogue, and partnership with others. But how to express these values without collapsing the distinctive elements of Catholicism itself? To develop Catholicism's teaching on other Christians (who formally share in the church of Christ), on the laity (who formally share in the priesthood of Christ), and on Mary (who formally shares in the mediatorship of Christ), the council turned to the analogy of attribution, which holds that attributes and "perfections" may be found across different, even widely distinct, entities.

These reflections should not be understood as an attempt to "translate" *Lumen gentium* or Vatican II into Thomist terms, as if such a project would be either possible or desirable. The council utilized several of Aquinas's axial ideas while purposefully jettisoning his vocabulary. Scholasticism had significant merits, undoubtedly, but it represented the legacy of the Middle Ages. Did scholastic thought allow the life-giving power of the gospel to speak to people of the twentieth century? How could the salt and light of Jesus Christ be unleashed to men and women of the contemporary age? Vatican II was convinced that a new approach was required. The substance of the Christian faith needed to be expressed in a more intelligible, attractive, and ecumenically oriented form.

---

62. Analogy was also on the minds of other influential members of the *De Fide* (besides Philips). Charue refers to analogical reasoning as helpful for solving theological issues. See *Carnets-AMC*, 150 and 153 (January 28, 1964, and February 1, 1964).

98

Ecumenism

Vatican II's Decree on Ecumenism, *Unitatis redintegratio*, is a document informed by rich theological themes: the importance of authentic pluralism within a fundamental unity, the hierarchy of truths and its crucial role in ecumenical dialogue, and the enduring significance of John XXIII's distinction between the deposit of faith and the mode of expression. In this section I would like, in the first place, to review the disputed theological issues that emerged with regard to *De oecumenismo* and, secondly, to show how participation and analogy are themes at the heart of the decree. Our examination will be conducted with the usual questions in mind: Is this document in material continuity with the prior tradition? Did its changes represent homogeneous growth *in eodem sensu*? Did the decree sanction reversals? And if so, do these constitute a collective *permutatio fidei*?

Times were tense in Rome in late November of 1964. This was so much the case that journalists dubbed the third week of November *la settimana nera*, "the black week," of the council. Why this doleful designation? Because of three decisions of Paul VI which, in the eyes of many, were injurious to the council's freedom and its fundamental intentions. First, the pope sustained the decision of the council presidents to postpone the voting on the Declaration on Religious Liberty, *De libertate religiosa* (or *Dignitatis humanae*), until the final session of 1965. This postponement was called for, so argued the conciliar presidents, because the text had been substantially rewritten.[63] Council rules required that significantly rewritten texts be allotted time for study and debate prior to any vote. Despite this, the postponement was considered an unmitigated disaster, particularly by the American bishops who ardently desired to bring back to the United States a strong conciliar endorsement of religious freedom.[64]

---

63. According to Giovanni Caprile, the new text was 55 percent longer than the original schema. See *Il Concilio Vaticano II*, vol. 4, *Terzo periodo, 1964–1965* (Rome: La Civiltà Cattolica, 1966), 476–78.

64. For details on this decision, see Jan Grootaers, "La crayon rouge de Paul VI," in *Les Commissions Conciliaires à Vatican II*, ed. M. Lamberigts, Cl. Soetens, and J. Grootaers (Leuven: Bibliotheek van de Faculteit Godgeleerdheid, 1996), 317–52, at 321–24. Also John O'Malley, *What Happened at Vatican II* (Cambridge, MA: Belknap Press of Harvard University Press, 2006), 240–42. Not long ago, Joseph Ratzinger (speaking as Benedict XVI) warmly praised Paul VI's "firmness" and "patience" in sustaining the presidents' decision to postpone the vote on *De libertate*. See Benedict's "Meeting with the Clergy of Rome," February 14, 2013, available at http://w2.vatican.va/content/vatican/en.html.

A second reason for the "black week" designation was that Paul VI, working through others, asked that a "note" be written explaining episcopal collegiality in juridical terms. This request resulted in the *Nota praevia explicativa* (discussed in the next chapter) that appears at the end of the dogmatic constitution *Lumen gentium*. The point of the Note was to allay the fears of some (including Paul himself) that since "episcopal collegiality" was a *novum* in the recent history of Catholicism, it needed to be expressed with juridical, as well as theological, clarity. At stake here was the relationship between the authority residing in the universal college of bishops and the authority resting in the Petrine office—a theological debate that went back centuries. Was supreme authority in the Catholic Church now divided between two "parties"? How was this authority to be exercised? Could there possibly exist an adversarial relationship between the pope and the bishops? To clarify matters, Paul VI insisted on an explanatory note. But this papal intervention—absent conciliar debate—was regretted by many, who saw it as a juridical imposition on *Lumen gentium*.

A third reason for the designation *la settimana nera*—and the most important one for our purposes—was that Paul VI made several last-minute changes to the Decree on Ecumenism, even though the document was ready for a final vote. What motivated these alterations? Paul himself was a strong proponent of ecumenism, as may be seen from his speech opening the second session of the council on September 29, 1963.[65] John XXIII had died in June, just a few months earlier. Paul VI's speech was carefully monitored for clues to determine the direction in which he would take the council. Would the new pope pull back on Vatican II's bold ecumenical intentions? In fact, Paul exhibited strong support for ecumenism from the outset of his pontificate.[66]

Although a vigorous supporter of the ecumenical movement, Paul also recognized that involvement in ecumenism constituted a new direction for Catholicism. Pius XI's encyclical *Mortalium animos* of 1928 had expressed

65. One council participant called this speech "almost a small summa of ecumenism." See Max Thurian, "Paul VI et les Observateurs au Concile Vatican II," in *Paolo VI e I Problemi Ecclesiologici al Concilio* (Brescia: Istituto Paolo VI, 1989), 249–58, at 253.

66. For concrete instances, see Pierre Duprey, "Paul VI et le Décret sur L'Oecuménisme," in *Paolo VI e I Problemi*, 225–48, at 230–32. Duprey, who at the time of the council was a staff member of the Secretariat for Christian Unity, says "it would not be difficult to establish a comparison between the decree on ecumenism and the different fundamental principles affirmed by Paul VI" in his September 1963 discourse opening the second session (231). Hereafter, page references from this work will be given in parentheses in the text.

grave reservations about the "movement" and had even banned Catholics from participating in it. The memory of this encyclical was so strong that on the eve of the council, Yves Congar wrote in his journal that he had low expectations for ecumenism. The bishops were not prepared for this moment. Indeed, Congar ruminated, as far as Christian unity is concerned, Vatican II was probably taking place twenty-five years too early.[67] Congar's concerns would prove unfounded. But the council's progress toward Christian unity did not come without obstacles.

On November 19, 1964, one day before the scheduled final vote on the decree, Paul VI mandated nineteen changes to the text.[68] Most of the changes were acceptable, not touching the essence of the decree. But number eighteen caused an immediate storm of controversy.[69] One clause in the original text of the decree (§21) read, "*Spiritu Sancto movente in ipsis Sacris Scripturis Deum inveniunt*" (By the movement of the Holy Spirit, [the separated brethren] discover God in these Sacred Scriptures). The change mandated by Paul VI read, "*Spiritum Sanctum* invocantes *in ipsis Sacris Scripturis Deum inquirunt*" (*Invoking* the Holy Spirit, [the separated brethren] *seek* God in these Sacred Scriptures). Duprey notes that the pope, in his own hand, had replaced the Latin word *inveniunt* with *inquirunt* (242). This served, of course, to weaken the straightforward affirmation that Protestant Christians *discover* God through their reading of the Sacred Scriptures. The pope let it be known that this alteration was not a matter for discussion; he was insisting that *inquirunt* replace *inveniunt* in the decree. Johannes Willebrands, the secretary of the Secretariat for Christian Unity, deeply regretted this alteration—not because the word *seek* could not be explained, but because the change from *discover* to *seek* would make "a detestable impression" (243). Why was this change made?

Duprey claims that by this alteration, "[Paul VI] wished to avoid saying that all reading of Scripture is made under the inspiration of the Holy Spirit and that in every case the reader encounters the Word of God." He

---

67. Congar, *My Journal*, 4.

68. For the changes, see *AS* III/8, 422–23. Also see Johannes Feiner, "Appendix," in Vorgrimler, *Commentary*, 2:159–60. At least some of the Pauline amendments correspond to *modi* (reservations) that had been submitted by certain bishops and had already been rejected by those composing the documents. See Caprile, *Il Concilio Vaticano II*, 480n22.

69. Philips noted in his journal, "The pope has made some modifications to the text of *De oecumenismo*, although, it appears, without anything too important. . . . [But] *the intervention of the pope is not judged favorably.*" See *Carnets-GP*, 141 (November 19, 1964); emphasis added.

continues, "[The pope] has in view here certain Protestant positions which would affirm that the individual reading of Scripture suffices, apart from the community and apart from its tradition" (246–47). To say *inveniunt*, without qualification, would be too absolute and definitive.

The change can also be explained by the fact that Paul VI always sought (and succeeded in achieving) virtually unanimous support for the conciliar documents. Accomplishing that goal demanded that he remain sensitive to the concerns of the more traditionalist minority. A large number of *non placet* votes (declaring the text unacceptable) would indicate that a significant segment of the bishops dissented from *De oecumenismo*. Paul no doubt reasoned that a few judiciously worded alterations would win the support of many bishops who had reservations about the decree and, indeed, about ecumenism in general. Ensuring virtual unanimity for each document—rather than a simple majority vote—was Paul VI's goal throughout the council.

The *theological* issue at stake in the alteration from *inveniunt* to *inquirunt* was, once again, the role of tradition in the life of the Catholic Church. Could one "find" God by searching the Sacred Scriptures alone? Did this formulation risk the conciliar endorsement of a *nuda Scriptura*? Did not one need the further complement of the church's life and tradition to understand the Scriptures fully? As we have seen, properly understanding tradition constituted an ongoing concern in the conciliar debates. Indeed, "the problem of the relationship between Scripture and Tradition is, from the very beginnings of Vatican II, at the center of ceaseless controversies."[70]

As noted, these papally mandated changes came at a tense time, for on the same day (November 19, 1964) the schema on religious freedom was pulled off the council floor. Many bishops were indignant at this turn of events. Some even wondered whether they should still vote in favor of the Decree on Ecumenism (244). But the members of the SCU urged the restive bishops to take the long view of matters. The decree was the result of unending hours of serious work. Despite the changes introduced by Paul VI, the document's substance remained untouched; it would establish a strong foundation for Catholic ecumenism for decades to come. If the decree were not formally promulgated, the SCU would receive a blow from which it would be difficult to recover. The staffers of the Secretariat argued that the decree remained acceptable, and they urged the bishops to vote *placet* without reservation (244).

70. Grootaers, "La crayon rouge," 328.

In the afternoon of that same day, November 19, there was a regularly scheduled meeting of the Protestant observers at the offices of the SCU, the last one scheduled for the council's third session. The agenda for the meeting was the draft schema on the missionary activity of the church. At the outset, however, the distinguished Lutheran theologian Oscar Cullmann asked if he could address another matter. Cullmann expressed his concern about the change from *inveniunt* to *inquirunt* in §21 of *De oecumenismo*, stating that while the new word is unobjectionable, the change itself makes a bad impression (245). Cullmann stated that he was well aware of Pascal's saying: one can only seek what one has already found. And he graciously added that *inquirere* is perhaps a more clearly Protestant word than *invenire*. Nonetheless, he regretted the change, thinking it would be difficult to explain to those not present at the council. The other observers applauded Cullmann's remarks (245).[71] Willebrands thanked Cullmann for his frankness, saying that he, too, regretted the alterations mandated by the pope, particularly the change to §21. He asked the observers for their prayers.

The vote on the Decree on Ecumenism took place the next day (November 20, 1964). Although tension still shrouded St. Peter's, the vote was overwhelmingly in favor of the decree: 2,054 *placet*, 64 *non placet*.[72] In retrospect, one can say that the members of the SCU saw clearly that *De oecumenismo* was built on a solid foundation and would have lasting importance for the ecumenical movement. The members of the Secretariat agreed that Paul VI's last-minute alterations, particularly the change from "find" to "seek," were unfortunate, but they recognized that the essence of the decree had not been touched.

Unitatis redintegratio remains a sterling affirmation of the Catholic Church's commitment to the ecumenical movement. With his changes, the pope slightly weakened the text. At the same time, one can understand Paul VI's desire that the decree receive the support of the entire council. A sizeable episcopal minority remained concerned that the interpretative light

71. Cullmann would later write, "Even the particularly unfortunate change introduced into paragraph 21 of the original text at the end of the Third Session, regarding Protestants and Scripture . . . can be understood, although not excused, in the light of the Catholic doctrine referred to in the following paragraph, where mention is made of the authority of the Catholic Church in expounding and preaching Scripture." See "Comments on the Decree on Ecumenism," *Ecumenical Review* 17 (April 1965): 94.

72. For the voting results, see *AS* III/8, 636–37. A final, formal vote was taken just prior to promulgation on November 21, 1964. The results were 2,137 *placet*, 11 *non placet*. See *AS* III/8, 781–83.

offered by Catholic tradition had not been affirmed with sufficient clarity; the pope altered this sentence to make that point more lucidly. Paul VI no doubt thought he was responsible for unifying the council behind a new direction for Catholicism and, indeed, behind what was in some ways a reversal of earlier magisterial teaching. A few judicious alterations would allay the fears of the minority, but without diminishing Catholicism's firm commitment to Christian unity.

Participation, Analogy, and Ecumenism

It would have been easy for Vatican II simply to proclaim Catholicism as the true church of Jesus Christ and to declare all churches and communities outside of it as ridden with corrosive error. But, as we have already seen in our discussion of *subsistit in*, the council wisely abjured that path, deciding instead to enter upon the complex issue of the analogical relationship between Catholicism and other Christian churches. Vatican II did, in fact, uphold the unique status of the Catholic Church, but it did so in a theologically sophisticated way, making clear that other churches truly, formally, and intensively participate in the church of Christ. In so doing, the council took the more difficult but decidedly more fruitful path, employing the tools of participation and analogy to argue that all Christian churches have a great deal in common.

Vatican II sought to emphasize the positive elements inhering in other churches. As Philips avers, the conciliar bishops gradually achieved ecumenical consciousness: "The divisions among Christians became a problem which they refused to avoid."[73] But how could Vatican II *theologically* incorporate this sense of partial unity and partial separation? Other churches firmly believed in the Holy Trinity, in Jesus Christ as the eternal Word made flesh, in the redemption, in the normative value of the Bible, and in the life of Christian discipleship. How could these elements be properly acknowledged and honored?

As previously noted, the council holds that Catholicism is the *per se* and *per essentiam* realization of the church of Christ, the prime analogue to which other churches are related. This is why Philips can say that the expression *subsistit in* "means that the Church of Christ is fully present [*pleinement présente*], it is 'en vigueur,' in the ecclesial organization of which the

---

73. Philips, "La Constitution," 190.

supreme head is Rome."[74] But fully does not mean exhaustively. Catholicism is not *exhaustively* the church of Christ, if one understands by that word the claim that other communities do not participate formally and substantially in Christ's church. They do so participate, even if in a limited manner. And this participation is not metaphorical or extrinsic; it is proper and intensive.

To hold otherwise would be a complete misunderstanding of what Philips, the Theological Commission, and Vatican II sought to accomplish. As *Lumen gentium* makes clear: just as the unique priesthood of Jesus—who is the *per se* realization of the priesthood—is not diminished by the participation in his priesthood by his ministers and his faithful; and just as the goodness of God—who is the *per se* realization of goodness—is not diminished by the participation in his goodness by other creatures; and just as the mediatorship of Christ—the one *per se* mediator between God and man—is not diminished by the prayers and accompaniment of Mary and the saints, so, in the very same way, the one church of Jesus Christ, while realized fully in Catholicism, is not diminished by the intensive participation of other Christian churches and communities.[75] These churches may be secondary analogates, yes, with limitations and imperfections, but they truly and intrinsically share in Christ's church. *Full* identification between Catholicism and the church of Christ, then, is not intended by Vatican II to mean *exhaustive* identification. Precisely here is where the council makes a significant ecumenical and doctrinal advance.

To support the claim that other churches formally participate in the church of Christ, I would like to return briefly to the topic of *subsistit in*. Not long ago it was discovered that this Latin phrase had been suggested by Sebastian Tromp, the conservative secretary of the Theological Commission. To the objection that the word *adest* (which had been used in the draft of November 1963) was imprecise, Tromp responded, "We are able to say then: [the church of Christ] subsists in [*subsistit in*] the Catholic Church, and this it does exclusively. And so it is said: the others possess only *elementa*. And this is explained in the text."[76] The American theologian Francis Sullivan has rightly argued that the "exclusivity" spoken of by Tromp was accepted by the Theological Commission only in a qualified way. In the first place, even the original draft of *De ecclesia* of 1962 spoke of the Orthodox churches as truly

---

74. Philips, "La Constitution," 190.

75. For the reasons why the council used the term *ecclesial communities*, see Philips, *L'Église*, 1:203–5.

76. Latin text cited in Becker, "Vatican II's *Subsistit In*," 517.

churches.[77] One may conclude from this that speaking of "only *elementa*," as Tromp does, in no way signifies an inability to participate formally in the one church of Christ.

Further, in the September 1964 draft of *De ecclesia*, we read that non-Catholics are "signed by baptism, by which they are joined to Christ, and they acknowledge and receive other sacraments in their own Churches or ecclesial communities."[78] Accompanying this draft was a *relatio* (explanatory note) from the Theological Commission explaining the changes made in this new draft. The *relatio* explains that in the separated churches, Christians receive "other sacraments" but not "all" the sacraments. It adds that the "elements" that have been enumerated—for example, baptism and other sacraments—do not refer only to the individuals but also refer to the communities themselves, and "in this one finds the *foundation* of the ecumenical movement."[79]

But how could these sacraments establish a "foundation" for ecumenism if their reception did not indicate a formal participation in Christ's church? The draft itself speaks of the "links" (*de nexibus*) between Catholicism and other Christian churches. Surely these links (both doctrinal and sacramental) point to the partial similarity existing between the Catholic Church and other Christian communities. Neither fully congruent nor utterly dissimilar, they are related analogically.[80]

Analogical reasoning allowed the council to achieve a new sense of unity with other Christians. The Catholic Church retained her traditional self-understanding, but this understanding does not exhaust the attribute or perfection of the church of Christ any more than occurs by saying that Christ is the one priest and the one mediator. The use of primary and secondary analogates allows for both full identity (Catholicism) and actual participation of other communities in Christ's church.[81] It is because of Protestant-

---

77. See *AS* I/4, 88, no. 6. This note makes clear, adducing several historical examples, that the word *church* has been "often and steadily" attributed to the Eastern communities.

78. *AS* III/1, 189.

79. *AS* III/1, 204, D; emphasis added.

80. This very point is displayed in the impassioned intervention of Bishop Léon Elchinger, speaking about the draft of *De oecumenismo* on November 19, 1963. He states that "*up to now*, the doctrines of the separated brethren that appeared false, we rejected as entirely false. *Now is the time* to recognize with greater reverence that in all the doctrines professed by our separated brother there is also a partial, and often a profound truth, and to profess it with him." See *AS* II/5, 562–66, at 564. In this speech, we see clearly the move to a new emphasis on analogical similarity. Further comments may be found in Elchinger's written text, *AS* II/5, 565, no. 10.

81. Affirming the uniqueness of the Catholic Church is the September 1964 *relatio* for *De*

ism's analogical similarity to Catholicism that Vatican II was able to reorient the Catholic Church toward the ecumenical movement, acknowledging the many elements of holiness and truth found in other Christian churches.

Concluding Reflections on *De oecumenismo*

In conclusion I would like to make two brief points. First, if participation and analogy are vital themes for understanding theological issues in *Lumen gentium*, including how the church of Christ is present in other Christian communions, then why have these topics been so often overlooked?

It is worth repeating that Vatican II did not want to invoke the conceptual arsenal of the thirteenth century at a time when Catholicism sought to bring a revivified gospel message to contemporary men and women and likewise sought to engage other Christians in serious ecumenical dialogue. Bishops often invoked John XXIII's call for a "pastoral" council in order to insist on widely accessible formulations.[82] There was little desire to use terms such as primary and secondary analogates or intrinsic and extrinsic attribution. Nonetheless, scholastic *ideas*, particularly participatory and analogical reasoning, were in plain sight at significant theological junctures. The linguistic shift at Vatican II—emphasizing conciliation and mutuality—indicates an underlying philosophical change, from dialectical to analogical reasoning. Such reasoning was prominent at the council, giving rise to an entirely different vocabulary. Once again, this helps substantiate Congar's assertion that "St. Thomas, the *Doctor communis*, furnished the writers of the dogmatic texts of Vatican II with the bases and structure [*les assises et la structure*] of their thought."[83]

---

ecclesia, which states, "The Church is only one [*unica*] and here on earth is present in the Catholic Church, although outside of her are found ecclesial elements" (AS III/1, 176). The same is true if we look at the response of the SCU to the concern of one bishop that the Catholic Church could be misunderstood as just one among various Christian communions. The SCU states, "Afterwards it is clearly affirmed that only the Catholic Church is the true Church of Christ" (AS III/7, 12).

82. For example, in the *relatio* distributed with the revised text of *De oecumenismo* (for discussion on September 23, 1964), the SCU states that the schema has a "pastoral nature, which generally does not admit the use of dogmatic, scholastic terminology, and this is especially the case inasmuch as ecumenism is a kind of movement, not a closed system" (AS III/2, 335). Several bishops appealed to John's desire for a "pastoral council" when criticizing the original schemas. For their interventions, see Jared Wicks, *Investigating Vatican II: Its Theologians, Ecumenical Turn, and Biblical Commitment* (Washington, DC: Catholic University of America Press, 2018), 158.

83. Congar, "La théologie au Concile," 53.

A second point is related to the questions we have been addressing throughout this volume: Is Vatican II's teaching on ecumenism in material continuity with the prior tradition? Is it a corrosive *permutatio fidei* or a legitimate *profectus*? If the Decree on Ecumenism had taught that the church of Christ, while present in Catholicism, is equally present in other Christian churches and communities, then, indeed, a major landmark of Catholic Christianity would have been transgressed and a Vincentian *permutatio* courted. This, however, is not what Vatican II affirmed—and no one at the time even suspected that such a teaching had been endorsed. If one studies the conciliar speeches, the writings of the Protestant observers, and the many journals kept by conciliar participants, one has no sense whatsoever that the decree intended to modify Catholicism's teaching on this point.

By preserving uniqueness—the church of Christ exists fully in the Catholic Church—Vatican II also maintained material continuity with the prior doctrinal tradition, *eodem sensu eademque sententia*. Catholicism is the place, as Philips states, where the church of Christ is found in all its plenitude and vigor.[84] That said, *De oecumenismo* also represents a *change* in Catholic teaching—both a crucial development and a reversal. As regards development, Vatican II teaches that the church of Christ is *also* found in other Christian churches and communities—with deficiencies (*UR* §3), it is true—but formally and substantially nonetheless. The council wished to leave behind the idea that other churches are the "church of Christ" metaphorically, called such only by extrinsic attribution as a kind of courtesy title. Terms such as *dissidents*, *heretics*, and *schismatics* are nowhere to be found in the conciliar decrees. As Philips stated soon after the 1964 promulgation of *Lumen gentium* and *Unitatis redintegratio*, "The [conciliar] accent is constantly placed on the positive aspect of the problem," that is to say, on the similarities between Catholicism and other churches. And as the aforementioned *relatio* of September 1964 insisted, these similarities constitute the foundation for Catholic participation in the ecumenical movement.[85]

As regards the reversal: How does one explain the difference between *Mortalium animos*, the 1928 encyclical of Pius XI, and the decree *Unitatis redintegratio* of Vatican II? Surely the council represents a significant volte-face on ecumenism. *Mortalium animos* casts doubt on the entire ecumenical enterprise, forbids Catholics from engaging in the movement, and comes close to calling Protestantism "a false Christianity, quite foreign to the one

84. Philips, *L'Église*, 1:119.
85. *AS* III/1, 204, D.

Church of Christ" (*ab una Christi Ecclesia admodum alienae*).[86] The Decree on Ecumenism, in contrast, warmly welcomes ecumenism, encouraging intelligent and active participation in it (*UR* §4). The discontinuity between the two documents is the source of consternation for some Catholics.[87]

I have already discussed the possibility of reversals of authentic magisterial teaching, but I would like to make two comments about this specific conciliar reversal—one formal, the other material. On the formal level, no theologian holds that teachings of the ordinary magisterium, although necessarily received by Catholics with *obsequium religiosum* (religious submission and respect), are irreversible or infallible. Ordinary magisterial teaching can always be adjusted in the light of new circumstances and may, on occasion, be reversed. On the material level, it should be recognized that Pius XI wished to make unmistakably clear that the claim that no church fully embodies the church of Christ was unacceptable. He further feared that the ecumenical movement would lead to a limp-wristed faith, absent specific Catholic teachings. In fact, both *Mortalium animos* and *Unitatis redintegratio* insist on the exceptional character of Catholicism. The difference is that the 1928 document evaluates all other Christian churches negatively, while the 1964 document insists on the *analogical similarity* of other Christian bodies to Catholicism. Just here we see the "combination of continuity and discontinuity at different levels" to which Benedict XVI referred in his 2005 speech.

The Decree on Ecumenism is a true development and advance over the prior tradition. While preserving the uniqueness of Catholicism, the council now surrounds this affirmation, in a positive way, with the authentic ecclesial elements found in other Christian churches. In this sense, there is a genuine *profectus*, a case of *res amplificetur*, of a reality growing within itself.

Judaism and World Religions

We now turn our attention to the declaration *Nostra aetate*, the shortest document promulgated by Vatican II, dealing with Judaism and world religions. Did the council maintain material continuity with the church's prior teaching on other religions? Or did *Nostra aetate*, regarded as one of the most

---

86. Pope Pius XI, *Mortalium animos* 8, http://w2.vatican.va/content/pius-xi/en/encyclicals/documents/hf_p-xi_enc_19280106_mortalium-animos.html.

87. See, e.g., Doorly and Nichols, *The Council in Question*, particularly Doorly's explicit appeals to the 1928 encyclical (69–74).

significant and impressive documents of the council, reverse fundamental Catholic teaching?

At the beginning of the third session in the fall of 1964, Gérard Philips confided to his conciliar journal that the declaration on Judaism remained in flux. Tension was in the air over several disputed schemas—*De Judaeis* (as the text was called), *De libertate religiosa*, and *De oecumenismo*—tension that would intensify over the next month. So contested was the issue of Judaism that some wished to abandon a separate document altogether, tossing the entire topic over to chapter 2 of *De ecclesia*, on the people of God.[88] Accounts of the schemata that ultimately culminated in *Nostra aetate* are readily available in the histories of Vatican II.[89] I would like to concentrate on certain foundational points that, I believe, will allow for a more penetrating understanding of the council's theological reasoning.

Participation and Analogy in *Nostra aetate*

In prior sections of this chapter, I have argued that participation and analogy are prominent themes at Vatican II—though scarcely visible on the council's terminological surface. Unsurprisingly, these same themes are at work when the council discusses the relationship of Catholicism to Judaism and other religions. Just as these principles allowed the council to express the deep unity existing between Catholicism and other Christian churches, so they permitted Vatican II to express solidarity between Christianity and world religions. By means of analogical reasoning, the council was able to accent "similarity in difference," a unity bespeaking neither congruent identity nor utter dissimilarity.

As in the Decree on Ecumenism, so also in the declaration *Nostra aetate*, Catholicism is presented as what has traditionally been called the *analogatum princeps*, the prime analogue where one finds the fullness of divine revelation. We have already seen this stated clearly in *Unitatis redintegratio*: "For it is only through Christ's Catholic Church, which is 'the all-embracing means of salvation,' that they [other Christian communions] can benefit fully from the means of salvation. We believe that Our Lord entrusted all the blessings of the New Covenant to the apostolic college alone, of which

---

88. *Carnets-GP*, 132 (October 11, 1964).

89. See Vorgrimler, *Commentary*, 3:17–136, and Alberigo and Komonchak, *History of Vatican II*, 4:546–59.

Peter is the head, in order to establish the one Body of Christ on earth to which all should be fully incorporated who belong in any way to the people of God" (§3). Similarly, in *Nostra aetate* the council declares that the Catholic Church "proclaims, and ever must proclaim, Christ 'the way, the truth, and the life' (John 14:6), in whom men may find the fullness of religious life, in whom God has reconciled all things to Himself" (§2). And in the conciliar decree *Ad gentes*, dealing with the church's missionary thrust, the council confirms the need for both Christ and his church: "'For there is one God, and one mediator between God and men, Himself a man, Jesus Christ, who gave Himself as a ransom for all' (1 Tim. 2:4-5), 'neither is there salvation in any other' (Acts 4:12). Therefore, all must be converted to Him, made known by the Church's preaching, and all must be incorporated into Him by baptism and into the Church which is His body" (§7).

I have combined these citations, chosen from innumerable others, to make clear that Vatican II presents Jesus Christ in a straightforwardly biblical manner as "the way, the truth, and the life" through whom men are saved. Further, the Catholic Church is presented as the "all-embracing means of salvation," Christ's body to whom has been entrusted the blessings of the new covenant. But, as was the case with other Christian communities, Judaism and other religions are now evaluated from the standpoint of their *proportional similarity to* and *intensive participation in* the truth proclaimed by the Catholic Church. Other religions are neither understood as nor described by the council as outcroppings of error, as entities riddled with flaws and faults. They are presented, rather, as secondary analogates embodying elements of grace and truth—with different levels of intensity, certainly—and, as such, profoundly related to Catholicism. Instead of accenting the *differences* between Christianity and other religions (as was common in the past), Vatican II stresses the *similarity* between Christianity and other faiths.

This emphasis on analogical reasoning allowed the council to say, even with regard to Hinduism and Buddhism, "The Catholic Church rejects nothing that is true and holy in these religions. She regards with sincere reverence those ways of conduct and of life, those precepts and teachings which, though differing in many aspects from the ones she holds and sets forth, nonetheless often reflect a ray of that Truth which enlightens all men" (*NA* §2). Hinduism and Buddhism, the council frankly admits, differ significantly from the Christian faith, but these religions nonetheless share, to some degree, in the truth that Christianity proclaims in its fullness. Even with only minimal similarity to the prime analogue—and likely with much greater difference—these faiths remain secondary analogates related to the church of Christ.

Of Judaism, of course, Vatican II speaks at greater length, stressing the much stronger bonds that link it with Christianity: "The Church keeps ever in mind the words of the Apostle about his kinsmen: 'theirs [Judaism's] is the sonship and the glory and the covenants and the law and the worship and the promises; theirs are the fathers and from them is the Christ according to the flesh' (Rom. 9:4–5), the Son of the Virgin Mary. She [the church] also recalls that the Apostles, the Church's main-stay and pillars, as well as most of the early disciples who proclaimed Christ's Gospel to the world, sprang from the Jewish people" (*NA* §4). In one sense, it would be entirely true to say that it is Christianity that participates in the covenant bestowed by God on Israel, the well-cultivated tree onto which the wild shoots of the gentiles have been grafted (Rom. 11:17–24). But, taking divine revelation in its totality, the council holds that Judaism *participates in*—even while under-girding—the revelation found fully in the light of Christ. Judaism is here a secondary analogate—though surely a unique one as the very *fons et origo* of Christianity. This is so clearly the case that we might say, borrowing language found in *Lumen gentium*, that Judaism's participation in the truth of divine revelation differs not only in degree but in essence from the participatory relationship of other religions.[90]

The analogical reasoning permeating *Nostra aetate* may also be found in *Lumen gentium*, chapters 14–16. Cast in the language of full and partial "incorporation" into the church, this section of the dogmatic constitution deals first with Catholics (who, if they are truly disciples of Christ, are "fully incorporated") and then with all those who are baptized in the name of Jesus. The council turns next to those "related" to Catholicism, with pride of place given to Judaism, "the people to whom the testament and the promises were given." From there the paragraph deals briefly with Muslims, who worship the one God; then with those who seek God "in shadows and images"; next with those who desire to follow the laws of conscience; and finally with those

---

90. A recent Vatican document comes close to this exact point: "Dialogue between Jews and Christians then can only be termed 'interreligious dialogue' by analogy." See Commission for Religious Relations with the Jews, "The Gifts and the Calling of God Are Irrevocable," no. 15 (December 15, 2015), http://www.vatican.va/roman_curia/pontifical_councils /chrstuni/relations-jews-docs/rc_pc_chrstuni_doc_20151210_ebraismo-nostra-aetate_en.html. The document goes on to say, "From the theological perspective the dialogue with Judaism has a *completely different character and is on a different level in comparison with other world religions*" (§20; emphasis added).

to whom God is unknown but who strive to live a good life: "whatever good or truth is found among them is looked upon by the Church as a preparation for the Gospel" (§16). Just here we see the deeply analogical structure of the document, with varying degrees of intensity (from *semina veritatis* to baptized Christians) characterizing the different levels of participation in the truth. This structure was carried over to *Nostra aetate*, which was promulgated in 1965, one year after *Lumen gentium*. In both *Lumen gentium* and *Nostra aetate*, then, Christianity is presented as the fullness of divine revelation. Other religions, insofar as they are vessels of God's truth and goodness, are *formally and intensively* related to the church of Christ. Or, to express it differently, Christianity is true *per se* and *per essentiam*. Other religions, with Judaism in an entirely unique position, are true *per participationem*.

To return to our original question: When treating Judaism and other religions, was Vatican II in material continuity with the prior doctrinal tradition, *eodem sensu eademque sententia*? Does conciliar teaching on this issue represent a legitimate *profectus* or a corrosive *permutatio*? I think an answer in favor of material continuity is clear, at least on the most foundational and crucial issue. The council unreservedly defends the centrality and uniqueness of Jesus Christ and of his body, the church. Christ himself is the way, the truth, and the life in whom "men find the fullness of religious life" (*NA* §2). Jesus is "the source of salvation for the whole world" (*LG* §17), and to him "all must be converted" (*AG* §7). Christ is described as "the one Mediator and the unique way of salvation" (*LG* §14). In these statements, and others like them, Vatican II upholds Christ as the fullness of truth, the source of salvation who must be ceaselessly proclaimed. Christianity, particularly as found within Catholicism, is presented as the exemplar or prime analogue embodying divine revelation in its totality. On both of these points, Vatican II is in direct continuity with the antecedent Catholic tradition.

However, in a significant change from the past, other religions are now evaluated positively, described according to their *proportional similarity* with Christianity. John O'Malley is right, then, to say that conciliar rhetoric about other religions indicated "not alienation from others but a search for communion with them, a quest for mutual understanding . . . and the common good."[91] But it needs to be added that this desire to forge links of communion with others was expressed theologically by a move from dialectical to analogical reasoning, thereby changing the lens through which other religions were viewed. Although truth and goodness are found in other

91. O'Malley, *What Happened*, 309.

religions (particularly Judaism), the council insists that other faiths need to be perfected by Jesus Christ. So one reads in *Ad gentes*,

> But whatever truth and grace are to be found among the nations, as a sort of secret presence of God, He frees from all taint of evil and restores to Christ its maker, who overthrows the devil's domain and wards off the manifold malice of vice. And so, whatever good is found to be sown in the hearts and minds of men, or in the rites and cultures peculiar to various peoples, not only is not lost, but is healed, uplifted, and perfected for the glory of God, the shame of the demon, and the bliss of men. (§9)

Truth and goodness, then, are certainly found elsewhere, but these must be purified, strengthened, elevated, and ennobled in Jesus Christ (*LG* §13). All religious practices, teachings, and virtues are related to the exemplar and prime analogue, Christian truth. Just as other Christian churches maintain certain *elementa ecclesiae*—sound doctrine, sacraments, creeds—so other religions maintain decisive elements that are congruent with the Christian faith.

Nostra aetate's positive evaluation of other religions was not long ago criticized by Benedict XVI, himself a participant at Vatican II as a theological expert. Benedict's concern is that the council's relentless accent on analogical similarity leads it to overlook the weaknesses that may be found in other religions: "In the process of active reception, a weakness of this otherwise extraordinary text [*Nostra aetate*] has gradually emerged: it speaks of religion solely in a positive way and it disregards the sick and distorted forms of religion which, from the historical and theological viewpoints, are of far-reaching importance."[92] Benedict's comment points to a danger inherent in any analogical approach: it may so emphasize the bonds existing among entities—the tight nexus between the exemplar (prime analogue) and those related to it (secondary analogates)—that differences and deviations are overlooked. Is this the case with *Nostra aetate*?

Vatican II in general and *Nostra aetate* in particular did not accent the differences existing between Christianity and other religions. We have already had occasion to cite the statement by Gérard Philips that "the [conciliar] accent is continually placed on the *positive aspect of this problem*."[93] In

---

92. For the text of Benedict's article "Fu una giornata splendida" in *L'Osservatore Romano* on the eve of the fiftieth anniversary of Vatican II (October 11, 2012), see http://www.vatican.va/special/annus_fidei/documents/annus-fidei_bxvi_inedito-50-concilio_en.html.

93. Philips, "La Constitution," 190; emphasis added.

a world weary of World War II, the Holocaust, and the Cold War, Vatican II wished to forge links among men. Yet the council documents are replete with affirmations about Jesus Christ as the savior of the world. While the council did not address the weaknesses of other religions, neither did it dissolve thick Christian faith and doctrine into the thin gruel of a universal religiosity.

Concluding Reflections on *Nostra aetate*

To return to our fundamental question: Given the novel accents and emphases in *Nostra aetate*, can we conclude that the document represents a *permutatio fidei*, a reversal of fundamental church teaching? *Nostra aetate* would indeed represent such a distortion if the council had abjured the necessity of Christ for salvation, or if it had mitigated the truth claims of Christianity. But the citations invoked earlier in this section (*NA* §2; *AG* §7; *LG* §17; *UR* §3) demonstrate that the council held neither of those positions. Jesus Christ is proclaimed as the source of salvation, the Christian faith as the fullness of truth, and the Catholic Church as possessing the all-embracing means of salvation. On all these counts, the council is undoubtedly in continuity with the prior doctrinal tradition.

We also recall the famous 2005 speech of Benedict XVI, who on the one hand ardently denounced a "hermeneutic of discontinuity and rupture" (in conciliar interpretation) yet on the other referred to Vatican II as containing a "combination of continuity and discontinuity at different levels." In 2012, in an article explicitly commemorating the fiftieth anniversary of the council, Benedict again railed against the idea that the council was a corrosive "rupture" with the earlier tradition, stating that the council fathers "neither could nor wished to create a different faith or a new Church. . . . This is why a hermeneutic of rupture is absurd and contrary to the spirit and will of the Council Fathers."[94] These citations indicate that Benedict was well aware that Vatican II was, on certain levels, discontinuous with the prior tradition; in his judgment, however, these discontinuities fall short of a pernicious rupture with the doctrinal teaching of the Catholic Church.

In contrast, Thomas F. Stransky, one of the original members of the Secretariat for Christian Unity, states that *Nostra aetate* represents for Catholicism "a 180 degree turnabout; indeed, it indicated and indicates 'radical

94. Benedict XVI, "Fu una giornata splendida": "*un' ermeneutica della rottura è assurda.*"

discontinuity.'"[95] In certain ways, there *does* exist radical discontinuity in *Nostra aetate*, particularly given its deeply irenic tone toward Judaism and other religions. It is no surprise that *Nostra aetate* contains few citations from the prior tradition to support its affirmations of friendship and respect for others, particularly the Jewish people. For Vatican II left behind an earlier Catholic emphasis on the unwillingness of the Jewish people to accept the Messiah. The conciliar stress was on the *analogical similarity* of Catholicism with Judaism and, to a lesser extent, with other religions. In this transformation, one does indeed observe a 180 degree turnabout in Vatican II's "form." But was there an equally severe reversal in content?

As earlier noted, Christian exceptionalism—and the centrality of Jesus Christ for salvation—was clearly maintained by *Nostra aetate*. Nonetheless, there *are* discontinuities in *Nostra aetate* beyond the rhetorical style of the document. The language of "supersessionism," for example, is entirely avoided. Like *Lumen gentium*, the declaration speaks positively of the first covenant: "Nevertheless, God holds the Jews most dear for the sake of their Fathers; He does not repent of the gifts He makes or of the calls He issues— such is the witness of the Apostle" (§4, citing Rom. 11:28–29). The ancient covenant has never been annulled; the promises of God to Israel have never been abrogated. Therefore, God's relationship with Israel is not to be regarded as having once existed but as now surpassed. A *living covenant* with God must be attributed to the Jewish people, even if Christ is that covenant's fulfillment.[96] For *Nostra aetate*, Judaism is now analogically related to—in fact, is the irreplaceable foundation of—the fullness of revelation found in the Christian faith.

Gerald O'Collins is right to conclude, then, that in "its style of language and the content of its teaching [Vatican II] firmly reversed [the council of] Florence."[97] Florence (1439–45) had taught that those remaining outside the Cath-

<hr/>

95. See Thomas F. Stransky, "Vatican II: Recollections of an Insider" ("Vatican II after Fifty Years" Symposium, Georgetown University, October 11, 2012), https://georgetown.app .box.com/s/n9kssnivy8ru3cr771bn. See also Stransky, "The Genesis of *Nostra Aetate*: An Insider's Story," in *Nostra Aetate: Origins, Promulgation, Impact on Jewish-Catholic Relations*, ed. Neville Lamdan and Alberto Melloni (Berlin: LIT, 2007), 29–53.

96. As a recent Catholic statement says, "On the part of many of the Church Fathers the so-called replacement theory or supersessionism steadily gained favor until in the Middle Ages it represented the standard theological foundation of the relationship with Judaism: the promises and commitments of God would no longer apply to Israel." See Commission for Religious Relations with the Jews, "The Gifts and the Calling," no. 17.

97. Gerald O'Collins, *The Second Vatican Council on Other Religions* (Oxford: Oxford University Press, 2013), 203.

olic Church, including Jews, heretics, and schismatics, would be cast into hell.[98] O'Collins insists that Vatican II, given its highly irenic teaching about the Jews (and adherents of other religions), engaged in a "dramatic change of doctrine" constituting a "massive shift in the official doctrine . . . of the Catholic Church."[99] He concludes that, on this point, one sees in Vatican II a case of "considerable discontinuity" and, when compared to Florence, "a case of reversal."

O'Collins is surely right that *Nostra aetate* is a reversal of the 1442 decree for the Jacobites (wherein the statement about Jews and heretics was made). And this reversal is one that all Christians now warmly endorse. But does this modification qualify as a *permutatio fidei*, a reversal of a fundamental landmark of the Catholic Church? Here I agree with Francis A. Sullivan, who, for a variety of reasons, speaks of the "very limited doctrinal authority" of the Florentine decree, which in fact was a decree of union with and instruction for the Coptic Church.[100] While formally belonging to an ecumenical council, this statement, Sullivan notes, is neither defined nor dogmatic teaching. In the case of Florence, then, one may speak of its glaring discontinuity with the teaching of Vatican II—but not of a reversal of a doctrinal landmark, of a *permutatio fidei*.[101]

To its lasting credit, Vatican II took the difficult but fruitful path of affirming that, while Catholicism possesses the fullness of divine revelation, other Christian churches, other religions (Judaism uniquely), and even unbelievers of goodwill have much in common with the Catholic faith. *Nostra aetate* can legitimately be called an organic development—a Vincentian *profectus fidei*—since it left intact the church's core theological beliefs about Jesus Christ, even while surrounding those beliefs with a positive and sensitive evaluation of other religions. But alongside this development are certain reversals and clearly identified discontinuities—in the church's rhetoric, in the theological construct of supersessionism, and in the statement in the decree for the Jacobites.

---

98. See Denzinger-Hünermann, *Enchiridion symbolorum*, ed. Robert Fastiggi and Anne Englund Nash (San Francisco: Ignatius, 2010), no. 1351.

99. O'Collins, *Second Vatican Council on Other Religions*, 204.

100. Francis A. Sullivan, *Creative Fidelity* (New York: Paulist Press, 1996), 78, 115–16. See also Sullivan, *Salvation outside the Church?* (Eugene, OR: Wipf and Stock, 2002), 66–69.

101. Along similar lines, Edward H. Flannery writes that the anti-Semitic tradition in Christendom "never became a universal dogmatic tradition, let alone a formal definition, of the Church; even though individual bishops, regional councils, and certain popes dealing in *ad hoc* applications of principle were disseminators of it." See *The Anguish of the Jews* (New York: Macmillan, 1965), 274.

The organic development in *Nostra aetate* can only partially be ascribed to *ressourcement*. The dearth of citations from earlier church teaching witnesses to the embarrassing paucity of positive statements about Judaism. Yet there is a significant recovery of certain Pauline passages, particularly Romans 9–11, in which Judaism is spoken of most favorably and not in a crassly supersessionist way.[102] This "development cum reversal" can also be ascribed to *aggiornamento* or updating. Historical events that formed the sociocultural horizon for Vatican II—the Holocaust, World War II, and a nuclear weapons–inspired Cold War—forced the bishops and theologians at the council to think beyond old animosities and divisions. The desire to forge strong links with other men and women constituted part of John XXIII's intentions for Vatican II from the outset. *Nostra aetate* went a long way toward fulfilling those hopes.

Continuing Questions Arising from Vatican II and *Nostra aetate*

By stressing participation and analogy—and so the similarity between Catholicism and other religions—Vatican II gave rise to theological questions that it did not directly ask and had no intention of resolving. I would like to mention a few of these questions (without examining them in detail) since they were not on the conciliar agenda and remain the subject of continuing theological investigation.

Nostra aetate speaks of other religions as reflecting a "ray" of that truth which enlightens all men (§2). It also says that "the Catholic Church rejects nothing that is true and holy in these [other] religions" (§2). These positive affirmations have led many to explore the precise relationship of other faiths to Jesus Christ and Christianity. The questions below provide a mere sampler of the debated issues arising out of *Nostra aetate* and the council at large.[103]

---

102. Building on Romans and *Nostra aetate*, a recent document states, "The Church is the definitive and unsurpassable locus of the salvific action of God. This however does not mean that Israel as the people of God has been repudiated or has lost its mission (see *NA*, no. 4). The New Covenant for Christians is therefore neither the annulment nor the replacement, but the fulfillment of the promises of the Old Covenant." See Commission for Religious Relations with the Jews, "The Gifts and the Calling," no. 32.

103. Some influential books in this ongoing discussion include Jacques Dupuis, *Christianity and the Religions: From Confrontation to Dialogue* (Maryknoll, NY: Orbis Books, 2002); Gerald O'Collins, *The Second Vatican Council on Other Religions* (Oxford: Oxford University

1. Although the council did not speak directly of revelation in other religions, may one assert that other religions (besides Judaism) are, to some extent, repositories of divine revelation?
2. If other religions possess God's truth in some manner, can it then be asserted that their adherents are saved *through* their religions rather than *despite* their religions? Do other religions have a positive value in God's plan of salvation? Do they offer a saving knowledge of God? Vatican II teaches that all men are saved through Jesus Christ: "[God] has constituted Christ as the source of salvation for the whole world" (*LG* §17). But if other religions reflect dimensions of truth and holiness, can the *practice* of these religions lead to salvation?
3. We read in *Ad gentes* §7, "God, in ways known to Himself, can lead those inculpably ignorant of the Gospel to find that faith without which it is impossible to please Him (Heb. 11:6); yet a necessity lies upon the Church (1 Cor. 9:16), and at the same time a sacred duty, to preach the Gospel." In this passage one sees the theological dilemma: the church must preach the gospel because all are saved through Christ. Yet God can lead others, in ways unknown to us, to the faith that saves. To what extent, then, is belief in Christ necessary for salvation?

Today, these three issues are ardently debated among theologians. I would simply add that the notions of participation and analogy, structural principles of the Vatican II documents, encourage a generally positive evaluation of other religions. But that evaluation is limited to those beliefs that other faiths hold in common with Judeo-Christian revelation.

Gaudium et spes

Vatican II's invocation of analogical reasoning is carried over to its Pastoral Constitution on the Church in the Modern World, *Gaudium et spes*. In its determined attempt to forge strong links between the Catholic Church and modernity, *Gaudium et spes* appears to reverse much papal teaching of the nineteenth and early twentieth centuries. This is so much the case that Joseph Ratzinger stated that the document gives the impression of being "a revision of the *Syllabus* of Pius IX, a kind of countersyllabus." He continues:

Press, 2013); and Gavin D'Costa, *Vatican II: Catholic Doctrines on Jews and Muslims* (Oxford: Oxford University Press, 2014).

The one-sidedness of the position adopted by the Church under Pius IX and Pius X in response to the situation created by the new phase of history inaugurated by the French Revolution was, to a large extent, corrected *via facti*, especially in Central Europe, but there was still no basic statement of the relationship that should exist between the Church and the world that had come into existence after 1789. . . . The text serves as a countersyllabus and, as such, represents, on the part of the Church, an attempt at an official reconciliation with the new era inaugurated in 1789.[104]

Describing *Gaudium et spes* as a "countersyllabus"—effectively a reversal of the affirmations of the nineteenth-century *Syllabus of Errors*—offers a forceful example of discontinuity between Vatican II and the prior magisterial tradition. Indeed, the difference between the two documents is at times pronounced. While the *Syllabus*, with its archly dialectical mode of expression, sought to distance the church as far as possible from liberal modernity, roundly condemning its errors, *Gaudium et spes* places a marked accent on the analogical *similarity* between Catholicism and the quest for truth and justice found in sectors of contemporary society.

John O'Malley, once again, highlights the conciliatory style characterizing Vatican II. The council's approach "reminds people of what they have in common rather than of what might divide them."[105] The pastoral constitution, in particular, is characterized by a vocabulary of "mutuality, friendship, partnership, cooperation—and dialogue."[106] As has been argued throughout this chapter, such "kinship" or "fraternal" language is undergirded philosophically by the conciliar emphasis on analogical reasoning and its (tacit) distinction between the prime analogue and secondary analogates. Christianity possesses the fullness of divine revelation. But even those who simply seek the truth with a sincere heart are intrinsically related to the Christian faith. They participate in a common human nature, which is made in the image and likeness of God, and display a desire for truth and justice. In this way, they formally and substantially share in the perfections found in Christianity.

104. Joseph Ratzinger, *Principles of Catholic Theology*, trans. Mary Frances McCarthy (San Francisco: Ignatius, 1987), 381–82.

105. John O'Malley, "Trent and Vatican II: Two Styles of Church," in *From Trent to Vatican II: Historical and Theological Investigations*, ed. Frederick J. Parrella and Raymond F. Bulman (Oxford: Oxford University Press, 2006), 313.

106. O'Malley, *What Happened*, 267.

This is why *Gaudium et spes* does not hesitate to adduce the anthropological links that bind together all human beings, whether or not they are religious believers. All participate in the same human nature and have the same divine vocation: "Since all men possess a rational soul and are created in God's likeness, since they have the same nature and origin, have been redeemed by Christ and enjoy the same divine calling and destiny, the basic equality of all must receive increasingly greater recognition" (§29).

In *Gaudium et spes* the council sought to reimage the relationship of Christianity to the surrounding culture. It was not a matter of fortifying the borders of the Christian faith—and condemning positions outside it. It was, once again, a matter of exploring the links that bind together men and women of very different backgrounds and beliefs. A good example of this is the way communism was handled by the council. Many bishops—some four hundred—had asked the Theological Commission to condemn atheism and communism in Schema XIII (as *Gaudium et spes* was called). Just such a condemnation had been issued by Pius XI in his encyclical *Divini redemptoris* of 1937. *Gaudium et spes* now offered an opportunity for the church to intensify that condemnation with the weighty authority of an ecumenical council. Bishop Charue, one of the vice presidents of the Theological Commission, noted that this proposal was explicitly discussed with Paul VI: "The pope says this [a condemnation] would be anti-pastoral and bad politics. . . . The text of Schema XIII ought to open doors, not close them. People, whether atheists or communists, ought to know that the Church loves them and is concerned with them."[107] We see here both Paul's and the council's desire to accent the similarities among men rather than their differences. All participate in a common humanity and a quest for a better world—including atheists and communists.

Spoils from Egypt

This stress on "commonality" also allowed Vatican II to invoke the ancient theme of spoils from Egypt. Since I have discussed this theme at some length, there is no need for a reprise here. Suffice it to say that in the Sacred Scriptures themselves, St. Paul makes appeals to the wisdom of the ancient Greek poets Epimenides (Titus 1:12) and Menander (1 Cor. 15:33). Similar employment of worldly wisdom may be found in Origen, Basil, and Augustine and

---

107. *Carnets-AMC,* 282–83 (November 8, 1965).

throughout the Christian tradition—always with the proviso, however, that such wisdom be measured and disciplined by the gospel.

Gaudium et spes stands squarely in that tradition when it says, "Faithful to her [the church's] own tradition and at the same time conscious of her universal mission, she can enter into communion with the various civilizations, to their enrichment and the enrichment of the Church herself" (§58). Similarly, "Just as it is in the world's interest to acknowledge the Church as an historical reality, and to recognize her good influence, so the Church herself knows how richly she has profited by the history and development of humanity. . . . From the beginning of her history she has learned to express the message of Christ with the help of the ideas and terminology of various philosophers, and has tried to clarify it with their wisdom, too" (§44).

These citations stand in a long tradition of the church taking "spoils" from the world. Given that ancient tradition, I hesitate before O'Malley's claim that *Gaudium et spes*, by affirming that the church learns from the world, is saying something "new and strange."[108] It may be unusual to find such a statement explicitly asserted by an ecumenical council. But *that* the church has been enriched by other cultures and philosophies is one of her *oldest* theological affirmations, attested from the time of St. Paul onward. As Newman says, the church ingests ideas from every culture, always stamping them with the image of the Master.[109]

Gaudium et spes's explicit reference, then, to the church's "profiting" from the world is simply the assertion of an old and well-founded Christian tradition. At the same time, the pastoral constitution does not endorse an *uncritical* appropriation of human wisdom. Ideas may be ingested from every quarter, but there is also care, in the words of Origen, not to build the golden calf of Bethel.

Nature and Grace

Some of the theological unease that has accompanied *Gaudium et spes* over the past fifty years is likely caused by the pastoral constitution's heavy accent on the autonomy of the natural order. This theme—intrinsically related to "spoils"—affirms that the world has its own *relative* autonomy, even apart

108. O'Malley, *What Happened*, 268.

109. John Henry Newman, *An Essay on the Development of Christian Doctrine* (London: Longmans, Green, 1894), 382.

from the transcendent truth of divine revelation.[110] In the following passage, for example, we see the council's unvarnished affirmation of the natural order: "If by the autonomy of earthly affairs we mean that created things and societies themselves enjoy their own laws and values . . . then it is entirely right to demand that autonomy. Such is not merely required by modern man, but harmonizes also with the will of the Creator. For by the very circumstance of their having been created, all things are endowed with their own stability, truth, goodness, proper laws and order" (§36). The natural order is here affirmed as having its own stability, its own excellence, its own autonomy. However, the pastoral constitution equally insists that this autonomy is not absolute. The natural order itself must be "bathed in the light of the Gospel" if earthly realities are to be properly understood: "Bishops . . . should, together with their priests, so preach the news of Christ that all the earthly activities of the faithful will be bathed in the light of the Gospel" (§43).

It is worth pointing out that *Gaudium et spes* uses some form of the word *simul* (at the same time) over forty times. While not all these instances refer to the conjunction between nature and grace, many of them display the council's attempt to balance the relative autonomy of the created order with the revealed order of grace and faith. The created order and divine revelation are not at antipodes; they are complementary realities, even if the former always requires, to reach its proper end, the light provided by divine truth.[111]

Given its attempt to balance the autonomy of the modern world with the truth of the gospel, Schema XIII was controversial even before it was presented to the bishops for discussion and voting. Was it too optimistic? Did it engage in an uncritical appropriation of modernity? Was it starkly discontinuous with Catholicism's nineteenth-century condemnations of modern rationalism?[112]

---

110. Understanding the precise relationship between the "natural" and the "supernatural" orders was at the root of deep theological tensions within the conciliar majority—and was clearly manifested in the redaction of *Gaudium et spes*. For a good analysis of this tension, see Joseph A. Komonchak, "Augustine, Aquinas or the Gospel *sine glossa*? Divisions over *Gaudium et spes*," in *Unfinished Journey: The Church 40 Years after Vatican II*, ed. Austen Ivereigh (New York: Continuum, 2003), 102–18. See also Wicks, *Investigating Vatican II*, 207–10.

111. This conciliar theme—the proper relationship between nature and grace—was later exploited by Pope Benedict XVI in his addresses to the civil authorities of various countries. For the council and Benedict on this theme, see Thomas G. Guarino, "Nature and Grace: Seeking the Delicate Balance," *Josephinum Journal of Theology* 18 (March 2011): 150–62.

112. Strongly defending the schema's balancing of nature and grace was the historian of Thomism M.-D. Chenu. For his comments on the schema, see Komonchak, "Augustine," 108–9. On the other hand, Wicks reports that Henri de Lubac's conciliar notes are filled with

Lukas Vischer, the Swiss Reformed theologian who was the designated observer from the World Council of Churches, strongly criticized the phrase "signs of the times," which was found in earlier drafts of *Gaudium et spes*. Was it truly the task of the church to respond to the signs of the times, as the document argued? Vischer contended that *signa temporum* was an ambiguous phrase. What was needed was a *critique* of the times by the gospel. Taking account of Vischer's comments, the council fathers used the phrase *signa temporum* only once in *Gaudium et spes*. And even then the word *perscrutandi* (scrutinize) was added, indicating the church's need to carefully examine the claims of the world. The final text reads, "The Church has always had the duty of scrutinizing the signs of the times and of interpreting them in the light of the Gospel" (§4). Vischer's criticisms helped to clarify the proper relationship between the church and the world.[113]

Nonetheless, theological concerns about the document persisted. Charue wrote in his journal that while Schema XIII was overwhelmingly approved in general form (by a vote of 2,111 *placet* to 44 *non placet*), there remained opposition "by a group of Germans, notably Cardinal Frings under the influence, so it is said, of Ratzinger."[114] A week later, Charue remarked that "Cardinal Frings . . . thinks that only part of the document is worthy of an [ecumenical] council."[115] Given this opposition, changes to the text continued. Unsurprisingly, Gérard Philips, who had labored over many of the conciliar documents, was given a crucial role in the editing.[116] It was

---

"concern and alarm" lest the "opening to the world" eclipse the gospel. Wicks, *Investigating Vatican II*, 208.

113. See Richard Schenk, "Officium signa temporum perscrutandi: New Encounters of Gospel and Culture in the Context of the New Evangelization," https://www.stthomas .edu/media/catholicstudies/center/ryan/conferences/2005-vatican/Schenk.pdf. Also Carmen Aparicio, "Contributo di Lukas Vischer alla *Gaudium et spes*," in *Sapere teologico e unità della fede: Studi in onore del Prof. Jared Wicks* (Rome: Editrice Pontificia Università Gregoriana, 2004), 3–19.

114. *Carnets-AMC*, 262 (September 23, 1965). See Brandon Peterson, "Critical Voices: The Reactions of Rahner and Ratzinger to 'Schema XIII' (Gaudium et Spes)," *Modern Theology* 31 (January 2015): 1–16. Some years later, Ratzinger described *Gaudium et spes* as breathing an "astonishing optimism." See *Principles of Catholic Theology*, 380. G. Alberigo speaks of the "facile historical optimism . . . that runs through so much of the constitution *Gaudium et spes*." See Alberigo and Komonchak, *History of Vatican II*, 5:611.

115. *Carnets-AMC*, 278–79 (September 30, 1965). For an exhaustive study of the redaction of *Gaudium et spes*, see G. Turbanti, *Un concilio per il mondo moderno: La redazione della costituzione pastorale "Gaudium et spes" del Vaticano II* (Bologna: Il Mulino, 2000).

116. Philips himself thought the pastoral constitution failed to reach the level of theological rigor found in *De ecclesia* and *De revelatione*. Writing on October 11, 1964, he states,

surely thought that Philips's own theological rigor would ease the concerns of the German contingent.[117]

At the end of the day, the council passed *Gaudium et spes* with overwhelmingly positive votes. But was the pastoral constitution in material continuity with the doctrinal tradition? Was it a development *in eodem sensu*? Or did the church bend the knee to modernity, courting a *permutatio fidei*?

Continuity and Discontinuity

At the start of this discussion, I mentioned Ratzinger's description of *Gaudium et spes* as a "countersyllabus," a term referring to the *Syllabus of Errors*, the list of deviations attached to Pius IX's 1864 encyclical *Quanta cura*. It would be difficult to express discontinuity more strongly than calling a conciliar document the polar opposite of nineteenth-century papal teaching. Where precisely does one find this discontinuity?

Part of it may be found in the analogical optic adopted by *Gaudium et spes* and by Vatican II as a whole. The Pian era of total hostility toward the culture of liberal modernity had come to an end. The conciliar accent, rather, was on the similarity between Catholicism and society at large. Contemporary men and women, even unbelievers, were often interested in truth, justice, and the search for a better world. In this way they participated in goals shared by, and central to, the life of Christianity. *Gaudium et spes* points to these similarities as the basis for continuing dialogue: "Everything we have [previously] stated about the dignity of the human person, and about the human community and the profound meaning of human activity, lays the foundation for the relationship between the Church and the world, and provides the basis for dialogue between them" (§40). It is precisely this accent on what the church *shares* with the world—not how it differs from it—that animates much of the pastoral constitution. And this change of philosophical style, from dialectical opposition to analogical similarity, caused much consternation in St. Peter's Basilica.

As noted, some four hundred bishops asked for an explicit condemnation of atheism and communism. In the internal discussions of the Theo-

---

"There is resistance . . . to schema XIII which is actually weak from the theological point of view and has been inadequately prepared." *Carnets-GP*, 132.

117. *Carnets-AMC*, 278 (September 30, 1965). But this scenario was not to pass without problems. In late October 1965, Philips suffered a serious cardiac incident, causing Charue to lament, "We are going to see the blow this is to the [Theological] Commission" (279).

logical Commission, Bishop Charue warned against such a condemnation, noting that the teaching of an ecumenical council "can block one for centuries." He added, "One thinks of our [present] difficulties given the condemnations of the nineteenth century which formally condemned liberalism and socialism."[118] Charue realized that the anathema of an ecumenical council could easily obstruct dialogue far into the future.

To circumvent the complaints of those asking for an explicit condemnation, a sentence was introduced into the *relatio* (theological explanation) of Bishop Garrone: "The Commission has attentively, and on several occasions, examined the question [of atheism and communism]. It has concluded that given the pastoral character of the council, and in view of the declared intentions of John XXIII and Paul VI, it ought to hold to those [conciliatory] principles."[119] Unsurprisingly, Garrone's comments failed to satisfy. Three weeks before the close of the council, Charue wrote: "Carli [a leader of the conservative minority] does not disarm."[120] In actual fact, Carli and his allies had raised an important theological point. To what extent could the council reverse prior magisterial teaching? The Coetus Internationalis Patrum was concerned that the 1937 encyclical of Pius XI explicitly condemning communism was now being reversed or, at best, ignored. Was prior magisterial teaching to be blithely abandoned by *Gaudium et spes*?

Paul VI took Carli's protests seriously and sought to defuse the situation by personally speaking with him. Throughout the council, Paul saw his role as uniting the bishops—and sought virtual unanimity in the voting for each of the documents. Having several hundred bishops vote *non placet* on a major conciliar constitution would surely call that statement's teaching into question. To forestall that possibility, the committee decided to mention *Divini redemptoris* in the footnotes in *Gaudium et spes*.[121] Was this simply a bone thrown to the barking Coetus? Was it an obvious case of "masking"—relegating the document to a footnote without explicitly adverting to its contents?

To some extent, masking was indeed at work. Vatican II's decision

118. *Carnets-AMC*, 250 (April 7, 1965).

119. *Carnets-AMC*, 286 (November 15, 1965). For Garrone's *relatio*, see *AS* IV/6, 560–63.

120. *Carnets-AMC*, 287 (November 16, 1965). Luigi Carli, bishop of Segni, Italy, was one of the leaders of the conservative group of bishops known as the Coetus Internationalis Patrum. For more on the Coetus, see Alberigo and Komonchak, *History of Vatican II*, 2:195–200. Charue adds that "the results of the votes are shockingly good, proving, one more time, the inanity of Carli and his group."

121. *Carnets-AMC*, 290 (November 19, 1965).

to stress the analogical similarity of all others to Catholicism—secondary analogates in relation to the prime analogue—did not leave much philosophical or rhetorical room for condemnations. Placing *Divini redemptoris* in the footnotes allowed the council to signal its recognition of the prior magisterial tradition, but without jeopardizing the newer, analogical approach. Vatican II certainly did not endorse atheistic communism but, once again, it was seeking to change the optic of the church-world relationship.

This continuity/discontinuity issue was also raised by another issue treated tangentially by *Gaudium et spes*: birth control. Once again, a prior papal encyclical was at the root of the discussion. Was the ban on contraception—clearly taught in the 1930 encyclical of Pius XI, *Casti connubii*—still binding on Catholics? If so, would the Pontifical Commission on Population, Family, and Birth, established by John XXIII and expanded by Paul VI, be given the freedom to examine the entire birth-control question?

Casti connubii is cited several times in the footnotes of *Gaudium et spes*. Of these, the most important is found in the section dealing with marriage: "Certain questions which need further and more careful investigation have been handed over, at the command of the Supreme Pontiff, to a commission for the study of population, family, and births, in order that, after it fulfills its function, the Supreme Pontiff may pass judgment. So with the doctrine of the magisterium in this state, this holy synod does not intend to propose immediately concrete solutions" (note 14).

Joseph M. Heuschen, auxiliary bishop of Liège, was a member of the Theological Commission and president of the subcommittee on marriage. In a postconciliar essay he notes that Paul VI had offered some "suggestions and counsels" on the marriage section of *Gaudium et spes*.[122] One of the pope's suggestions, no doubt out of deference to the council's more conservative minority—who zealously sought to preserve ordinary magisterial teaching—was that references to *Casti connubii* be included in the text. When this was resisted by the subcommittee, Paul insisted on inserting mention of the encyclical into *Gaudium et spes*.[123]

Heuschen's careful analysis of this footnote reminds us that while development *in eodem sensu* was important at Vatican II, material continuity with the tradition did not forestall the *possibility of reversals* of prior teach-

122. See J. M. Heuschen, *"Gaudium et Spes*: Les Modi Pontificaux," in Lamberigts, Soetens, and Grootaers, *Les Commissions Conciliaires*, 353–58, at 354.
123. Heuschen writes that on December 4, 1965, Mgr. Haubtmann told him that "he had received the order from on high . . . to insert the citations from *Casti connubii* into note 14." "Les Modi Pontificaux," 357.

ing. As Heuschen points out with regard to note 14, it "does not include a modification of doctrine, but it does not exclude its possibility."[124] Vatican II "did not exclude that an evolution in the teaching of the Church is possible. The council has therefore left the door open."[125]

Heuschen's comments are important because he clearly envisions the possible reversal of the ordinary teaching of the Catholic Church. In this instance, of course, a reversal (Heuschen uses the softer word "evolution") did not occur, either at the council or afterward. But the *possibility* was clearly anticipated. Once again, material continuity *in eodem sensu* is not demanded by ordinary magisterial teaching. And if a reversal of *Casti connubii* had indeed occurred, it would not have amounted to a *permutatio fidei* in the sense condemned by Vincent of Lérins. As I have noted several times, material continuity with the tradition does not necessarily entail the irreformability of prior authentic teaching.

Some may conclude, however, that the relegation of *Casti connubii* to the footnotes was another instance of masking in *Gaudium et spes*, comparable to the similar relegation of *Divini redemptoris*. But that may not be entirely the case. There was legitimate concern about the freedom of the Pontifical Commission on Population, Family, and Birth. If Pius XI's encyclical had been cited in a straightforward fashion, it could easily have given the impression that the Commission's conclusions had been dictated a priori by Vatican II itself. Citing *Casti connubii* in the note was a way of indicating that the council was mindful of prior authentic teaching, while not insisting on its binding nature.[126]

Concluding Reflections on *Gaudium et spes*

Any fair reading of *Gaudium et spes* will conclude that, doctrinally speaking, the document is in material continuity with earlier Catholic teaching. Indeed, it is the only conciliar document that explicitly repeats the crucial statement of John XXIII insisting on such continuity: "The *depositum fidei* or truths of the faith are one thing; the manner in which they are expressed is another, *eodem sensu eademque sententia*" (§62).

124. Heuschen, "Les Modi Pontificaux," 355.
125. Heuschen, "Les Modi Pontificaux," 358.
126. Another interesting example of masking is the way *Gaudium et spes* dealt with the Galileo affair. For details, see *Carnets-AMC*, 250 (April 7, 1965).

Perhaps the most telling indication of the continuity of the pastoral constitution with the prior doctrinal tradition is found in Charue's journal: "[Rosaire] Gagnebet and [Umberto] Betti were charged by Ottaviani to review the texts [the various parts of *Gaudium et spes*] from the doctrinal point of view. They have pointed out only some details."[127] Gagnebet and Betti were conservative Roman theologians, experts on the Theological Commission. It is no surprise that Ottaviani, the president of the *De Fide*, asked these two men to comb *Gaudium et spes* for errors and inconsistencies. If there had been any, they would have immediately and loudly announced them.

Nevertheless, like the other documents of Vatican II, *Gaudium et spes* has an organizing principle that differs from that of prior councils: it seeks to stress the similarity between Catholicism and the modern world, with the accent placed on the attributes and "perfections" shared between the two. Christianity is upheld as the fullness of divine revelation, while the modern world is regarded as sharing in the quest for truth, justice, and peace. The structuring principle of the text—here as elsewhere—is the relationship between the prime analogue (Catholicism) and the "participating" secondary analogates.

Because of this relentless accent on similarity, *Gaudium et spes* betrays some embarrassment about past papal denunciations of modernity. The pastoral constitution passes over the church's nineteenth-century condemnations of liberalism in silence, "as if they had never happened."[128] One finds nothing in *Gaudium et spes* remotely similar to the *Syllabus*'s condemnation of this position: "In the present day it is no longer expedient that the Catholic religion should be held as the only religion of the State, to the exclusion of all other forms of worship" (§77). Or more famously: "The Roman Pontiff can, and ought to, reconcile himself, and come to terms with progress, liberalism and modern civilization" (§80). Vatican II ignored these assertions and, in fact, tacitly reversed them. This was the basis for Ratzinger's description of *Gaudium et spes* as a kind of "countersyllabus."

As we have seen in prior sections, reversals of ordinary teaching do not constitute, in and of themselves, corruptions of the faith, *permutationes fidei*. But neither can these obvious reversals be called "developments," as if they were in homogeneous continuity with the antecedent tradition. Such reversals are more properly regarded as part of the *process* of development, wherein the church gradually reaches a conclusion that it judges to be more in harmony with the gospel than prior ordinary teaching. Of course, it goes

---

127. *Carnets-AMC*, 287 (November 16, 1965).
128. O'Malley, "Trent and Vatican II," 312.

without saying that *Gaudium et spes* did not endorse every aspect of modernity. Even a cursory reading of the constitution will reveal its strong critiques of atheism, of a worldly progress without God, and of an anthropology unmoored from Jesus Christ. But, as with other themes at Vatican II, the accent was on the similarity of the church with the modern world, rather than on the world's errors, faults, and deficiencies.

Conclusion

In this chapter we have examined several of the topics treated at Vatican II that are still disputed fifty years later. I have sought to bring several points to the fore:

1. Analogical reasoning was the crucial structuring principle of many of the most important conciliar texts. Indeed, the traditional metaphysical tools of participation and analogy provided the philosophical basis for several of Vatican II's documents. This claim is supported by Congar's assertion, surprising at first sight, that "St. Thomas, the *Doctor communis*, furnished the writers of the dogmatic texts of Vatican II with the bases and structure of their thought. We do not doubt that they themselves would make this confession."[129]

2. In accordance with this conciliar employment of participation and analogy, Catholicism is presented as the fullness of divine revelation, while other belief systems formally share, with different levels of intensity, in the attributes and "perfections" that Catholic Christianity possesses. While not using traditional terminology—which in fact is scrupulously avoided—the council teaches that the Catholic Church is the prime analogue to which others (secondary analogates) are profoundly related.

3. The deeply irenic rhetorical style of the council, pointed to again and again by John O'Malley, is itself undergirded by a philosophical shift from dialectical and equivocal approaches to an analogical one. This latter perspective emphasizes similarity rather than difference, and this, indeed, is the structure of the entire council.

4. These principles allowed Catholicism to express its deep unity with other Christians, with the adherents of other religions (particularly

129. Congar, "La théologie au Concile," 53.

Judaism), and with all seekers after truth and justice. There is no dif-
fusion of Catholic uniqueness in the conciliar texts, but neither is
there an affirmation that Catholicism *alone* purveys the truth. Other
churches and other religions possess and convey the truth, with varying degrees of intensity.

5. This shift from dialectical (or equivocal) to analogical reasoning
   changed the optic through which other realities were seen and understood. Protestantism was viewed not as a heresy but as a deeply
   Christian reality, strikingly proximate to the Catholic faith. The Jewish
   religion was no longer viewed as a superseded covenant but as the
   sine qua non foundation for Christianity and itself the exemplar of
   a living covenant. Nonreligious seekers after truth were viewed not
   as condemnable atheists and Marxists but as partners in building a
   society where justice reigns. In all of this, Catholicism did not change
   its self-understanding—but it did stress its close proximity to others.

6. As we have seen, Vincent of Lérins argues that the church always undergoes change over time; indeed, he tells us, this change occurs *plane
   et maximus*. For Vincent, it is the *type* of change that is truly important:
   profectus or *permutatio*. Vatican II generally developed earlier ecclesial
   teaching in a harmonious, organic, architectonic way. Such changes
   preserve the material continuity and identity of earlier Christian doctrines even while developing them *in eodem sensu eademque sententia*.

7. At the same time, Catholic theology allows for reversals of ordinary
   magisterial teaching, and such reversals certainly took place at Vatican II. But these were not reversals of fundamental dogmatic landmarks and so do not represent, in Vincent's terminology, *permutationes fidei*—pernicious corruptions of the Christian faith.

Let us now examine some other theological issues that remain disputed long after the close of Vatican II, again asking whether they represent
advances or corruptions of the prior Christian tradition.

CHAPTER 5

Disputed Topics and Material Continuity

In the previous chapter, we examined various teachings of Vatican II that remain disputed even after more than fifty years. Were these teachings homogeneous and organic developments, indicating growth *in eodem sensu?* Or were they corruptions, additions *in alieno sensu?* We concentrated on those conciliar teachings that clearly utilize participation and analogical reasoning as structuring principles, arguing that such use resulted in a significant modification of approach—from difference and dialectic to proximity and similarity. In this final chapter, we will examine several other critical conciliar issues that remain in dispute. While not employing analogical reasoning in every instance, these topics are important because they raise the foundational theological question of our study: Were the changes enacted by the council in material continuity with the prior tradition of the Catholic Church?

Primacy and Collegiality

One of the fiercest battles at Vatican II had to do with the relationship between the papal office and the universal Catholic episcopacy. Just here we have one of the most striking instances of both doctrinal development and *ressourcement* reasoning.

This issue of the collegial authority of the episcopacy arose right at the outset of the council. Indeed, several authors point to this initial incident as a decisive turning point for Vatican II. For only when the bishops who were gathered in St. Peter's insisted that they would nominate their own candidates for the conciliar commissions—and not simply accept the lists prepared in advance by Roman officials—did Vatican II become a council of *bishops* and not simply a synod controlled by the curia.[1] This assertion of episcopal authority so unnerved certain curial figures that Cardinal Ottaviani, the head of the Holy Office and president of Vatican II's Theological Commission, was later reported as saying that "evil [*le mal*] is found in the very composition of the Theological Commission."[2]

A second significant event involving episcopal authority occurred on October 15, 1962, just a few days after the council had opened. Dissatisfied with the schema on the church, Cardinal Suenens of Brussels asked the Louvain professor Gérard Philips, an expert on the Theological Commission, to write a new redaction of *De ecclesia*.[3] Philips acceded to the request, although the production of a new text—when the original one had not yet been debated—seemed treasonous. When the new draft became known, Philips was challenged for his actions; he defended himself by claiming that he "was not able to refuse this service requested by the Belgian episcopacy."[4] Nevertheless, Cardinal Ottaviani was furious that other schemas on *De ecclesia* were circulating privately. The cardinal attacked Philips in a speech in St. Peter's (December 1, 1962), although without naming him.[5]

As is well known, the original schema *De ecclesia* was criticized by several bishops on the first day of discussion—namely, Liénart, Elchinger,

1. Benedict XVI, in his speech of February 14, 2013, stated that this action was an "act of responsibility" on the part of the conciliar bishops. For the voting, see *AS* I/1, 225–29. See also L. Declerck and M. Lamberigts, "La role de l'épiscopat belge dans l'élection des commissions conciliaires en octobre 1962," in *La Raison par Quatre Chemins*, ed. Jean Leclercq (Louvain: Peters, 2007), 279–305.

2. *Carnets-GP*, 120 (July 12, 1964). Philips continues, "It is the only time that he [Ottaviani] spoke to me frankly, telling me what he has thought from the beginning." Ottaviani made a similar remark to Charue, who was astounded that he was speaking this way almost two years after the original event. See *Carnets-AMC*, 198 (June 3, 1964).

3. "In a letter to Veronica O'Brien, Suenens stated that on October 13, 1963, on leaving St. Peter's Basilica, Cardinal Cicognani said to him: 'Why don't you write your own schema *De Ecclesia*?'" See *Carnets-GP*, 157–58n16, with reference to the Suenens archive. The year noted should be 1962. By October 1963 the new text of *De ecclesia* had already been approved by the Theological Commission.

4. *Carnets-GP*, 84 (April 8, 1963).

5. *Carnets-GP*, 86 (April 9, 1963). The entire incident was painful for Philips. He writes, "Card. Ottaviani said [in aula]: '*Audiant omnes*. Even before the text of *De Ecclesia* was made public, there was already another text that was widespread!'" For Ottaviani's speech, see *AS* I/4, 121–22 (December 1, 1962).

and especially De Smedt, who famously stated that the schema displayed little of an ecumenical spirit and was rife with triumphalism, clericalism, and juridicism.[6] After several days of strident episcopal criticisms, the originally prepared schema *De ecclesia* was withdrawn from the council floor without a formal vote. As Philips would later remark, the prepared texts on revelation and the church corresponded neither to the exigencies of the contemporary world nor to the ecumenical spirit proposed by John XXIII. In fact, the original schemas represented "surpassed theological opinion."[7]

By early 1963, several new schemas on the church were circulating among bishops and theologians.[8] A subcommittee of the Theological Commission was established to choose a base text suitable for discussion. Philips relates in his conciliar journal that on February 24, 1963, members of the subcommittee (absent Browne and Parente, the two most conservative members) held a meeting with several theologians to discuss the various alternative schemas. It was decided that, among the circulating drafts, Philips's text of *De ecclesia* had the best chance of winning the approval of both the Theological Commission and the bishops gathered in St. Peter's Basilica.[9]

A couple of days later, Charue phoned Philips to inform him that his text would indeed be taken as the basis for discussion, although he should also take account of various other projects (the drafts submitted by Parente and by the German theologians, as well as the long Chilean text). Each bishop on the subcommittee would name a theological expert, and together the experts would establish the text and present the reasons for their positions. Philips notes that two of the most conservative theologians, Gagnebet and Schauf, had no real objection to his schema. He adds of Karl Rahner,

6. For the various speeches, see *AS* I/4, 126–48. Congar remarked that De Smedt's criticisms "seem to me excessive." Yves Congar, *My Journal of the Council*, trans. Mary John Ronayne and Mary Cecily Boulding (Collegeville, MN: Liturgical Press, 2012), 226 (December 1, 1962). Philips notes that De Smedt was regularly applauded by the assembly and that he made a great impression by saying that the Theological Commission had several times refused the request for collaboration made by the Secretariat for Christian Unity. *Carnets-GP*, 90 (April 9, 1963).

7. *Carnets-GP*, 82 (April 8, 1963).

8. *Carnets-GP*, 91 (April 10, 1963). Of the text written by German theologians, circulating in January 1963, Philips says, "The text of the Germans is long, heavy and written in bad Latin. All the clarity of the Latin language is lacking." He adds, "It would be an immense labor to make this text usable."

9. *Carnets-GP*, 92 (April 10, 1963). Charue notes that Bishops König, Garrone, and Seper, along with theologians Moeller, Daniélou, and Rahner, were present at this meeting. *Carnets-AMC*, 88–89 (February 24, 1963).

"Rahner is very meticulous, but at bottom very orthodox and always available for consultation; he has offered to help me to the maximum. For him, it is clear that our text cannot reflect his personal opinions, but neither should it exclude them. This will suffice for him."[10]

Philips relates that the theologians worked well together. On March 5, 1963, their revised schema of *De ecclesia* was presented to the full Theological Commission with Philips, the principal author, as spokesman. The text was immediately attacked by Ottaviani, who called the new schema "too pompous, non-pastoral, and non-theological."[11] Philips ascribes Ottaviani's description to the fact that his revised schema lacked scholastic explanations, precisely because John XXIII had called for new modes of expression. After an hour and a half of sustained resistance to the new schema, Ottaviani finally relented, telling Philips to introduce his text. Philips recognized that this was the crucial turning point: "If I am able to speak," he records, "I have a serious chance of having my text accepted."[12]

But things started off badly. First, in the new schema the word *sacramentum* was applied to the church—a term unfamiliar in this context. On top of this, the draft spoke of the church from the Holy Trinity (*Ecclesia de Trinitate*)—once again, an unfamiliar phrase. As he carefully explained the text, Philips recognized that opposition would gradually diminish. But at the start of the discussion there was distrust of his work. The bishops were generally amenable to his explanations, but at times the theologians, according to Philips, advanced "mere quibbles and even nonsense." However, Philips was careful not to wound anyone's vanity, for this would serve only to derail the project. He acknowledges in his journal that theologians of the "left" feared that he made too many concessions, but he adds, "It is not a question of forcing the right to a capitulation, but of rendering the text equally acceptable to them, without giving them a complex of losers."[13]

Philips recognized that the schema *De ecclesia* needed to be acceptable to both the progressive majority and the more conservative minority. This desire to establish an appropriate *via media*, a text supported by all members of the *De Fide*, characterized Philips's approach during his entire time leading the Commission's discussions. After the memorable session of March 5, 1963—when the Louvain theologian successfully defended

10. *Carnets-GP*, 93 (April 10, 1963).
11. *Carnets-GP*, 98 (April 11, 1963). Charue remarks, "Voilà! It is now he who speaks of pastoral!" *Carnets-AMC*, 99 (March 5, 1963).
12. *Carnets-GP*, 98 (April 11, 1963).
13. *Carnets-GP*, 99 (April 11, 1963).

his new schema—friends assured him that "the text [was] now 'on the rails.'" Indeed, he notes, "They tell me that I alone am able to pass the best text [through the Theological Commission]; but this privilege is hardly enviable!"[14]

Nonetheless, Philips understood that he had achieved no small success in this conciliar drama. He had managed to rally support for a successor document to the original *De ecclesia*, despite the acrimony that attended the discussions in the basilica. This had not been done without tears: "I have not been able to give complete satisfaction to either the 'left' or the 'right'; I am exposed to blows from both sides." Nonetheless, the Theological Commission gradually placed its confidence in Philips, impressed by his serene exposition of the matters at hand.[15] As the moderator of the Theological Commission, Philips proceeded carefully, especially given the various theological proclivities represented on the *De Fide*. Early on, even individual words were the source of heated argument, leaving Philips to remark that such skirmishes were an indication of "how close the fighting [was], just as the fights still to come [would] be."[16]

By March 13, 1963, the Theological Commission had examined and approved chapters 1 and 2 of *De ecclesia*—on the church as mystery and on the hierarchy (this order would later change). Several bishops congratulated Philips on his labors, causing him to remark that this was quite a turnabout from December 1962, when he was considered guilty of treason for having composed a new schema on the church. He notes, "At bottom, 'the right' is now equally convinced that the text has been sensibly improved, and that it will have a good chance of passing at the Council."[17] At this point *De ecclesia* was still a torso, with only the first two chapters completed. Much work

14. *Carnets-GP*, 99 (April 11, 1963).

15. *Carnets-GP*, 99 (April 11, 1963). Even Ottaviani gradually became less combative, giving Philips the freedom to edit the text. Philips remarks that the cardinal is likely impressed by "my eloquence in Latin." *Carnets-GP*, 101 (April 11, 1963). Later, Archbishop Pietro Parente, a conservative member of the curia and of the Commission, congratulated Philips on his *signorilità* (gentlemanliness) toward all members of the *De Fide*.

16. *Carnets-GP*, 100 (April 11, 1963).

17. *Carnets-GP*, 103 (April 11, 1963). Philips considered himself something of a conciliator between the two theological tendencies present at the council. While his theological sympathies lay with the majority—and so with the advances in exegesis, ecumenism, and theological reflection that had occurred since the 1940s—he nonetheless understood the concerns of the minority and was gradually able to gain the confidence even of very conservative thinkers such as Tromp and Ottaviani. Congar was impressed by Philips's ability to win the trust of disparate personalities; see *My Journal*, 509.

remained to be done over the next year and a half before the final voting in St. Peter's.[18]

After Pope John XXIII's death in June 1963 (and so before the second conciliar session), attention turned to the coming conclave. Would there be an attempt to reverse the gains already achieved by the council? Philips speculated that this was highly unlikely: the bishops were exercising leadership, free discussion was taking place on crucial issues, and several schemas were in the process of being rewritten. Vatican II was well on its way to renewing the church. Philips concludes, "At bottom, the shift in the Church has taken place; there can be no backtracking. May the Lord guide the Church!"[19] Although himself a moderate theologian, Philips supported the change in perspective that had taken place at the council. He pointed to the revival of ideas such as collegiality and the priesthood of the baptized that had fallen into desuetude in Catholic thought. No matter the pope elected to replace John XXIII, it was clear that theological development would continue. Revealingly, Philips writes, "From the first to the fourth and last chapter of *De ecclesia* [at this point, the document was four chapters long], the 'new' tendency [*tendance 'nouvelle'*] has obtained substantially what it wished. . . . I have personally written or rewritten the general project [*De ecclesia*]. In November [1962], people did not expect this evolution and, still less, that the 'older' tendency [*tendance 'ancienne'*] would have submitted to it."[20]

How did Philips understand this "new tendency"? We have already had occasion to examine an article he wrote at the end of the first session, giving us a window into the theological thinking of the conciliar majority and minority.[21] Philips continued to reflect on the two theological trajectories present at the council, remarking in late 1963, "The tensions and the oppositions between the Curia and above all the Holy Office on one side, and the majority of the Council on the other side, have been intense. At the root of this conflict, one finds the opposition between a juridical notion of theology and an open theology of revelation which takes account of modern

---

18. It is an indication of Philips's humility that he left Rome almost immediately after the *De Fide* approved his text, remarking, "If I had remained at Rome, I would have inevitably courted a certain triumphalism, which would be to no benefit." *Carnets-GP*, 104 (March 15, 1963).

19. *Carnets-GP*, 112 (June 2, 1963).

20. *Carnets-GP*, 113 (June 2, 1963).

21. Gérard Philips, "Deux tendances dans la théologie contemporaine," *Nouvelle revue théologique* 85 (March 1963): 225–38.

scientific work."[22] By "modern scientific work" Philips was referring to the advances that had taken place in exegesis and in historical studies—and in the continuing project of *ressourcement*. Such labors gave theology its vibrancy and immediacy. As Philips would later say, theology needs "more of life, more of reality, more that truly grips the believer—so it is not so notional."[23] He pointed to chapter 4 of the draft of *De ecclesia*—with its emphasis on the call to holiness of all the baptized—as an example of implementing recent studies on the Bible and the early church. The schema's accent on the laity's vocation to sanctity, as well as its emphasis on the episcopal role in church governance, did not reverse any significant church teaching, but it undoubtedly recovered ancient themes that had become obscured over time, integrating them more fully into the life of the church.

As the second session drew to a close, Philips noted that the schema *De ecclesia* still needed much work. Further, in response to Paul VI's request that each Commission elect a second vice president and a second secretary, the *De Fide* had elected Bishop Charue and Philips himself, respectively, with Philips garnering sixteen votes against six for the more conservative Dominican Rosaire Gagnebet. From this point forward, Philips would have a leading role in all the deliberations of the Theological Commission. Although he already had the principal role in *De ecclesia* and was working on *De revelatione* and Schema XIII (ultimately *Gaudium et spes*), Philips believed the voting indicated that the more conservative members of the *De Fide* regarded him as a "party man," a progressive. "Nevertheless," he writes in his journal, "I hope this will change nothing in my spirit of openness."[24]

The Debate on Collegiality

Episcopal collegiality—the authority of bishops acting together with the pope in the governance of the Catholic Church—was an issue that surfaced at the beginning of the council and remained controversial until *Lumen gentium* was formally promulgated in late 1964. Three crucial points emerged on the subject that would be debated throughout the council.

First, some argued that Peter *alone* is the rock on which the church was founded. The apostles are not the foundation; they themselves *rest* on

22. *Carnets-GP*, 114 (November 14, 1963).
23. *Carnets-GP*, 147 (May 27, 1965).
24. *Carnets-GP*, 116 (December 2, 1963).

the Petrine foundation. This issue even troubled Paul VI: Can one say, on the basis of Scripture, that the church was founded on the Twelve? Where does one find the biblical foundations of collegiality?[25]

Second, while everyone agrees—and history attests—that bishops have authority when gathered together *in* ecumenical councils, can it be likewise affirmed that they exercise real authority, indeed supreme apostolic authority, *outside* of a council? If pushed too far, does this thesis of supreme episcopal authority lead inexorably to conciliarism—to an ugly standoff between dueling authorities, pope and council? Cardinal Browne, thinking within Thomist categories, argued that if supreme power were to be attributed to the episcopacy, it could not be considered an *active* power, since such a power is naturally oriented toward action and this would force a competition with the authority of the pope. Rather, episcopal authority must be a *passive* power, a capacity that can be *activated* by the pope.[26]

Third, how should one interpret the phrase from Vatican I that the pope exercises his infallible authority *ex sese non ex consensu Ecclesiae* (by himself alone, not needing the consent of the wider Church)? Philips himself had suggested that the schema should read, "The Pope expresses the faith of the Church." But this was taken to have an unsavory modernist flavor.[27]

What theological concerns swirled around these three issues? The main source of unease, undoubtedly, was that an emphasis on the collegial authority of the episcopacy would jeopardize papal primacy. That, in turn, would compromise and undermine the "landmark" dogmatic teaching of Vatican I. Philips writes of Cardinal Browne, a vice president of the Theological Commission, "[He] fears above all a definition of the collegiality of

---

25. *Carnets-GP*, 101 (April 11, 1963); *Carnets-AMC*, 162 (March 6, 1964).

26. Browne's objection would carry weight. The *Nota praevia explicativa* (appended to *Lumen gentium*) reads, "In his consecration a person is given an ontological participation in the sacred functions [*munera*]; this is absolutely clear from Tradition, liturgical tradition included. The word 'functions' is used deliberately instead of the word 'powers' [*potestates*], because the latter word could be understood as a power fully ready to act" (§2). The *Nota praevia* will be discussed below.

27. *Carnets-GP*, 102 (April 11, 1963). Philips will later write that when we see the "*ex sese*" cited in *Lumen gentium* §25, we see how a "subsequent council *maintains intact and reinforces* the doctrine once proclaimed, while, at the same time, adding some clarifications, marking better the nuances and intentions, and preventing misunderstandings." See Gérard Philips, *L'Église et son mystère au IIe Concile du Vatican: Histoire, texte et commentaire de la Constitution "Lumen Gentium,"* 2 vols. (Paris: Desclée, 1967–68), 1:329; emphasis added. Philips's point, of course, is that the *idem sensus* (the same meaning) is maintained but now placed within a wider horizon.

the episcopate so that there would be established, next to the Curia, a permanent committee of bishops in Rome."[28] In other words, there would be a permanent attempt to limit the power and authority of the papacy.

Similarly, Bishop Charue, the other vice president of the *De Fide*, recounts his visit to Paul VI in early 1964: The pope "appeared shocked" when Charue told him that collegiality had been approved unanimously by the Theological Commission, *etiam Praeses* (even by the president, Ottaviani himself). To Paul's concerns about episcopal authority Charue responded, "The college [of bishops] is only able to exist if it is *sub et cum Petro*: without the pope, it dissolves." He continued, "Whatever may be the *potestas* [power] of the bishops, its *exercitum* [exercise] can only exist in communion with the Pope and under his primatial authority."[29]

But it was not only the more conservative minority who had complaints about *De ecclesia*. In an August 2, 1964, journal entry, Philips remarks, "Yesterday, I had a long meeting with the Cardinal [Suenens] on Mariology and ecumenism in *De ecclesia*. In what concerns collegiality, he was affected by the reactions of a certain number of Orthodox who see in this matter [the relationship of Pope and bishops] a reinforcement of Roman juridicism concerning the primacy of the Pope." Philips regrets that the "two worlds" of Orthodoxy and Catholicism do not meet, especially since there has not been permanent contact between the two churches for a long time. "We are still far from each other," he ruefully concludes.[30] But Philips does not concede that the text is weak on synodality: "It is clear that in the schema *De ecclesia* a certain number of affirmations remain very juridical and Western. After all, one thinks and writes according to one's own nature. But one finds equally several considerations (and probably many more than the Orthodox think) on the Church as communion. Between *communio* and 'juridical' structure there is certainly a difference, but not a contradiction. And is it not a distinctive sign of Catholicism that it reconciles two 'different' conceptions—not for the sake of an artificial harmonization, but for the sake of a more profound understanding?"[31]

Philips's comments are important on several levels. First, while the genre of *De ecclesia* is not scholastic, neither is it missing the necessary juridical elements to ensure that the proper relationship between primacy and

---

28. *Carnets-GP*, 94 (April 10, 1963).
29. *Carnets-AMC*, 176 (March 16, 1964).
30. *Carnets-GP*, 123 (August 2, 1964).
31. *Carnets-GP*, 123 (August 2, 1964).

collegiality is maintained. Second, Philips insists that the dogmatic constitution purveys a *communio* ecclesiology—envisioning the universal church
as a communion of local churches around the world. That aspect is present,
even if not as intensely as some Orthodox observers desired. Third, one
sees in Philips's remarks the true Catholic sense of *semper simul* (always
at the same time). Complementarity, synthesis, and conjunction were the
characteristic theological traits of the council, rather than unilateralism. One
sometimes hears the comment, in a disparaging tone, that the Vatican II
documents are the result of "compromise." But it is often the case that several strands of the tradition are artfully woven together. This was certainly
Philips's intentional methodology in *De ecclesia*.

Five Questions of Orientation

The issue of episcopal collegiality became so heated that the council modera-
tors (Cardinals Lercaro, Suenens, Agagianian, and Döpfner) took an unusual
procedural step in order to orient the future discussion of the schema *De
ecclesia*. Given the large number of speeches in St. Peter's and the mass of
written emendations submitted to the *De Fide*, several votes would be taken
on chapter 2 (on the hierarchy) of the schema. These votes would reveal
more clearly the mind of the conciliar fathers and provide direction to the
Theological Commission in its continuing redaction of the text.[32]
    Five crucial questions were voted on in St. Peter's on October 30, 1963.
Among the inquiries were the following: Does the college of bishops, in
teaching, governing, and sanctifying, succeed the apostolic college so that
this body, in union with its head, the Roman pontiff, and never without its
head, possesses plenary and supreme power in the universal church? And
does this power belong to bishops by divine right (rather than by papal
mandate)? If answered in the affirmative, these questions would assert the

32. For a full discussion of these five questions, along with the voting tallies, see Claude
Troisfontaines, "À propos de quelques interventions de Paul VI dans l'élaboration de 'Lumen
gentium,'" in *Paolo VI e I Problemi Ecclesiologici al Concilio* (Brescia: Istituto Paolo VI, 1989),
97–143, at 103; Philips, *L'Église*, 1:29–31; John O'Malley, *What Happened at Vatican II* (Cambridge, MA: Belknap Press of Harvard University Press, 2006), 180–85; and Alberto Melloni,
"The Beginning of the Second Period: The Great Debate on the Church," in *History of Vatican II*, ed. Giuseppe Alberigo and Joseph A. Komonchak (Maryknoll, NY: Orbis Books, 2000),
3:70–91. For the official text of the five questions and the introduction made by the general
secretary, see *AS* II/3, 573–75 (October 29, 1963).

supreme authority of the episcopal college—an authority, however, that can only be validly exercised in union with the bishop of Rome.

Unexpectedly, the votes on the five questions were overwhelmingly in favor, indicating a desire by the bishops to return to an earlier understanding of ecclesial authority, and ending the increasingly solipsistic papacy of the nineteenth century. The pope governed the church *together with* the universal episcopacy, which exercised its authority *de jure divino*, not by papal mandate. As Philips was fond of saying: in the Gospels, Peter is *protos* (Matt. 10:2), but he is never alone.

The voting tallies of October 30, 1963, came as something of a shock to the theologian Edward Schillebeeckx.[33] He was astounded by the impressive majorities on each of the questions, noting that "no one expected such a resounding yes." The speeches on the floor of St. Peter's had given the impression that the bishops were split down the middle, leading the Dominican theologian to remark, "Thus, *interventions in the Aula* can give a totally distorted picture!" Indeed, Schillebeeckx saw in the votes on the five questions a resounding affirmation of episcopal authority as a *de jure divino* structure of the church: "Christ did not give responsibility over the entire church to *one person*, the Pope, but to an *Apostolic College* with Peter by divine right as its head. Thus: the obligation to proclaim the Good News *with authority* and to *sanctify* humanity . . . falls *collegially* to the college of bishops, united with their head, the Pope."

Philips, for his part, thought the votes of October 1963 simply confirmed what was well attested in church history: the *de jure divino* authority of the college of bishops. Without such a juridical-ontological understanding of episcopal authority, the bishops would be reduced to mere apparatchiks. How could the episcopacy possibly exercise supreme authority in an ecumenical council if the body of bishops did not already *possess* that authority by divine mandate? In other words, bishops cannot simply be "conceded" or "delegated" authority for the sake of an ecumenical council, in a one-time fashion. Such authority must be possessed from the beginning, as a *constitutive* dimension of the church. It was precisely through the recovery of the church's traditional understanding (a clear example of *ressourcement* thinking) that Philips hoped to overcome the one-sided papalism that had emerged from Vatican I.

---

33. The following quotations are taken from *The Council Notes of Edward Schillebeeckx, 1962–1963*, ed. Karim Schelkens (Leuven: Maurits Sabbebibliotheek Faculteit Godgeleerdheid, 2011), 34–36.

The votes on the five questions had made clear that the *munus* (power or function) of episcopal governance comes with consecration, not with papal delegation. Yet Pope Pius XII had taught, and indeed well before Pius it was generally held, that bishops received their power of jurisdiction directly from the Roman pontiff.[34] The common theological opinion was that while episcopal consecration conferred the power of sanctifying, this was not true of the power of jurisdiction and governance. This latter authority could only be bestowed by the pope through a canonical mission. This very thesis was ardently defended by the more conservative theologians on the *De Fide*, Tromp, Gagnebet, and Schauf.[35]

Philips, on the other hand, was intent on showing that the power of jurisdiction (and so the theological foundation for collegiality) is necessarily rooted in episcopal ordination—not dependent on any canonical determination.[36] Once again, he argued, if governance and jurisdiction were not bestowed with episcopal consecration, how then could one explain the authority bishops exercised in an ecumenical council? Did it make sense that such solemn authority was simply *delegated temporarily* by the pope? The five votes of October 30, 1963, answered these questions with crystal clarity. In this instance, the light shed by research into church history—*ressourcement* thinking—allowed for the reversal of ordinary magisterial teaching.

In a surprising statement from a man involved with virtually every conciliar document, Philips wrote soon after the council ended, "The link established between sacramentality and episcopal collegiality constitutes, in our eyes, *the most important theological progress advanced by the council*."[37] Beyond the extraordinary advances that the council achieved on ecumenism, on Judaism, on revelation, and on religious freedom, Philips singles out *this* issue as the most significant one theologically. The reason for this is surely that the link between sacramental consecration and gov-

---

34. Pius XII wrote in the 1943 encyclical *Mystici corporis*, "Yet in exercising this office they [bishops] are not altogether independent, but are subordinate to the lawful authority of the Roman Pontiff, although enjoying the ordinary power of jurisdiction *which they receive directly from the same Supreme Pontiff*" (§42; emphasis added).

35. *Carnets-AMC*, 162 (March 7, 1964).

36. Philips, *L'Église*, 2:306. On this point Philips, and the majority on the *De Fide*, received unexpected help from the curialist Archbishop Parente, who argued that the separation of order and jurisdiction was an opinion of later medieval canonists, not well founded in the earliest tradition. Troisfontaines remarks that it took courage for Parente to maintain this position. See "Quelques interventions," 107n19.

37. Philips, *L'Église*, 2:306; emphasis added.

ernance provided the *essential theological basis* for a robust doctrine of collegiality. Only if the power of jurisdiction was strictly linked with episcopal consecration was there a *sacramental basis* (and not simply a canonical or legal basis) for the collegial authority of bishops. And only a vigorous doctrine of collegiality could overcome the one-sided papal solipsism inherited from Vatican I, thereby providing the church with *universal leadership* in the future.

Although the votes of 1963 were decisive, they certainly did not end the debate on collegiality, which would continue for another year. For the more conservative bishops and theologians, collegiality continued to threaten papal primacy as well as the papal magisterium, which was exercised *ex sese*, without the consent of the church. Did the votes of 1963 threaten the dogmatic landmarks of the Catholic Church? Was Vatican II unwittingly courting a *permutatio fidei*? Precisely because of these concerns, the debate on collegiality extended far into 1964.[38]

Paul VI's *Suggerimenti*

In his visit to Paul VI in March of 1964, Bishop Charue had assured the pope that "the College [of bishops] is only able to exist if it is *sub et cum Petro*: without the pope, it dissolves." Despite these assurances, concerns about collegiality continued to cause anxiety to both Paul VI and the conciliar minority. This was so much the case that in May of 1964 the pope offered thirteen *suggerimenti* (suggestions) to improve the schema, although leaving the Theological Commission the freedom to discuss them.[39] Speaking about these suggestions, Philips remarks, "[Archbishop] Parente has reacted strongly, which largely facilitates the task for us."[40] Having a conservative member of the Holy Office express reservations about Paul VI's proposed modifications allowed the other members of the *De Fide* to breathe more freely. Philips continues, "We accept most of the 13 propositions which are,

38. Jared Wicks notes that the five votes of October 30, 1963, galvanized the more conservative minority bishops. From that day forward, they "fused together" to propagate their point of view. See "Vatican II's Turn in 1963," *Josephinum Journal of Theology* 19 (2012): 194–206, at 203.

39. For Paul's suggestions, contained in his letter of May 19, 1964, see Jan Grootaers, ed., *Primauté et collégialité: Le dossier de Gérard Philips sur la Nota explicativa praevia* (Leuven: Leuven University Press, 1986), 125–32.

40. *Carnets-GP*, 120 (July 12, 1964).

at base, some repetitions and precautions. We avoid, however, the texts that are too sharp."[41]

One of the "sharp" texts strongly resisted by the Commission was Paul's proposal that the pope is answerable "to the Lord alone."[42] The *De Fide* responded that the formulation risked excessive simplification. Parente himself stated that this formula was "a blunder."[43] In actual fact, the pope is answerable to many dimensions of divine revelation: the basic structure of the church, the sacraments, the definitions of councils, and other elements too numerous to mention.[44]

Paul VI was fearful that the schema's accent on episcopal authority would cast a shadow on papal primacy. If that occurred, then *De ecclesia* would have called into question the material continuity of the Catholic faith as defined by Vatican I. Further, the pope was under tremendous pressure from the bishops and theologians of the more conservative minority, with Parente—himself a traditional theologian—stating that there had been an "assault" on the pope.[45] With his thirteen suggestions, Paul VI was hoping to achieve two goals: (1) to calm the anxieties of the minority bishops by showing that Vatican II was a harmonious development of Vatican I, and (2) to achieve moral unanimity in the voting on the dogmatic constitution. Paul was convinced that any new direction in the church—as collegiality surely was, at least in recent centuries—needed to be supported by a vast majority of the world's Catholic bishops.

Philips was not convinced that Paul's gambit would be successful. Despite the revisions to *De ecclesia*, "experience teaches us one more time that

---

41. *Carnets-GP*, 120 (July 12, 1964). Paul VI thought he had every right to make suggestions and, at times, to demand changes to the conciliar texts. As he is reported to have said, "The pope is not simply the council's notary. He has a responsibility to God and to the Church." See Carlo Colombo, "Paolo VI: Il Papa non può essere il semplice notaio del concilio," in *Inchiesta sul Concilio*, ed. Gian Franco Svidercoschi (Rome: Città Nuova, 1985), 34.

42. For Paul's suggested addition, "*Ipse, uni Domino devinctus*," see Grootaers, *Primauté et collégialité*, 130.

43. Indeed, Parente stated that Paul VI's formulation "*sapit haeresim*" (smacked of heresy). See *Carnets-AMC*, 202 (June 5, 1964). Charue adds that the pope's formulation risked being a new "*ex sese*," referring to the assertion of Vatican I (1869–70) which taught that the dogmatic definition of a pope is of itself, and "not because of any consent of the church," irreformable. *Carnets-AMC*, 204 (June 5, 1964).

44. The response of the Theological Commission to this papal suggestion may be found in *AS* III/1, 247. The Commission further argues that the suggested phrase would induce new anxieties, particularly in the Easterners, as has been historically the case with the *ex sese* clause.

45. *Carnets-AMC*, 193 (June 1, 1964).

the resistance [to collegiality] will manifest itself until the last moment."[46] Philips was not mistaken—the assault on the pope and the schema would continue. But the majority of bishops and theologians on the Theological Commission were committed to the idea that episcopal collegiality was well attested in the life of the early church and that a one-sided papalism was both recent and deeply detrimental to the life of Catholicism.

Continuing Discussions on Collegiality

Although the five questions of 1963 had given clear direction to the Theological Commission—and although the Commission successfully handled the thirteen modifications proposed by Paul VI—pressure on the *De Fide* continued from several quarters. Philips writes in his journal, "Certain of those on the 'left' or on the 'right' have said that I have been too indulgent. In all cases, I have tried to keep the peace. But not peace at any price. I have never said or defended what I did not consider to be true. In brief, I have tried to be honest."[47] Philips *was* criticized for being too indulgent toward the more conservative minority, but he never relented on two crucial points at the heart of *De ecclesia*: (1) that the collegial authority of bishops was well attested in the history of the church, and (2) that the *munus* of governing comes not from papal delegation but is bestowed with episcopal consecration. On both of these points, *ressourcement* thinking, in its twin manifestations, was at work. On the first point, one finds a *supplement* to the Catholic doctrinal tradition; on the second, one finds a *reversal* of the ordinary magisterial teaching of *Mystici corporis*.

Philips was entirely opposed to those who tried to reduce the collegial authority of bishops to "charitable solicitude" (a mere offering of advice) to the pope. This was the kind of "collegiality" favored by many in the more conservative minority. Philips countered this position with his most significant and weighty theological argument: if the bishops' authority were reduced to charitable solicitude, they would not have the authority to teach *even in an ecumenical council*. For if the bishops were truly to *exercise* authority, then they needed to *possess* authority in a juridical sense. It could never be a matter of the pope "delegating" authority to them for a delimited period of time. Further, bishops acting together—as a group—must have a

---

46. *Carnets-GP*, 120 (July 12, 1964).
47. *Carnets-GP*, 124 (August 2, 1964).

juridical form as a college. In other words, there must be a unique episcopal *ordo* that possesses authentic authority in and of itself and that is capable of acting with authoritative force.[48] In fact, this body is a locus of *supreme authority*, even if, in exercising such authority, it must act in consonance with the bishop of Rome.[49]

But the more conservative minority continued to resist Philips and the Theological Commission on these points: "From the side of the 'right' they are very happy with 'charitable solicitude' for they do not accept [episcopal] authority: this last would belong only to the Pope."[50] To this Philips tirelessly responds: the very fact of an ecumenical council militates against the minority position, for "the lived theology of the conciliar event would become impossible [without authority belonging *de jure* to the episcopal college]." Indeed, "the Council would not be able to be convoked, if there did not exist a body of bishops by full right [*plein droit*]."[51] But even though the episcopal college can only teach authentically *with the pope* and never without him, several in the minority found distasteful the idea that supreme authority resides *also* in the college of bishops. Cardinal Ottaviani, for example, continued to insist that there cannot be two subjects of infallibility (pope and episcopal college). The pope alone is the subject of authority, and bishops receive their infallibility through him; Peter alone is the *vicarius Christi*. To speak otherwise, for Ottaviani, was to distort settled Catholic doctrine.[52]

Toward a Final Vote on *De ecclesia*

Paul VI opened the third session of the council on September 14, 1964, with a ringing endorsement of collegiality.[53] The pope insisted that the present council must teach about the apostolic office of bishops, thereby completing the work of Vatican I. Of the many important issues addressed by the council, this one was of the greatest gravity and delicacy. Indeed, Paul continued, Vatican II's deliberations on the role of the bishops would be its dis-

---

48. *Carnets-GP*, 128–29 (August 14, 1964).

49. It is for this reason that one of the questions of orientation (of October 30, 1963) spoke of "*duplex forma supremae potestatis*" (the dual form of supreme power).

50. *Carnets-GP*, 128 (August 14, 1964).

51. *Carnets-GP*, 129 (August 14, 1964).

52. *Carnets-AMC*, 112 (March 12, 1963).

53. Of Paul's speech Charue says, "The discourse of the pope is remarkable, and notably open to collegiality." *Carnets-AMC*, 214 (September 14, 1964).

tinguishing mark far into the future. Ever alert to the issue of homogeneous development, the pope made clear that *De ecclesia* would certainly confirm Vatican I's teaching on the unique authority of the Petrine office. But its principal task was to honor the prerogatives of bishops. What was required was a clarification "congruent with the doctrine of the papacy." As throughout the council, Paul VI was here a champion of harmonious development, change that is consonant with earlier doctrinal landmarks.

Despite these positive papal remarks, the battle for collegiality was not over. In fact, Philips relates, "The offensive against chapter three [on the hierarchy] continues even more strongly."[54] On September 21, 1964, Bishop Franič, a leading member of the minority, delivered a strong *relatio* (theological explanation) against collegiality, arguing that the Roman pontiff cannot be reduced to a *primus inter pares*.[55] Bishop Carli of Segni urged that the issue of collegiality be left to free theological debate, just as the council had decided not to enter into controversies over the Blessed Mother. Charue worried that Carli's suggestion might be gaining traction among some of the bishops.[56]

The decisive votes on *De ecclesia* took place in late September 1964. The votes were overwhelmingly in favor of the schema, causing Charue to remark that the "results are staggering, surpassing all hope."[57] Bishop Colombo, Paul VI's friend and advisor, had predicted that the number of negative votes would not exceed three hundred. Charue thought this entirely too optimistic, but the Italian bishop proved prescient. The maximum number of *non placet* votes was 328 out of 2,200.[58] Only 574 bishops voted *juxta modum* (with reservations) on the most controversial part of chapter 3, on the hierarchy. The critical number of two-thirds in favor—essential for approving a text—had been achieved.

Carli, one of the leading voices of the minority, was appalled at the overwhelmingly positive vote, causing Charue to remark that the opponents of collegiality, while loud and noisy, had no great influence on the bishops.[59]

---

54. *Carnets-GP*, 130 (September 17, 1964).

55. *AS* III/2, 193–201, at 194.

56. *Carnets-AMC*, 216 (September 14, 1964). Charue urged Archbishop Parente, a member of the Holy Office and a supporter of collegiality, to respond to Carli on the floor of St. Peter's using Paul VI's speech opening the third session. (Charue's remarks, while listed as September 14, 1964, clearly were made at a somewhat later date.)

57. *Carnets-AMC*, 216 (September 14, 1964).

58. *Carnets-GP*, 131 (October 11, 1964); *Carnets-AMC*, 217 (September 14, 1964).

59. *Carnets-AMC*, 217 (September 14, 1964). Again, this entry was written several days later than dated.

Paul VI was deeply relieved by the results of the voting, even calling these days "the most beautiful of his life."[60] Despite the efforts of a determined minority, the vast majority of bishops believed that the teaching authority of the episcopal college was a homogeneous development—not a distortion—of the prior dogmatic tradition.

In the last month before the final vote on *De ecclesia*, which would take place in November 1964, there was a flurry of activity. Over 5,500 *modi* (proposed amendments) had been submitted by the bishops for chapter 3.[61] The Theological Commission began to make small alterations to the text in hopes of winning over the schema's remaining opponents. On October 21, 1964, just a month before the final vote, Paul VI—still under pressure from the minority—received Philips in audience. Several authors mention the meeting, although with differing accounts of what precisely transpired.[62] Philips relates, unsurprisingly, that he defended before the pope the two theological propositions he regarded as essential: (1) the power (or function) of episcopal jurisdiction is bestowed with consecration, and (2) the episcopal college is a locus of supreme authority, although only with and under the pope (*cum et sub Petro*). On these two essential points, Philips never wavered. Indeed, he thought they constituted the most important theological advance of Vatican II. Although the meeting may have been a bit testy, the Louvain theologian later reflected, "I had spoken to him [Paul] with much frankness, above all during our second audience. He was, at base, in agreement with me."[63]

Philips worked hard—on the Theological Commission and with Paul VI himself—to show that the episcopal college (and so collegial authority) neither owes its existence to the pope nor is the result of a pragmatic papal decision. The college is a constitutive structure of the church. Paul VI may indeed have pushed back a bit on Philips, as several accounts of that October meeting (although not Philips's own) indicate.[64] The pope was under

60. Troisfontaines, "Quelques interventions," 116n36.

61. *Carnets-GP*, 132 (October 11, 1964).

62. For a list of versions, see *Carnets-GP*, 164–65n146.

63. *Carnets-GP*, 142 (May 24, 1965). Philips adds, "In what concerns the doctrine of collegiality, he [the pope] never hesitated, but he seemed to have been very sensitive to safeguard the primacy, especially since he had said with great insistence that this primacy is now in great danger."

64. Albert Prignon, rector of the Belgian College, states in his journal that Philips had the impression, after his meeting with Paul in October 1964, that the pope "had classed him as belonging to the party of the left and that he had lost his credibility." Prignon, *Journal*, 152 (October 12, 1965), cited in *Carnets-GP*, 164n146.

enormous pressure. He wanted to be certain that papal primacy was clearly preserved in *De ecclesia*, precisely to ensure that any change enacted by the council would be in continuity with the prior doctrinal tradition. Philips himself was sympathetic to Paul's anxieties. There had been great progress at the council, but some theologians had spoken as if Vatican II had shaken the very foundations of Catholic doctrine. This had made the pope's task more difficult. As Philips remarks, "The evolution of ideas in the Church, even if it has slowed down under pressure, is no longer able to be stopped. It is a pity that 'all' has been placed into question and rendered uncertain for many believers. The extremists of the left have made our task very difficult."[65]

This revelatory sentence causes us to recall the statement made by the French minister of education to Bishop Elchinger: "You are doing a bad job at the Council. You are calling everything into question. What was true yesterday is no longer true today." Congar thought the cause of this unfortunate sentiment was the headline-hungry media. Philips, for his part, casts blame upon certain (unnamed) extremists who cannot distinguish between a legitimate "evolution"—which Philips fully sanctions—and the desire to place "all" into question, thereby stressing discontinuity and rupture with the antecedent tradition.[66]

Nota praevia explicativa

Up until the eleventh hour, the idea of collegiality was contested. Philips relates that on the evening of November 10, 1964, he received a note from Paul VI with a request to examine an enclosed letter. The letter, written by the Dominican theologian Gagnebet, an expert on the Theological Commission, once again attacked the very notion of collegial authority, arguing that the episcopacy cannot be a locus of supreme authority in the church, even

---

65. *Carnets-GP*, 133 (October 11, 1964). Later Philips will remark, "Certain expressions (from the 'left') according to which Vatican I 'was nonetheless left standing' seemed to have been the cause of this [Paul VI's] concern." *Carnets-GP*, 142 (May 24, 1965). Philips saw his own tendencies as centrist: "My intervention has not been revolutionary and there are probably some people who regret it." *Carnets-GP*, 124 (August 2, 1964).

66. While occasionally taking extreme leftists to task, Philips is equally wary of those conservative bishops and theologians who resist collegiality, ecumenism, and other conciliar advances. As he says, "Something that always strikes me about 'Roman' theologians—they listen so little. They know all and judge all from their own point of view which they confuse with the faith." *Carnets-GP*, 124 (August 2, 1964).

cum et sub Petro.[67] After reading Gagnebet's comments, Philips remarked, "Practically everything is called into question once again. I ask myself if he [the pope] might decide to postpone [the final voting on] chapter III. These are some difficult hours."[68]

Indeed, Paul VI remained concerned that a core group of conservative bishops and theologians still believed that collegiality would undermine the papacy. And the pope feared that a significant minority might publicly dissent from *De ecclesia*. Even two to three hundred *non placet* votes would be unacceptable, particularly for a dogmatic constitution. While the vast majority of bishops were in favor of collegiality, the pope wanted to achieve unanimity. This desire gave birth to the famous *Nota praevia explicativa*.

Hoping to mollify the opponents of collegiality, Paul VI asked the *De Fide* to prepare a note that would be appended to the end of *Lumen gentium*. This *Nota praevia* (explanatory note) would explain in juridical language the precise relationship between the pope and the bishops. There is no need to go through all the twists and turns connected with its composition.[69] The Note was written by Philips at the request of Bishop Colombo, the pope's friend and theological advisor.[70] But Colombo himself had also prepared a text. The two drafts were in competition until November 10, 1964, when the Theological Commission voted to retain Philips's work as the base text even while introducing modifications.[71] On November 13, 1964, word came that Paul VI had approved the *Nota praevia* and that the final votes on *De ecclesia* would take place on November 17 and 18, 1964. Philips refers to the whole process as something of a Calvary. Yet, with the passage of the dogmatic constitution now in sight, he says his "dominant sentiment is gratitude towards God."[72]

On November 16, 1964, the general secretary, Pericle Felici, introduced

---

67. Gagnebet argued that supreme power belongs to the episcopal college only *ratione capitis* (by reason of its head, the pope). For Gagnebet's letter, see Grootaers, *Primauté et collégialité*, 119.

68. *Carnets-GP*, 135 (November 14, 1964).

69. Philips offers a blow-by-blow account, from October 30 to November 16, 1964, in his *Carnets-GP*, 136–39. He offers even more detailed information in Grootaers, *Primauté et collégialité*, 85–119. Another detailed account may be found in Troisfontaines, "Quelques interventions," 97–143.

70. Troisfontaines writes: "It ought to be said . . . that the principal redactor of the *Nota praevia explicativa* was Philips, assisted and approved by the Theological Commission." See "Quelques interventions," 121.

71. The texts of both Philips and Colombo may be found in Grootaers, *Primauté et collégialité*, 98–104.

72. *Carnets-GP*, 135 (November 14, 1964).

the *Nota praevia* in St. Peter's Basilica. As mentioned in the previous chapter, this was a tense time at the council, so much so that journalists dubbed it *la settimana nera*, the black week of Vatican II. A confluence of events had caused profound unease: the pulling off the floor of *De libertate religiosa* by the council presidents, the imposition of nineteen changes to the Decree on Ecumenism by Paul VI, and now the addition of an extended note to *De ecclesia*. While the pope saw the Note as a chance to soothe those who opposed collegiality, other bishops regretted the addition, seeing it as a needless juridical imposition on the dogmatic constitution.

Not that the *Nota praevia explicativa* changed much. Douglas Horton, one of the Protestant observers at the council, remarked that the Note reminded him of one of those face-saving devices that, in fact, "change nothing." Similarly, Yves Congar said of the Note, "As far as I can see, it changes nothing."[73] Despite these assurances, the Note's mere existence disturbed many bishops and theologians. Congar thought the negative reactions were unnecessary, as the Note's purpose was clearly to appease the minority, playing the same part "that the speech of Zinelli had played at Vatican I."[74]

In a vote on the *modi* (amendments) to the disputed chapter 3 of *De ecclesia* (November 17, 1964), there were only forty-six negative votes (out of over two thousand). This landslide caused Philips to remark, "The pope has attained his objective of winning over the minority." Two of the most conservative Italian cardinals, Ruffini and Siri, "have passed on the instruction to vote for [*De ecclesia*]. The experts and the Fathers on the 'right' have obtained satisfaction."[75] Paul VI must have been deeply satisfied with the result. He had worked hard to ensure the moral unanimity of the conciliar bishops—and so the unity of the church. The *Nota praevia* served the purpose of reassuring the minority that the doctrinal landmarks defined at Vatican I had not been placed in jeopardy by *De ecclesia*. The supreme authority of the episcopal college must always be exercised *cum et sub Petro*, and so never without the college's head. Even Cardinal Browne, an ardent

---

73. Congar, *My Journal*, 682 (November 17, 1964). For Horton, see his *Vatican Diary*, 163, cited in O'Malley, *What Happened*, 367n140.

74. Congar, *My Journal*, 679 (November 16, 1964). At Vatican I, Bishop Zinelli spoke of the "four limits" that must be placed on the jurisdiction of the pope. These limits have become important in contemporary ecumenical discussion. See, e.g., Group of Farfa Sabina, *Communion of Churches and Petrine Ministry: Lutheran-Catholic Convergences*, trans. Paul Misner (Grand Rapids: Eerdmans, 2014), 45–47.

75. *Carnets-GP*, 140 (November 17, 1964).

supporter of the papacy and the curia, "declared himself 'almost' satisfied. The relief is great."[76]

The final vote on *De ecclesia* took place on November 19, 1964, with only ten votes against the dogmatic constitution. Philips notes that there was still some grumbling against the *Nota praevia*, but at this point the fight was over. *De ecclesia* had been overwhelmingly approved by the council.[77]

Given the controversy it caused, we may ask: Did the *Nota praevia* damage or modify the theological affirmations found in *Lumen gentium*? Not in Philips's judgment. He consistently argued that the Note was nothing more than a response to the most significant and weighty amendments submitted by the bishops. Indeed, Philips originally prefaced the Note with the phrase *pro facilitate lectoris* (to aid the reader). These words were, unfortunately, suppressed; without them the Note tends to have "an absolute character," which was not intended.[78] John O'Malley argues that Paul VI did indeed achieve virtual unanimity in the voting for *De ecclesia*, but "the price for that virtual unanimity was high." With the *Nota praevia*, Paul "gave those who opposed collegiality a tool they could—and would—use to interpret the chapter as a reaffirmation of the status quo."[79] But did the Note truly exact a high theological price? Philips often stated that there was nothing in the *Nota praevia* that was not to be found in *Lumen gentium* itself. Congar had made the same point about the Note: "It changes nothing." With or without the *Nota praevia*, the teaching of Vatican I on the primacy and infallibility of the papal magisterium had been preserved, but the primacy was now embedded within a collegial structure understood as a constitutive dimension of the church. It was precisely because of this structural element that Philips saw collegiality (and its basis in sacramental consecration) as the most significant *theological* advance of the council. It was a true *profectus*, a recovery and homogeneous development of the prior doctrinal tradition.

Despite the important advances found in both the Dogmatic Constitution on the Church and the Decree on Ecumenism (both formally promulgated on November 21, 1964), Philips was convinced that the turmoil surrounding the last week of the third session (*la settimana nera*) had obscured Vatican II's extraordinary theological achievements: "The good impression

76. *Carnets-GP*, 140 (November 17, 1964).

77. *Carnets-GP*, 140 (November 19, 1964).

78. Grootaers, *Primauté et collégialité*, 76. Philips responds to "inexact" interpretations of the *Nota praevia* in *L'Église*, 2:307–10.

79. O'Malley, *What Happened*, 245.

of the final vote on the Church is lost in great part because of all this turmoil. It is a pity."[80]

Writing in May 1965, between the third and fourth sessions, Philips looked back with some justifiable pride on the achievements of *Lumen gentium*. But he also recognized defects, stating that the controversial chapter 3 (on the hierarchy) "suffered from innumerable additions destined to guarantee the primacy. The text would have been able, for example number 22 on collegiality, to be a declaration of great amplitude, above all for relations with the East. The doctrine [on collegiality] remains without doubt the same, but there is a rampart of sharp precautions, of the sort that what would have made a good impression is now largely wasted."[81] Despite these flaws, Philips is still able to say that "the idea of communion is one of the most beautiful restorations that *Lumen gentium* has made to Catholic ecclesiology, which has been for too long stiffened by the idea of law."[82] At the distance of six months after promulgation, Philips asks himself, "Maybe I should have been more energetic? And refused all these additions [to chapter 3]? . . . Perhaps. But this would have probably provoked the failure of the whole thing. Further, what one finds there [in *Lumen gentium*] is true and exact. The greatest difficulty came from the preoccupation of the Pope."[83]

Philips knew that he had to make concessions in order to achieve unanimity in the Theological Commission and, ultimately, in St. Peter's Basilica. Despite inevitable defects, what is said in the document is "true and exact," uncompromising on fundamental principles. Philips never yielded on either the theological importance of collegiality or the fact that the *munera* (teaching, governing, and sanctifying) are given with consecration, not by delegation of the pope. Further, the pope is set *within* the church—as head of the college of bishops—not outside it or above it.[84]

---

80. *Carnets-GP*, 141 (November 19, 1964).

81. *Carnets-GP*, 142 (May 24, 1965).

82. Grootaers, *Primauté et collégialité*, 207. Philips adds that *Lumen gentium*, while preserving the solemn definitions of Vatican I, overcomes the solitude of the monarchical papacy with a lively doctrine of communion.

83. *Carnets-GP*, 142 (May 24, 1965).

84. Some wanted the pope spoken of as "head (*caput*) of the church," but Philips and the *De Fide* refused this, generally reserving "head of the church" for Christ and "head of the college" for the pope. See Troisfontaines, "Quelques interventions," 111. This is also why Philips, in number four of the *Nota praevia*, replaced "dependent" on the Roman pontiff with the "consent of" the pontiff. "Dependent" also gives the sense of someone "outside" the church. See Grootaers, *Primauté et collégialité*, 75. Also Philips, *L'Église*, 1:294–95.

Concluding Reflections on Primacy and Collegiality

Having reviewed some of the conciliar debates on the relationship between papal primacy and episcopal collegiality, let us now return to the questions at the center of this volume: Was Vatican II's teaching on collegiality in material continuity with the prior teaching? Did it constitute growth *in eodem sensu*? Or was the council's teaching a distortion of Christian doctrine? In sum, was Vatican II's teaching on collegiality an authentic *profectus* or a corrosive *permutatio fidei*?

The more conservative conciliar bishops were deeply concerned that the dogmatic landmarks defined at Vatican I would be undermined, or at least placed in jeopardy, if the present council taught that the universal body of bishops also constituted a locus of supreme authority in the Catholic Church. Could there be two such authorities? If so, would not the primacy of the bishop of Rome be compromised? In fact, *Lumen gentium* preserved the primacy of the pope—indeed, in chapter 3 of the dogmatic constitution this primacy is defended at great length—but it is defended *together with* the actual governing authority of the college of bishops, an authority that comes from episcopal consecration and not from any delegation by the Roman pontiff. Nonetheless, the supreme authority of the college can only be legitimately exercised *cum et sub Petro*—that is, together with the pope, the head of the college. As *Lumen gentium* teaches, "But the college or body of bishops has no authority unless it is understood together with the Roman Pontiff, the successor of Peter as its head" (§22).

There was not, then, in the council's teaching on collegiality, any overturning or, in Vincent's terms, transgression of prior doctrinal landmarks. The dogmatic definition of Vatican I remained intact even while this teaching was embedded in a more global vision of the teaching authority of the church's leaders. *Lumen gentium* would indeed have transgressed prior conciliar landmarks if it had taught that the exercise of the infallible papal magisterium was dependent on the consent of the episcopal body, or if it had taught that the universal episcopacy could exercise supreme teaching authority *without or even against* the bishop of Rome. But neither of those positions was sanctioned by Vatican II. With its strong emphasis on the teaching authority of bishops, *De ecclesia* clearly entailed growth—considerable growth—and even the reversal of prior ordinary teaching in service to such growth.[85] But no

---

85. I refer here to our earlier discussion of *Mystici corporis* of Pius XII. A discussion of the reversal of the encyclical may also be found in Philips, *L'Église*, 1:274–75.

dogmatic landmarks of the Catholic tradition were contravened by *Lumen gentium*. Paul VI was determined to satisfy the minority (and himself) by ensuring that the Petrine office and its unique magisterial authority was fully guarded by the dogmatic constitution. This, indeed, he accomplished.[86]

The homogeneous development that occurred on the issue of episcopal collegiality represents the triumph of *ressourcement* in a dual sense—as both supplement and reversal. As we have seen, the dogmatic constitution did not supplant papal primacy and infallibility; rather, it surrounded them with the teaching authority of the episcopal college, *cum et sub Petro*.[87] Philips—with other theologians—pointed again and again to the fact that episcopal collegiality was well attested in the history of the church. But Philips unwaveringly insisted that collegiality must itself rest on bishops receiving their jurisdictional authority with consecration and *not* through papal delegation. If the bishops were to *exercise* authority, they needed to *possess* it in a juridical sense. It could not simply be delegated to them by papal mandate. Bishops constitute a unique *ordo* within the church—and authority belongs to the college *de jure*. If this were not the case, then how could bishops teach authoritatively in an ecumenical council?

As already noted, Philips called the link between sacramental consecration and episcopal collegiality "the most important theological progress advanced by the council." That is an extraordinary statement from a man who worked on virtually every major document issued by Vatican II. The reason is surely that this link provided the *essential theological basis* for a robust doctrine of collegiality, which in turn affected the *very structure* of the Catholic Church by overcoming a one-sided papal absolutism. But to hold this position required a reversal of prior ordinary teaching—and precisely here one sees the other use of *ressourcement*. The 1943 encyclical *Mystici corporis* had taught that bishops receive their ordinary power of jurisdiction "directly from the same Supreme Pontiff." But this teaching was reversed by the Theological Commission and the council itself. The *munera* are received in episcopal consecration, thereby providing the sacramental foundation

86. On the day of promulgation (November 21, 1964), Paul VI insisted that the dogmatic constitution had not changed traditional doctrine in any way (*nullo modo immutata est*). Using words reminiscent of Vincent's teaching on continuity, the pope declared, "What Christ wished, we also wish. What was, still remains. What has been taught for centuries in the church, we still teach the same [*eadem et nos docemus*]."

87. As Philips states, "The praise that an Eastern bishop will attribute to the Church of Rome is as the one who presides in charity. In juridical terms, this will become *sub et cum Petro*." Grootaers, *Primauté et collégialité*, 214.

for collegiality. Of course, as with all the reversals of prior teaching that took place at Vatican II, this one, too, is "masked," with no mention made of it. The *Nota praevia* simply states, rather coyly, that the teaching of recent pontiffs must be interpreted according to "the necessary determination of powers" (§2).[88]

As Vincent of Lérins taught long ago, change always occurs in the church of Christ. The crucial issue is the *kind* of change. While some conciliar bishops wanted no change whatsoever—with every jot and tittle of ordinary magisterial teaching preserved—the majority of bishops and experts, along with Paul VI himself, sanctioned homogeneous, organic growth over time, with the recognition that occasional reversals are part of the *process* of legitimate development. Through its use of *ressourcement* in both senses— as supplement and, on occasion, as reversal of ordinary teaching—*Lumen gentium* accomplished this goal.[89]

Revelation

Vatican II placed a marked emphasis on the role of the Bible in the life of the Catholic Church. The council also thought seriously about the relationship between Scripture and tradition, long a thorny theological and ecumenical issue. We begin this section by again posing our fundamental questions: Did the council's teaching on these crucial issues mark a break with the antecedent tradition? Was the material continuity of the Catholic faith protected? Was there development *in eodem sensu* or reversal *in alieno sensu*?

88. Troisfontaines refers to this as a "sibylline" utterance. See "Quelques interventions," 126n57.

89. Another significant instance of *ressourcement* at Vatican II concerned the role of the laity. Inserting the chapter on the people of God (chapter 2 of *De ecclesia*) before the chapters dealing with offices or states in the church was an explicit attempt to overcome an image of the church as a *societas inaequalis*. See Yves Congar, *Le Concile de Vatican II: Son Église, Peuple de Dieu et Corps du Christ* (Paris: Beauchesne, 1984), 109–22. The idea for moving the chapter had been suggested by Cardinal Suenens in July 1963 and was brought to the council floor by Bishop Joseph Gargitter on September 30, 1963. See *AS* II/1, 359–62.

Scripture and Tradition

As has been well documented, the initial session of Vatican II, held during the fall of 1962, defined the struggle for the council.[90] Many regard October 13, 1962, as a significant turning point because the bishops, led by Cardinals Liénart and Frings, rejected the pre-prepared lists for the various conciliar commissions, insisting that they choose their own candidates from among the world's bishops. Benedict XVI, in one of his last speeches before retiring from the papacy, pointed to this event as a crucial moment in the council's unfolding: "It was not a revolutionary act, but an act of conscience, an act of responsibility on the part of the Council Fathers."[91]

A second decisive moment, more important theologically, was the debate on the schema *De fontibus revelationis* (On the sources of revelation), in which the prepared schema on the relationship between Sacred Scripture and the church's subsequent tradition was roundly rejected by the gathered bishops. I do not intend to summarize the episcopal interventions on this issue; they have been amply chronicled.[92] Building on that research, I seek, rather, to examine the conciliar advances in revelation theology and to answer the questions about continuity and discontinuity posed at the beginning of this section.

Not long after the schema *De fontibus* was introduced on November 14, 1962, the "assault" against it began. This aggressive polemic, Philips observes, was principally against the Scripture-tradition duality and was led "above all by the Germans who have read Geiselmann."[93] The invocation of Josef Geiselmann's seminal work is important because the Tübingen theologian had challenged the post-Tridentine consensus—which had become deeply rooted in Catholic theology and catechesis—that Scripture and tradition are

90. For the opening days of the council, see Alberigo and Komonchak, *History of Vatican II*, 2:1–106. See also Joseph A. Komonchak, "The Struggle for the Council during the Preparation of Vatican II (1960–1962)," in *History of Vatican II*, 1:167–356.

91. Speech of February 14, 2013, to the clergy of Rome: http://w2.vatican.va/content/ben edict-xvi/en/speeches/2013/february/documents/hf_ben-xvi_spe_20130214_clero-roma.html.

92. The document *De fontibus* was presented on November 14, 1962. The text of the original schema may be found in *AS* I/3, 14–26, followed by days of speeches. The speeches may be found in *AS* I/3, 32–297. The translation of several interventions may be found in Joseph A. Komonchak, "The Conciliar Discussion on the Sources of Revelation," https://jakomonchak .files.wordpress.com/2012/10/debate-on-de-fontibus.pdf.

93. *Carnets-GP*, 85 (April 8, 1963). Charue adds that the German bishops are particularly active, but the French, the Dutch, and even the Spaniards speak against the schema. *Carnets-AMC*, 47 (November 13, 1962).

two separate sources of divine revelation.[94] Geiselmann argued that this disjunctive separation into two distinct sources was *not* based on the Council of Trent's decree on revelation but was itself a later interpretation. Philips wryly notes that on the basis of Geiselmann's research the bishops now identified a problem—the Scripture-tradition relationship—that would have been unimaginable for them in the past.

An example of the criticism aimed at the schema may be found in the speech of Cardinal Frings, who states, "This mode of speaking about two sources of revelation is not ancient. It was alien to the holy Fathers, alien to the scholastics and even to St. Thomas, alien to all the Ecumenical councils."[95] In this speech and others like it, we have a good example of *ressourcement*, with a retrieval of earlier ecclesial teaching—including the teaching of the sixteenth-century Council of Trent itself—now calling into question a later theological consensus on Scripture and tradition as two independent "sources." But not only was the language of *duplex fontes* (two sources) not traditional; it was, as several bishops pointed out, deeply detrimental to the cause of ecumenism. The proposed schema, then, not only suffered from theological defects; it was also abstract and ecumenically deficient, lacking the pastoral character called for by John XXIII.

After several days of attacks on the schema, the bishops voted (on November 20, 1962) on whether debate should continue. The majority voted to discontinue discussion, with 62 percent voting against *De fontibus*. This was just short, however, of the two-thirds that was required by conciliar regulation to end the debate.[96] Nevertheless, in light of the widespread discontent with the document, Pope John XXIII pulled the schema off the floor, establishing a *Commissio mixta de divina revelatione*.[97]

The rejection of the schema *De fontibus* was a major turning point of Vatican II.[98] It demonstrated that the conciliar bishops would not un-

94. Josef Rupert Geiselmann, *Die lebendige Überlieferung als Norm des christlichen Glaubens: Die apostolische Tradition in der Form der kirchlichen Verkündigung—das Formalprinzip des Katholizismus, dargestellt im Geiste der Traditionslehre von Joh. Ev. Kuhn* (Freiburg: Herder, 1959).

95. *AS* I/3, 34–36, at 35. Also see Komonchak, "Conciliar Discussion," 4. For his part, De Smedt lamented the scholastic style of *De fontibus*, saying that it constituted "a great difficulty for non-Catholics." *AS* I/3, 184–87.

96. For the voting, see *AS* I/3, 254–55.

97. *AS* I/3, 259. This "mixed commission" was composed of members from the Theological Commission and the Secretariat for Christian Unity.

98. As Congar says of the vote to reject the schema, "I never would have believed that." See *My Journal*, 195. See also O'Malley, *What Happened*, 152, and Jared Wicks, "Augustin

questioningly accept the schemata prepared by the Preparatory Theological Commission under the leadership of Cardinal Ottaviani. One theological problem with the schema was that it had not taken account of a considerable amount of new research on the relationship between Scripture and tradition.[99] By speaking of some truths found only in tradition—an idea deeply rooted in numerous theology textbooks—the schema went beyond the affirmations of the Council of Trent (as Geiselmann had pointed out).[100] Reflecting on the rejection of *De fontibus*, Philips states that the Bible and tradition cannot be understood as two independent witnesses, as happens when we speak carelessly of "two sources." He adds that some theologians "consider as novelties ideas belonging to a tradition that is more authentic and more ancient [than the recent one], but which has become somewhat obscured."[101] Ratzinger criticized the original schema as defective because all the questions relevant to a theology of revelation—inerrancy, historicity, and the Scripture-tradition relationship—"were decided in a purely defensive spirit."[102]

After several false starts at a redrafted schema, frustration started to build.[103] Some even suggested that the major theses on revelation could be tossed over to the dogmatic constitution *De ecclesia*. But this suggestion was strongly resisted by Paul VI, who, at the close of the second session (December 4, 1963), spoke of the need for a conciliar document on revelation. Ratzinger asserts that Paul's decision was well founded. Not only did a document on revelation prevent ecclesio-monism; it also made clear that the church needs, in the first place, to *listen* to the Word of God.[104]

Continually hounding the drafting process was the precise role of tradition in the life of the Catholic Church, an issue that "from the very beginnings of Vatican II [was] at the center of ceaseless controversies."[105] Charue

Cardinal Bea, SJ," in *The Legacy of Vatican II*, ed. M. Faggioli and A. Vicini (New York: Paulist Press, 2015), 185–202.

99. The Scripture-tradition relationship was not the only issue raised by the bishops. There were also concerns about the inerrancy of Scripture and the historicity of the Gospels. See Joseph Ratzinger, "Dogmatic Constitution on Divine Revelation," in *Commentary on the Documents of Vatican II*, ed. Herbert Vorgrimler (New York: Herder and Herder, 1969), 3:163.

100. See *AS* I/3, 14–26, at 15 (no. 4).

101. Philips, "Deux tendances," 228.

102. Ratzinger, "Divine Revelation," 3:159.

103. For the redrafted schema of February 1963, see *AS* III/3, 782–91.

104. Ratzinger, "Divine Revelation," 3:162.

105. Jan Grootaers, "La crayon rouge de Paul VI," in *Les Commissions Conciliaires à*

confirms this sentiment, noting that, even after the rejection of *De fontibus*, Ottaviani still strenuously defended the claim that there are revealed truths in tradition that are not found in Sacred Scripture.[106] Ultimately, a new subcommittee of the *De Fide* was convoked, with Charue himself as president, to prepare a new draft on revelation. This committee produced a thoroughly revised schema that was presented to the full Theological Commission in June 1964.[107] Charue was pleased with the result, calling it "remarkable progress." The new text had gone beyond "the passionate and painful stage of 'two sources.'" "One now has a substantial exposé of revelation and tradition," Charue writes. "One could have hoped for better, but this is good, even very good."[108]

Despite Charue's optimism, the exchanges grew more impassioned when the new draft was discussed in the full Theological Commission in June 1964. While the Commission agreed on most points, there was, unsurprisingly, "a heated discussion on the question of the extra material provided by tradition."[109] The conservative expert H. Schauf completely disagreed with the new draft's understanding of the Scripture-tradition relationship, especially its bewildering "opposition to the ordinary teaching of the church as this is displayed in various catechisms."[110] So contentious was the topic of tradition that even *papal* statements were called into question. One member of the *De Fide*, following Leo XIII, proposed speaking of Holy Scripture as the "soul of theology." Others argued, however, that this phrase—left unattended—slights the church's tradition. Philips suggested an acceptable compromise: Scripture will be called the "soul of theology," but the written Word of God and tradition *together* are the "foundation of theology."[111] A vote on the suitability of this draft resulted in a 17–7 majority in favor of it.

Since the Theological Commission could not present a completely unified response to the draft, it decided to present two *relationes* (reports)

Vatican II, ed. M. Lamberigts, Cl. Soetens, and J. Grootaers (Leuven: Bibliotheek van de Faculteit Godgeleerdheid, 1996), 328.

106. See *Carnets-AMC*, 89 (February 25, 1963). Ottaviani even chided Rahner for admitting privately (but not publicly) that there were truths found only in tradition. *Carnets-AMC*, 94 (March 1, 1963).

107. For details on the redaction of this document, see Umberto Betti, ed., *Commento alla costituzione dogmatica sulla divina rivelazione* (Milan: Massimo, 1966).

108. *Carnets-AMC*, 185 (April 25, 1964).

109. Ratzinger, "Divine Revelation," 3:162.

110. *Carnets-AMC*, 198 (June 3, 1964). Schauf was well aware of the common teaching of the church on this matter, having published a 1963 book titled *Die Lehre der Kirche über Schrift und Tradition in den Katechismen*.

111. *Carnets-AMC*, 201 (June 5, 1964). See *Dei verbum* §24.

to the bishops gathered in St. Peter's—a majority report written by Rahner and a minority report written by Schauf. The *relator* for the majority was Archbishop Florit, a rather conservative biblical scholar. Precisely because of this reputation, his defense of the draft was crucial. In fact, Ratzinger calls Florit's *relatio*, delivered on September 30, 1964, "one of the most important events of the Council."[112] The *relator* for the minority, Bishop Franić, citing a variety of papal documents, argued that tradition has always had primacy in Catholic teaching. The failure of the proposed text to indicate this primacy was a "*defectum notabilem.*"[113]

On the floor of St. Peter's, Franić's strong critique of the schema was echoed by other bishops. Cardinal Ruffini, for example, objected to two sentences in the schema. One read, "This living (*viva*) Tradition advances (*proficit*) in the Church with the assistance of the Holy Spirit." Another read, "The understanding of the realities and the words that have been handed down grows (*crescit*)."[114] The *relatio* accompanying the schema explained that, with the assistance of the Holy Spirit, the church progresses and grows, "always retaining, however, its original identity."[115] In fact, these sentences closely parallel the thought of Vincent of Lérins, who argued that there is *always* growth and development in the church's faith, but without betraying the original meaning.

For Ruffini, however, the schema's use of the words *vivere* and *crescere* were deeply troubling.[116] His implication was that the terms *living* and *growing* were entirely incompatible with the stability of Catholic doctrine. In a last-ditch attempt to insist on the material identity of doctrinal teaching over time, 175 fathers (many aligned with the Coetus Patrum) submitted a written request asking the Theological Commission to add "*eodem sensu eademque sententia*" to the final text of *Dei verbum*. The Commission refused, remarking simply that the "interpretation of Vincent of Lérins is controverted."[117]

112. Ratzinger, "Divine Revelation," 3:163. For Florit's *relatio*, see *AS* III/3, 131–41.

113. For Franić's *relatio*, see *AS* III/3, 124–29.

114. *AS* III/3, 69–105, at 80.

115. *AS* III/3, 85 n. H: "semper tamen originaria identitate retenta." It is no surprise that Cardinal Florit, in his *relatio*, refers specifically to this phrase. See *AS* III/3, 137. On Vatican II's appeals to Vincent, see Thomas G. Guarino, "Vincent of Lérins and the Hermeneutical Question," *Gregorianum* 75 (1994): 491–524, at 511–18, and Thomas G. Guarino, "Tradition and Doctrinal Development: Can Vincent of Lérins Still Teach the Church?," *Theological Studies* 67 (2006): 34–72.

116. *AS* III/3, 142–45 (September 30, 1964).

117. *AS* IV/5, 696. For details, see Guarino, "Tradition and Doctrinal Development."

What is of keen theological interest is that the more conservative bishops, deeply taken with Vincent's accent on the material continuity of doctrine (the *idem sensus*), entirely overlook the Lerinian's equally emphatic stress on homogeneous *growth* over time. Vincent freely uses phrases indicating change: *res amplificetur* (the matter grows within itself) and *dilatetur tempore* (it is expanded with time). He also uses a host of verbs indicating development in the life of the church: *crescere, proficere, maturescere, florere,* and *enucleare*. Of course, this growing, advancing, ripening, flourishing, and unrolling must always preserve the fundamental doctrinal landmarks that the church has sanctioned—but that is precisely what the *relatio* says: that the "original identity" of doctrine is always maintained.

Bishops like Ruffini, who objected even to phrases like *viva traditio* and *crescit intelligentia*, had incompletely digested Vincent's thought on development. They accepted doctrinal stability and continuity—surely part of Vincent's brief—but they ignored growth and development, which the theologian of Lérins subtly intertwines with material identity. For Vincent, change is not the enemy of divine truth. Indeed, change is *inevitable* in Christ's church—just as it is in nature and in life generally. The truly crucial issue is the *kind* of change sanctioned. Failing to see this, Ruffini speaks of *viva traditio*—living tradition—as if it were indistinguishable from a relativizing modernism.[118]

Continuing Debate: Three Disputed Issues

The revised text—with further emendations based on the speeches and written comments of the bishops—was voted on in the next conciliar session (starting on September 20, 1965). The various chapters of *De revelatione* were passed with huge majorities.[119] But the bishops also submitted a vast number of *modi* (amendments), many, once again, coming from the Coetus Patrum, the group of conservative bishops that was deeply concerned about

118. The more conservative minority bishops were not the only ones to misconstrue Vincent. The theologians of the more progressive majority also misunderstood him. Congar and Ratzinger, for example, thought that Vincent and his famous canon—*semper, ubique, et ab omnibus*—would block the *dynamic* notion of tradition Vatican II sought to uphold. See Thomas G. Guarino, *Vincent of Lérins and the Development of Christian Doctrine* (Grand Rapids: Baker Academic, 2013), 2–3.

119. For the voting on the chapters, see the tallies in *Carnets-AMC*, 259–61 (September 20, 1965).

the continuity of Vatican II's teaching with prior magisterial statements. Had tradition been given an adequate place in the schema? Was the historical nature of the Gospels properly protected?

Philips relates that when discussions on the *modi* began, the atmosphere on the Theological Commission was tense.[120] The *modi* on "tradition" and on the phrase *veritas salutaris* (the truth of salvation) had sparked vigorous debates. So heated were the discussions that Philips remarks, "The ambiance resembles a bit of the 'black week' of the third session." For a man not given to exaggeration, the comparison with *la settimana nera* indicates the disputatious atmosphere that had pervaded the council. The primary issue, once again, was the precise nature of tradition. *That* tradition is central to Catholicism was never in doubt at Vatican II. But determining the *precise relationship* between Scripture and tradition became a pivotal and decisive issue. After the rejection of *De fontibus*, the language of "two sources" was no longer available, having been buried under the historical recovery of Trent and the earlier tradition. But crucial questions remained: How could the council enshrine "tradition" in a way that was not injurious to relations with the separated brethren? Could Catholics speak of the material sufficiency of Scripture for the truths of salvation, thereby confirming the similarity between Catholicism and Protestantism on the written Word of God? If so, would this be in continuity with the church's doctrinal tradition? Could the council adopt a Catholic notion of "Scripture alone"?

We have already seen, in our discussion of *De oecumenismo*, that Paul VI mandated an important change to that decree in order to give a more prominent role to tradition—thereby mollifying the conservative minority and winning virtually unanimous support for *Unitatis redintegratio*. Would the pope once again intervene, to ensure that tradition had a stronger role?

Although the initial voting on *De revelatione* had been overwhelmingly positive, Paul VI sent a letter to the Theological Commission, asking it to consider, once more, the role of tradition in the church's life. Charue observed, "The poor Pope is under assault and he searches for unanimity."[121] A small but significant group of bishops (about 15 percent) remained unsatisfied with *De revelatione*—particularly on the question of tradition—and the pope was insistent that their concerns be addressed. Paul did not want to risk a few hundred *non placet* votes; such would call into question the authority

---

120. *Carnets-GP*, 151 (October 12, 1965).
121. *Carnets-AMC*, 262 (September 24, 1965).

of the dogmatic constitution—and the claim that it was in homogeneous continuity with prior teaching.

Three major issues came to the fore and were vigorously debated in the *De Fide.* The first was the precise relationship between Scripture and tradition. The second was the meaning of the term *veritas salutaris,* "saving truth" (treated in §11 of the final document, *Dei verbum*). What does it mean to say that everything in the Bible is true that God has taught *for the sake of our salvation?* The third was the kind of "historical truth" that is proper to the Bible (discussed in §19 of *Dei verbum*). Does the entire Bible teach historical truth?[122] Both Philips and Colombo (the pope's theological advisor) worked hard to find acceptable formulations for these three theological issues in hopes of avoiding a papal intervention.

As regards the first issue, Philips, as was so often the case, proposed a compromise formula. Intended to be placed in §9 of *De revelatione,* his proposed addition read, "Therefore not all Catholic doctrine is able to be proven directly from Holy Scripture alone."[123] This formula was immediately supported by Yves Congar and some other experts. But Cardinal Florit (who had delivered the crucial *relatio* in favor of the text in 1964) and the expert closely aligned with him, Umberto Betti, wished to suppress both *sola* and *directe.* To suppress these words, however, would have defeated the precise purpose of Philips's proposal: to leave open the possibility of speaking about the material sufficiency of Scripture for the truths related to salvation. If those words were suppressed, one would no longer be able to speak of *sola Scriptura* in a Catholic sense—and so ecumenical opportunities would be lost. Philips's formulation allowed for the sufficiency of Scripture while acknowledging that tradition has an essential role in the formulation of Catholic doctrine. Ultimately, both Florit and Betti relented, agreeing to Philips's sentence.[124]

Archbishop Parente attacked Philips's formula on the grounds that it failed to deal adequately with the "two sources." Parente proposed an alternative: "Sacred Tradition and Sacred Scripture, while fully distinct, form one

122. *Carnets-AMC,* 265–66. After September 25, 1965, Charue remarks that he has abandoned his day-by-day notes. He offers, rather, a summary of events over the last two months of the council, probably written in October and November 1965.

123. *Carnets-AMC,* 266: "quo fit ut non omnis doctrina catholica ex sola S. Scriptura directe probari queat."

124. Betti explains that one concern with Philips's formula was that every Catholic teaching would now need to find an "indirect" foundation in Scripture. See *Commento alla costituzione dogmatica,* 56–57.

sacred deposit."[125] Of this attempt, Charue writes, "It is already evident that this formula has no chance of success."[126] Bishop Colombo then advanced still another proposal: "The Church does not draw her certitude about Divine Revelation from Sacred Scripture alone."[127] The Theological Commission voted on Philips's original formula, rejecting it by a vote of 13–11. Philips then proposed a compromise, with a sentence closer to the one proposed by Colombo: "Sacred Scripture contains the full ensemble of Christian mysteries, without all the revealed truths being expressly propounded in them."[128] Colombo accepted this formulation, which then passed by a vote of 14–10.

At this point, four proposals describing the Scripture-tradition relationship had come before the Theological Commission:

1. Philips: "Therefore not all Catholic doctrine is able to be proven directly by holy Scripture alone" (rejected by the Theological Commission).
2. Parente: "Sacred Tradition and Sacred Scripture, while fully distinct, form one sacred deposit."
3. Colombo: "The Church does not draw its certitude about Divine Revelation from Sacred Scripture alone."
4. Philips-Colombo: "Sacred Scripture contains the full ensemble of Christian mysteries, without all revealed truths being expressly propounded in them."

Although the Philips-Colombo formula was approved, the tight vote indicated discontent in the Theological Commission. In fact, the *De Fide's* acceptance of this last formula would not survive.

The second issue had to do with the meaning of the term *veritas salutaris*. The schema of *De revelatione* §11 stated that the books of Scripture "teach certainly and faithfully, integrally and without error, the entire *truth of salvation*."[129] But was this formulation adequate? A significant number of bishops were concerned that the truth of Scripture appeared to be *limited* by this phrase. Are the Scriptures infallibly true *only in those matters directly*

---

125. "S. Traditio et S. Scriptura, quamvis invicem plane distinctae, unum sacrum depositum constituunt."

126. *Carnets-AMC*, 267.

127. "Quo fit ut Ecclesia certitudinem suam de S. Revelatione non per solam S. Scripturam hauriat."

128. "Sacrae Scripturae complexum mysterii christiani referent, quin omnes veritates revelatae in eis expresse enuntientur."

129. *AS* IV/1, 355 (September 20, 1965); emphasis added.

affecting our salvation? Are they not truthful in other matters as well? Despite some misgivings, the Theological Commission voted to retain the term with a strong 19–5 vote. Charue argued that the expression is stated "*assertive non exclusive*"—that is, the phrase does not exclude those verses not directly concerned with redemption. Nonetheless, Charue himself concedes that "it is regrettable that the schema says so little to explain the expression '*veritas salutaris.*'"[130]

The historicity of the Gospels was the third hotly disputed issue in the Theological Commission. In §19 of *De revelatione* (September 20, 1965), the term *history* was not used except for the subtitle of the section: "The Historical Nature of the Gospels."[131] In fact, the *relatio* accompanying the text states that the words *historia* (history) and *historice* (historically) have been avoided precisely because of their ambiguity.[132] The schema states, rather, that the four Gospels truly hand on (*vere tradere*) what Jesus, the Son of God, did and taught among men, for the sake of their eternal salvation.

Once again, questions were posed in the Theological Commission: Did these sentences adequately protect the historical events recorded in the Gospels? Or was the historical truth of the New Testament in some way limited and even undermined? Charue remarks that the 1964 decree of the Pontifical Biblical Commission (PBC) had systematically avoided the use of the word *history*.[133] After a brief skirmish over this word, the *De Fide* "approved our text by a strong majority. In fact, the context shows that the historicity [of the Gospels] is accepted."[134] Charue adds that "in order to avoid that historicity would appear to be limited to the time when Christ lived here below," the *De Fide* added to the text "until the day in which he was taken up into heaven."[135] In other words, the *historical character* of the Gospels is preserved not only for Christ's life but also after his death and resurrection, until he ascended to his heavenly Father.

The Theological Commission had now examined three of the most disputed issues in the schema: Scripture and tradition, the truth of the Bible, and the historical character of the Gospels. Charue affirms, "We were pleased with the results, but we awaited an intervention from on high [the pope]."

130. *Carnets-AMC*, 267.

131. *AS* IV/1, 367.

132. *AS* IV/1, 369, D.

133. *Carnets-AMC*, 267. Charue is referring to the PBC document titled "On the Historical Truth of the Gospels."

134. *Carnets-AMC*, 266–68.

135. *Carnets-AMC*, 268: "usque in diem quo assumptus est."

And then: "Voilà . . . a telephone call came from the Vatican . . . telling me that the pope wished to receive me the next day [October 12, 1965]."[136]

Paul VI spoke frankly to Charue about his anxieties over *De revelatione*. The pope reproached the Theological Commission for not having had contact with Cardinal Bea and the Secretariat for Christian Unity. Charue responded that the text on revelation had been submitted to Cardinal Bea last year (1964) and the latter had decided that it was not necessary to meet as a "mixed commission." Paul was dissatisfied with this remark, saying that his "predecessor [John XXIII] had established this commission and it had never been suppressed. I had nothing to respond to this."[137] The pope was particularly anxious about the phrase *veritas salutaris*, fearing that it gave the impression that Scripture is not reliable in all matters, only those directly pertaining to salvation. Paul continued, "The danger of varying interpretations is serious and it does not suffice to invoke the meaning intended by the Commission. It is necessary that the text can defend itself. The same is true for historicity. It is necessary to be attentive."[138] Addressing Charue directly, the pope asked, "And you, what do you think?" The vice president of the *De Fide* responded, "I am moved to be questioned by the Pope with such trust, but before God, I must say that, personally, I do not have these fears." Paul replied, "*Bien*. Your advice is precious to me. But the Pope has a heavy responsibility and all do not speak as you do."

In this exchange, one sees something of the "assault" under which Paul VI labored. Bishops had come to him with theological fears: about tradition, about the "truth of salvation," and about the historical character of the Gospels. Were these adequately defended in the dogmatic constitution? For a significant minority, the text was not in obvious continuity with the tradition. Charue, however, a very moderate bishop, thought the schema was adequate, represented homogeneous development, and did not require any papal intervention.

Nonetheless, Paul told Charue that he wished to intervene on *De revelatione* before the text was sent to the bishops gathered in St. Peter's. On October 18, 1965, the expected letter was sent to the Theological Commis-

---

136. *Carnets-AMC*, 268. Because of the concerns expressed by the minority, the *De Fide* expected that the pope would offer "suggestions." Ottaviani had even asked Paul VI to add a "*Nota praevia*" to *De revelatione*, such as the one that had appeared with *Lumen gentium*. Suenens, on other hand, worked to convince the pope to avoid anything resembling the "black week" of 1964. See Riccardo Burigana, *La Bibbia nel concilio* (Bologna: Il Mulino, 1998), 415–16.

137. *Carnets-AMC*, 269.

138. *Carnets-AMC*, 269.

sion, indicating that Cardinal Bea would join the *De Fide* with the pope's suggestions. The next day Ottaviani summoned the vice presidents (Browne and Charue) and secretaries (Tromp and Philips) to a meeting. It was decided that the *De Fide* would address the pertinent issues that evening; the *periti* would be present, but neither the bishops nor the experts would speak; and after some minutes of reflection, the voting on the pope's suggestions would begin.[139] In fact, at 6:00 p.m. on October 19, 1965, the Theological Commission was joined by Cardinal Bea.[140] Charue wrote in his journal, "Something abnormal is happening. But, when convened, all are quiet and Cardinal Bea is invited to offer his advice. He does this in an unexpected manner which clearly weighs on the group. Rahner complains openly about it after the meeting, while Philips himself is outraged. He adds that he has never had more than limited confidence in Bea."[141]

Did the papal *modi* of October 19, 1965—as transmitted by Bea—help ensure the material continuity of *De revelatione* with the prior tradition of the Catholic Church? Would such continuity have been jeopardized without this intervention? As noted, Charue had told Paul VI that he harbored no fears whatsoever about the orthodoxy of the text. In response, the pope mentioned the "heavy responsibility" of his office, which surely involved satisfying the minority's concerns. If the minority mustered even a couple hundred negative votes, this would give the impression that there existed a significant group of dissenters from a dogmatic constitution of an ecumenical council. This was a risk Paul was not willing to take.

---

139. *Carnets-AMC*, 270.

140. A continuing question is, How did Cardinal Bea, not a member of the Theological Commission, become the pope's emissary at this crucial moment for the dogmatic constitution? Paul had argued to Charue, just a week before, that the mixed commission for *De revelatione* had never been suppressed. Therefore, Bea could still claim to be a member. Nonetheless, as Charue had stated to the pope, Bea had approved the text in November of 1964, stating that a meeting of the commission would not be necessary. In any case, Paul considered the mixed commission as still alive—with Bea, therefore, as co-president. See Grootaers, "Le crayon rouge," 327.

141. *Carnets-AMC*, 271. Albert Prignon relates that Bea spoke about some "ambiguities" in the schema. Philips saw this as calling into question the integrity of the text and Philips's own good faith as *De Fide*'s secretary. For the only time during the council, Ottaviani did not allow Philips to respond, leading the latter to remark: "Because these men wear some red on their chest [as cardinals], they are able to treat you as a liar and even take away your right to defend yourself." See A. Prignon, "Évêques et Théologiens de Belgique au Concile Vatican II," in *Vatican II et la Belgique*, ed. Claude Soetens (Louvain-la-Neuve: Collection Sillages, 1996), 174–75.

In the dramatic meeting of October 19, 1965, Bea returned to the three disputed issues that had been under discussion in the Theological Commission for several weeks. To everyone's relief, Bea started by explaining that it was not necessary to reopen the question of the "two sources." Indeed, he himself had defended this point with the pope.[142] A sheet was then distributed with seven formulas dealing with tradition (including the four noted above and some variants). Bea rejected the Philips-Colombo formula from the outset while strongly encouraging the members of the Theological Commission to vote for a revised formula that read, "It is not from Sacred Scripture alone that the church draws her certitude about all that has been revealed." The second round of voting achieved the necessary majority, with nineteen votes for Bea's choice as opposed to eight for Philips's first formulation.

Notwithstanding the pressure from Bea, the chosen formula is a theologically sound one, allowing for a Catholic understanding of *sola Scriptura*—thereby keeping ecumenical unity always in sight—even while still insisting on a crucial role for tradition in the life of the church. The formula had the further advantage of satisfying those bishops who believed that tradition had been slighted in the schema.

With regard to the phrase *veritas salutaris*, Bea was very firm, saying, as Charue reports, that "the expression is dangerous, inadmissible and against which he [Bea] had struggled his entire life." Charue remarks, "That may be the case, but he had approved this text last year! Unless he had read it only superficially."[143] Of course, the *theological* issue at stake was that, if misconstrued, the phrase could be used to limit the truth of Scripture to a relatively few matters—to those directly concerned with salvation and redemption.

Responses to Bea's comments were not allowed. Instead, Ottaviani called immediately for a vote: *Maneat aut tollatur textus?* Does the phrase *veritas salutaris* remain in the text as is, or should it be omitted? Changing the text at this point required nineteen votes, two-thirds of the *De Fide*.[144] When this number was not achieved, Philips proposed an alternative, using a formula submitted by seventy-three members of the minority: "the truth

142. In much of the narrative that follows, I am relying, unless otherwise indicated, on Charue's journal. See *Carnets-AMC*, 271. Also important is Burigana, *La Bibbia*, 415–30.

143. *Carnets-AMC*, 272. Philips similarly notes that Bea had explicitly approved of the text in 1964. See *Carnets-GP*, 153 (November 1, 1965). Indeed, Philips had noted in his journal, "Cardinal Bea accepts the text without a new meeting of the *Commissio Mixta*." *Carnets-GP*, 119 (July 12, 1964).

144. The vote totals are recounted in *Carnets-AMC*, 272–73.

which God wished to consign to the sacred writings for the sake of our salvation." This compromise formula immediately achieved the necessary votes.[145] At this very moment, Charue relates that he heard Archbishop Parente whisper to Franič, "*Quod ejecimus per portam, reintroducunt per fenestram*" (What we kicked out the door, they have brought back through the window). There was some basis for Parente's comment since the new formula did not significantly change the meaning of the text. But the fact that Philips used a "minority" formulation (drawn from the *modi*) likely resulted in its acceptance by the necessary two-thirds of the Commission. Charue notes appreciatively that, while making strong recommendations, "even for *veritas salutaris*, the Pope left the decision to the Commission."[146]

Finally, concerns remained about the historical character of the Gospels. Did the Gospels in every case report a historical event? Or, in some instances, did the biblical account reflect the post-resurrection faith of the church? Should *De revelatione* (§19) assert that the Gospels are "history," or should something else be said?

Philips had proposed the term *historicitas* (historicity) in order to avoid the problems connected with the terms *historia* (history) and *historicus* (historical). This would allow the council to assert the "historical character" of the Gospels without entering into technical questions disputed by exegetes and historians. For his part, Paul VI suggested to the Commission the use of the term *historica fides* (historical faith)—but Philips argued that this term could be taken in the sense popularized by Bultmann and was best avoided.[147] Philips offered as an alternative: "*quorum historicitatem incunctanter affirmat*"—that is, the Gospels "whose historical character [the church] unhesitatingly affirms." Bea expressed his approval of this formula, and it was overwhelmingly passed by the *De Fide* with a vote of 26–2.[148]

At the end of this tension-filled meeting, Charue concluded, "Overall, the result is beneficial, since it reassures many of the Fathers."[149] Charue is referring, of course, to the more conservative group of bishops who were fearful that tradition was being slighted in the schema and that the historical character of the Bible had not been affirmed with sufficient clarity. Charue relates that during the final voting, a "good, old missionary bishop"

---

145. *Carnets-GP*, 153 (November 1, 1965): "quam Deus nostrae salutis causa, litteris sacris consignari voluit."

146. *Carnets-AMC*, 273.

147. *Carnets-GP*, 154 (November 1, 1965).

148. *Carnets-AMC*, 273.

149. *Carnets-AMC*, 273.

asked if he could vote *placet* for *De revelatione* with a clear conscience. "My affirmative response left him visibly relieved." In these remarks, one sees the benefit of Paul VI's quest for unanimity. A few judiciously worded changes in the document—on the role of tradition and on the historicity of the Gospels—assured many bishops that the teaching of Vatican II was in continuity with, even while making homogeneous advances upon, the prior doctrinal tradition. A few days later, Bishop Colombo reported to both Charue and Philips that the pope was very satisfied with the outcome.[150]

The voting on *De revelatione* took place in St. Peter's on October 29, 1965. Charue relates, "The result [of the final vote] was splendid. There was fear that there would be numerous departures before the feasts [All Saints Day and All Souls Day], but the Pope had recalled the obligation of all bishops to be present. In fact, each time the majority surpassed 2,000 votes."[151] For the entire text of the schema, the votes were 2,081 *placet*, 27 *non placet*, and 7 *nul*. Charue was astounded by the overwhelming numbers by which *De revelatione* was passed, remarking, "And to think that this was a schema that divided the Fathers into two blocs in 1962!" He is referring, of course, to the acrimony in St. Peter's three years earlier, when tensions were high over *De fontibus*. "This [new document]," Charue continues, "will be called the dogmatic constitution *Dei Verbum* (a recent and happy change). *Deo gratias*."[152]

On November 18, 1965, in a solemn ceremony, Paul VI formally promulgated *Dei verbum*. Charue was deeply touched: "My emotion is great when the results of the vote are published and when the Pope pronounces the text of promulgation." Thinking back to those acrimonious debates at the beginning of the council, Charue again exclaims, "What a path we have travelled since November, 1962!"[153] As was customary, a vote was taken just prior to the formal promulgation of the document: 2,344 *placet*, 6 *non placet*. The results were indeed extraordinary: only six *non placet* votes out of all the

---

150. *Carnets-AMC*, 274. Philips was sensitive to the fact that, throughout the council, some theologians accused him of being too accommodating toward the minority bishops and theologians. That this was on his mind is revealed by the surprising way he ends his conciliar journal: "I was happy that the theologians assisted at the last session of the Theological Commission [referring to the October 19 meeting with Bea]. In this, they are not able to accuse me of being too accommodating. I have sought to accomplish my work with honesty. *Sed Dominus est qui iudicat*." *Carnets-GP*, 156 (November 1, 1965).

151. *Carnets-AMC*, 275–76.

152. *Carnets-AMC*, 276.

153. *Carnets-AMC*, 276.

Catholic bishops of the world. Paul VI had achieved his goal of unanimity for the two most important documents—indeed, the only dogmatic constitutions—of Vatican II: *Lumen gentium* and *Dei verbum*. A few judicious changes had convinced almost everyone that these documents were in clear continuity with the prior doctrinal tradition: not *permutationes*, but a collective *profectus fidei*.

Concluding Reflections on Revelation

Let us conclude this section by reflecting on the questions central to this volume: Is the text of *Dei verbum* in material continuity with the antecedent tradition, *in eodem sensu eademque sententia*? Are there significant doctrinal changes? Vincent of Lérins, we remember, taught that change was endemic to the life of the church. But were there changes in *Dei verbum* resulting in the kind of distortions decried by Vincent?

First, the discussions on *De revelatione* that transpired in the *De Fide* reveal the exceeding care that was taken with every word of the text. Any point that was even slightly controversial was the subject of animated debate. A clear example is Leo XIII's statement compressed in the phrase that Scripture is the "soul of theology" (*DV* §24). One would expect that this papal assertion would pass the Commission without controversy.[154] But some members thought the phrase, left unadorned, slighted the role of tradition in the life of the Catholic Church. It needed to be added, therefore, that Scripture and tradition *together* form the "primary and perpetual foundation" of sacred theology. Such care indicates that the document was carefully examined for its relationship with prior dogmatic teaching.

Second, as previously noted, the precise role of tradition was deeply disputed throughout the council, beginning with the debate over *De fontibus* in November 1962. Certainly, Scripture was given a new prominence at Vatican II—of that there is no question. But this increased emphasis on Scripture was relatively uncontroversial. The truly contentious issue was the exact role of tradition. Would Catholicism abandon the central part that tradition had played in its dogmatic teachings? In fact, the importance of tradition was intensified by several crucial interventions of Paul VI.

---

154. Leo XIII, *Providentissmus Deus*: "eiusdem Scripturae usus in universam theologiae influat disciplinam eiusque prope sit anima." This passage was cited by Pope Benedict XV in his 1920 encyclical, *Spiritus Paraclitus*.

As we saw with the Decree on Ecumenism, Paul mandated a controversial change (from *inveniunt* to *inquirunt*) to make clear that one "finds" Christ only with the help of tradition. Similarly (although without the same degree of insistence), the pope, through his intermediary Cardinal Bea, required of the *De Fide* the addition of one sentence that would strengthen the importance of tradition in *De revelatione*. While Paul VI gave the members of the Commission the freedom to choose one among several possible formulations, Bea, as we have seen, urged the *De Fide* to vote for the one that was finally chosen: "Consequently it is not from Sacred Scripture alone that the Church draws her certainty about everything which has been revealed" (*DV* §9).

This simple sentence was a brilliant addition to the text, deftly accomplishing two goals: it indicated the indefeasible importance of tradition for Catholicism, and, at the same time, it preserved the material sufficiency of Scripture for the truths of divine revelation. By maintaining biblical sufficiency, Vatican II moved much closer to a fundamental affirmation of the Reformation, but did so in a Catholic way. All the truths necessary for salvation may be found in Scripture—but to understand them in their amplitude, one needs the further complement of ecclesial tradition. This was both a traditional thesis (as testified by the two masters of doctrinal development, Vincent of Lérins and John Henry Newman) and a significant ecumenical step forward.

Paul VI's addition to paragraph 9 represented a return to the church's earliest roots. Tradition is indeed essential to a full understanding of Sacred Scripture. But tradition is at the *service* of Scripture rather than a competitor to it. Or, as Cardinal Florit explained in his *relatio* before the voting on October 29, 1965: where Scripture alone (*Scriptura sola*) does not suffice for certitude, tradition is able to bring forth a decisive argument.[155] The text of *De revelatione* had been unchanged in its substance, Florit added, but perfected in its manner of expression. In other words, the written Word of God remained prominent in the dogmatic constitution, but the *meaning* of Scripture was to be clarified by the church's doctrinal tradition.

In one of his last speeches before he retired as bishop of Rome, Joseph Ratzinger, who served on the Theological Commission as an expert, paid homage to Paul VI on this crucial addition to *De revelatione*:

> Here the [conciliar] battle—as I said—was difficult, and an intervention of Pope Paul VI proved decisive. This intervention shows all the delicacy of a father, his responsibility for the progress of the council, but

---

155. *AS* IV/5, 741.

also his great respect for the council. The idea had arisen that Scripture is complete; everything is found there; consequently, there is no need for Tradition, and so the Magisterium has nothing to say. At that point the Pope transmitted to the Council, I believe, fourteen formulae. . . . I remember more or less the formula "*non omnis certitudo de veritatibus fidei potest sumi ex Sacra Scriptura*," in other words, the Church's certainty about her faith is not born only of an isolated book, but has need of the Church herself as a subject enlightened and guided by the Holy Spirit. Only then does the Scripture speak with all its authority. This phrase . . . is decisive, I would say, for showing the Church's absolute necessity, and thus understanding the meaning of Tradition, the living body in which this word draws life from the outset and from which it receives its light, in which it is born.[156]

Third, through its recovery of earlier Catholic thinking on tradition, including the careful rereading of the Council of Trent, *Dei verbum* became an exercise in *ressourcement* in both senses in which the council utilized that term: to supplement and enhance prior teaching, and—in a qualified sense—to underwrite a reversal. On the one hand, the notion of tradition was given a new vitality and dynamism, being understood as living and growing (precisely as Vincent and Newman had taught) even while protecting the stable continuity and identity of the faith over time. This was clearly *ressourcement* as recovery and enrichment of antecedent teaching. On the other hand, *Dei verbum* reversed a long catechetical and manualist point of view, wherein tradition added, quantitatively, to the truths taught by Sacred Scripture. As noted earlier in this chapter, H. Schauf, one of the experts on the *De Fide*, threatened to speak publicly against the council if it departed from the ordinary theological and catechetical teaching on Scripture and tradition. But the dogmatic constitution handled the issue deftly—with the addition mandated by Paul VI quelling any concerns that the notion of tradition had been shortchanged by Vatican II.[157] In this sense,

---

156. Speech of February 14, 2013. While Benedict alludes to fourteen formulae, the younger Ratzinger correctly noted that Paul VI sent *seven* formulae, with the charge to choose one. See "Divine Revelation," 3:194–95. The number seven is confirmed by two experts on the *De Fide*: Umberto Betti, *Diario del Concilio* (Bologna: Dehoniane, 2003), 77, and Philips, *Carnets-GP*, 153 (November 1, 1965).

157. Indeed, *Dei verbum* straightforwardly cites Trent's affirmation that "both sacred tradition and Sacred Scripture are to be accepted and venerated with the *same sense* of loyalty and reverence" (§9; emphasis added).

one may say that *Dei verbum* represented a reversal of previous ordinary teaching—although obviously not a dogmatically defined landmark of the Catholic Church. Here, as elsewhere in the council documents, no mention is made of the reversal, indicating something of the "masking" that attended all the conciliar changes of course.

Fourth, throughout *Dei verbum* one sees a determined attempt to take account of the positive aspects of the Reformation, particularly its forceful accent on the primacy of Scripture. Congar pointed out that such primacy had been a theological theme long before the sixteenth century—but it needed to be recovered for Catholicism by Vatican II.[158] As so often occurred throughout the council, *Dei verbum* stressed the *analogical similarity* between Catholics and Protestants, incorporating themes significant for Reformation theology whenever possible.

Fifth, sometimes much is made of the claim that *Dei verbum* does not speak of revelation "propositionally." But care needs to be exercised on just this point. While the dogmatic constitution emphasizes biblical witness and salvation history, in no sense is the truth of Christianity—as expressed in dogmatic propositions—denied. On the contrary, *De revelatione* speaks of the continuity, perpetuity, and material identity of the Christian faith in direct terms: the Christian dispensation is the "new and definitive covenant that will never pass away" (§4). And God has seen that what he has revealed will "abide perpetually in its full integrity and be handed on to all generations" (§7). Of course, one obvious way of handing on divine revelation in its full integrity is through the articulated propositions of Christian doctrine.[159] As John XXIII indicated at the council's outset, the *meaning* of these doctrines was to be retained even while seeking expressions intelligible to contemporary men and women. This was the point of his crucial distinction between the *depositum fidei* and the *modus quo veritates enuntiantur.*

Was the teaching of *Dei verbum* materially continuous with the prior tradition of the Catholic Church? It is clear that while *Dei verbum* certainly offered new accents and emphases, its material continuity with the antecedent dogmatic tradition is not in doubt. Thus the dogmatic constitution represents a *profectus non permutatio fidei.*

158. See Yves Congar, *Tradition and Traditions*, trans. Michael Naseby and Thomas Rainborough (New York: Macmillan, 1967).

159. This point, of course, is not limited to Catholicism. Much the same position is held by distinguished Protestant theologians such as Geoffrey Wainwright and Robert Jenson. See Wainwright, *Is the Reformation Over?* (Milwaukee: Marquette University Press, 2000), 39; and Jenson, *Systematic Theology*, vol. 1 (New York: Oxford University Press, 1997), 20.

Religious Freedom

The Declaration on Religious Freedom (ultimately *Dignitatis humanae* but referred to throughout the council as *De libertate religiosa*) tests many of the themes we have been discussing in this book: the meaning of development, the possibility of reversals, and how change takes place in the Catholic Church. As John Courtney Murray forthrightly states in his introduction to the document, "It was, of course, the most controversial document of the whole Council, largely because it raised with sharp emphasis the issue that lay continually below the surface of all the conciliar debates—the issue of the development of doctrine."[160] Murray is correct. *De libertate* raised several questions with crystal clarity: May any change whatsoever be called a development? Is there any difference between a development and a reversal? Or have these two terms been silently and surreptitiously conjoined—and this because Catholics have a well-known "allergy" to change?[161]

Joseph Ratzinger, who would later (as Benedict XVI) make a crucial distinction between a "hermeneutic of discontinuity and rupture" and a "hermeneutic of reform," did not hesitate to say, when *De libertate* was formally promulgated by Paul VI in December 1965, that "there was in St. Peter's the sense that here was the end of the Middle Ages, the end even of the Constantinian age."[162] There could hardly be a stronger expression of discontinuity than the claim that a teaching that had been almost coincident with the church's life—from Emperor Constantine in the fourth century to the Catholic Church of the mid-twentieth century—had been abrogated by Vatican II. This comment, made soon after the council ended, gives us a sense of why the debates on the declaration have been so heated. This document—more clearly than any other conciliar teaching—appears to have reversed centuries of magisterial teaching. And if it does engage in such a significant reversal, does it not fall under the condemnation of Vincent of Lérins as a *permutatio fidei*? After all, Vincent insisted that an infallible mark of heretics was their traitorous plea: "Condemn what you used to hold and hold what you used to condemn. Reject the ancient faith and the dictates of

160. John Courtney Murray, "Religious Freedom," in *The Documents of Vatican II*, ed. Walter M. Abbott (New York: Herder and Herder, 1966), 673.

161. John O'Malley, "Trent and Vatican II: Two Styles of Church," in *From Trent to Vatican II: Historical and Theological Investigations*, ed. Frederick J. Parrella and Raymond F. Bulman (Oxford: Oxford University Press, 2006), 316.

162. Joseph Ratzinger, *Theological Highlights of Vatican II*, trans. Henry Traub, Gerard C. Thormann, and Werner Barzel (New York: Paulist Press, 2009), 144.

your fathers and the deposits of the ancients" (*Comm.* 9.8). It is no surprise, then, that even the validity of the council has been called into question on the basis of this declaration's teaching.[163]

As we have seen, Vincent taught sixteen hundred years ago that change is endemic to the church of Christ. But legitimate change must be homogeneous growth, development that builds on that which preceded it. Was the change sanctioned by *De libertate* in the Vincentian tradition? Was it architectonic development *in eodem sensu*? Or was it, as its critics have incessantly charged, a *permutatio fidei*, a corruption of the faith that deformed Catholic doctrine?

1964

In late September 1964, things seemed to be going well for the schema on religious freedom. On the strength of the American bishops' ardent interventions, Charue remarked, "The tide is favorable for religious liberty." More importantly, "one heard a magisterial exposition by bishop Colombo in which one suspected the *vox Petri*!"[164] Through Colombo, his friend and collaborator, Paul VI made it clear that he, too, was in favor of the schema. But the conciliar waters would not remain calm. A few weeks later, Gérard Philips wrote in his journal, "There is also [along with *de Judaeis*] great resistance to the text on religious liberty and one [even] speaks of a new commission."[165] Many bishops had concluded that the proposed schema on religious liberty was not, in fact, a true development—homogeneous growth—but a naked reversal of the magisterial tradition. The word *development* seemed wholly inaccurate when describing *De libertate*.

Even in 1963 the theological issues of development and reversal had been on the table. The 1963 schema *De oecumenismo* had included a chapter on Judaism and a chapter on religious freedom.[166] Bishop De Smedt, in his *relatio* for the chapter on religious freedom (November 18, 1963), stated that

---

163. Along with changes to the liturgy, *De libertate* has always been the primary problem with Vatican II cited by Marcel Lefebvre, who broke with the Catholic Church after the council. See his book *Open Letter to Confused Catholics*, trans. Society of St. Pius X (Kansas City, MO: Angelus Press, 1986).

164. *Carnets-AMC*, 219–20 (dated September 14, 1964, but noted as September 25 in Charue's journal).

165. *Carnets-GP*, 132 (October 11, 1964).

166. *AS* II/5, 433–41.

non-Catholics suspect the church of "Machiavellianism," because Catholics argue *for* religious freedom when they are few in number but *against* it when they constitute the majority. More to the theological point, De Smedt appealed to the evolution (*terminus evolutionis*) of the church's doctrine on the dignity of the human person. He also squarely faced the prior papal magisterium, from Gregory XVI onward, arguing that these statements (against religious freedom) needed to be understood in their proper context.[167] But, as O'Malley rightly states, De Smedt "had a difficult task," because the document seemed not to be a development and a continuation of the past "but a deviation from it."[168] And while De Smedt's reasoning was persuasive to many bishops, a significant group regarded his arguments as slippery. Calling a "reversal" a "development" had the appearance of theological legerdemain. Despite his valiant attempt, De Smedt's ringing affirmation of religious freedom was not easily harmonized with prior papal teaching.

A year later (September 23, 1964) *De libertate religiosa*—now its own schema but still attached to *De oecumenismo*—again came to the floor.[169] De Smedt again introduced the text, avoiding any extended treatment of "development" but arguing in favor of the schema's affirmation that the state does not even have the *capacity* to judge the truth about religion.[170] How then, he strongly implied, could the state possibly recognize the true religion? After De Smedt had finished speaking, Cardinal Ruffini immediately attacked the declaration, homing in on the state's essential role in fostering and protecting religion. If the state were relieved of this task, then significant agreements between the Holy See and various nations would need to be dissolved. Ruffini encouraged the bishops to proceed with the greatest caution.[171] Several subsequent episcopal speeches echoed the passionate objections of the Sicilian cardinal.

On September 28, 1964, the episcopal interventions ended and work began on revisions. Ultimately, the declaration was given to five members of the *De Fide*, who, on November 9, 1964, presented the reworked schema to the full Theological Commission. A positive vote by the Commission allowed the schema to proceed to the bishops gathered in St. Peter's.[172] Just a

---

167. *AS* II/5, 485–95.

168. O'Malley, *What Happened*, 196.

169. *AS* III/2, 317–27 (*declaratio prior*).

170. *AS* III/2, 348–53, at 352. The schema speaks of the state as "*ineptam esse*" regarding the truth about religion. See *AS* III/2, 321.

171. *AS* III/2, 354–57.

172. *Carnets-GP*, 138 (November 16, 1964). See also Vorgrimler, *Commentary*, 4:52. The schema distributed on November 17, 1964 (*textus emendatus*), may be found in *AS* III/8, 426–49.

few days later, however, the council presidents pulled the text of *De libertate* off the floor, prior to any voting. This, of course, was one of the incidents precipitating the "black week" of 1964. The American bishops, in particular, ardently desired a strong conciliar affirmation of religious freedom—especially since Catholicism had been repeatedly accused of wavering on this fundamental human right. The decision of the council presidents seemed to the Americans—and not to them alone—ill-founded, shortsighted, and entirely unnecessary. Despite this widespread consternation, Philips agreed with the decision: "The vote on religious liberty that had been announced for today has been adjourned by the superior authority. The text, which is to a great extent new, ought to be re-discussed."[173]

In retrospect, the removal of the schema was a wise decision. If the declaration had passed (as was likely the case), it would surely have been claimed that *De libertate*—despite signaling a new direction for Catholicism when compared to prior magisterial teaching—had been rushed through the council without adequate reflection and debate. Looking back at Vatican II fifty years later, Benedict XVI did not hesitate to commend the decision to pull the schema: "In the third session, the Americans told the Pope: we cannot go home without bringing a declaration on religious freedom voted by the Council. The Pope, however, had the firmness and the decision, the patience, to take the text to the fourth session, for the sake of greater discernment and the fuller consent of the Council Fathers."[174] Although the vote had been postponed, the *relatio* was nonetheless delivered by De Smedt and "was received by frenetic applause during and after his report."[175] This strong show of approbation emboldened the American bishops: "The Americans are very dissatisfied and collect some signatures in order to write a letter of objection to the Pope. Four cardinals: Spellman, Ritter, Léger and König meet with the Pope who asks for their trust. What this means is not clear."[176]

Paul VI had made it known—through the speech of Colombo just a couple of months earlier—that he was in favor of the declaration. Foremost on the pope's mind, however, was the unity of the council, and so the unity

173. *Carnets-GP*, 141 (November 19, 1964).

174. Benedict is referring to the fact that Paul VI supported the decision of the council presidents. See Benedict XVI, speech of February 14, 2013, http://w2.vatican.va/content/benedict-xvi/en/speeches/2013/february/documents/hf_ben-xvi_spe_20130214_clero-roma.html.

175. *Carnets-GP*, 141 (November 19, 1964). Tagle refers to "thunderous and prolonged applause" that interrupted De Smedt's speech. See Luis Antonio G. Tagle, "The 'Black Week' of Vatican II," in Alberigo and Komonchak, *History of Vatican II*, 4:395–406, at 401.

176. *Carnets-GP*, 141 (November 19, 1964).

of the Catholic Church. Paul was well aware that the schema had roiled the more conservative bishops, and he was determined to give them an opportunity to dispute the text. But he simultaneously assured the cardinals that he did not intend to abandon the cause of religious freedom. The schema would be debated at the beginning of the fourth session, in September 1965.

While the decision to pull *De libertate* off the floor was controversial, there were cogent reasons to do so. The newly edited schema only came to the bishops on November 17, 1964, with a vote scheduled for two days later. The more conservative bishops asked for a postponement, garnering 441 signatures in support of their petition.[177] Their request was based on two principles: (1) conciliar rules (art. 30) stipulated that the bishops should have time to come to a mature judgment on any distributed text,[178] and (2) the schema distributed on November 17 had been entirely rewritten. Several paragraphs were completely new; taken as a whole, the text was 55 percent longer than the earlier schema.[179] Could such a significantly altered text be voted on without study and debate? The minority had made telling points. But because of the tense atmosphere already existing in the basilica (over the pope's changes to *De oecumenismo* and his insistence on the *Nota praevia*), the withdrawal of *De libertate* "provoked bitterness."[180]

There was so much dismay over Paul VI's actions at the end of the third session that Philips believed they had, regrettably, overshadowed the extraordinary achievements of *Lumen gentium* and *Unitatis redintegratio*.

1965

Although the council was hurrying toward its conclusion, significant questions about *De libertate* remained.[181] The primary theological issue was the schema's deviation from prior magisterial teaching. The more conservative

---

177. See Giovanni Caprile, "Aspetti positivi della terza sessione del concilio," *La Civiltà Cattolica* 116, no. 1 (February 20, 1965): 317–41.

178. For the rules of Vatican II, see Philippe Levillain, *La Mécanique Politique de Vatican II* (Paris: Beauchesne, 1975), 449–64.

179. Caprile, "Aspetti positivi," 328, 329n16. Elsewhere it has been noted that "the text had been radically revised under the considerable influence of John Courtney Murray." See Alberigo and Komonchak, *History of Vatican II*, 4:533.

180. Caprile, "Aspetti positivi," 327.

181. See Ricardo Burigana and Giovanni Turbanti, "The Intersession: Preparing the Conclusion of the Council," in Alberigo and Komonchak, *History of Vatican II*, 4:533–45.

bishops lodged "the now-standard objections that it [the text] contravened the long tradition of the church and the explicit teaching of recent popes."[182] But these objections were entirely true—and they raised a thorny theological problem. Where was continuity and material identity? Where was teaching *in eodem sensu*? Was Catholicism courting a *permutatio fidei*? It is no wonder that Cardinal Siri, speaking on September 14, 1965, warned that if the bishops contravened the solid teaching of earlier popes—Leo XIII, Pius IX, and Pius XII—then their own teaching authority would be weakened and discredited.[183] After all, Siri reasoned, if prior teaching could be discarded, why should anyone adhere to the assertions of Vatican II? Others, such as Cardinal Urbani of Venice, tried to mitigate the objections of Siri and Ruffini, claiming that the teachings of earlier popes—from Gregory XVI to John XXIII—showed a certain "progress" regarding the primacy of the human person and his or her rights.[184]

Although there were several dramatic speeches on the schema, this tension is not reflected in the journals of either Philips or Charue. The former notes, laconically, that the discussion is on course: "The greatest opposition comes from Spain, less so from Italy. The discussion is not very lively."[185] Even more blasé is Charue: "Interventions continue on '*de Libertate*.' The succession [of speeches] is rather monotone and one feels that the game is over."[186] A few days later Charue does not hesitate to remark, "The success [of the schema] is certain."[187]

On September 21, 1965, and after the intervention of the pope, the following question was submitted to the council's bishops: "Does it please the Fathers to take the newly emended text on religious liberty as the definitive base text for the declaration, although with further added perfections such as the Catholic doctrine on the true religion and the amendments proposed by the Fathers in debate, according to the norms of the council?" The result of the voting was 1,997 in favor with only 224 opposed—almost 90 percent positive.[188] Surely it pleased many of those uneasy about the document that the schema would be perfected "according to the Catholic doctrine on the

182. O'Malley, *What Happened*, 249.
183. *AS* IV/1, 207–9. Siri is speaking about the schema of September 14, 1965 (*textus reemendatus*). *AS* IV/1, 146–67.
184. *AS* IV/1, 211–15 (September 14, 1965).
185. *Carnets-GP*, 151 (September 16, 1965).
186. *Carnets-AMC*, 256 (September 16, 1965).
187. *Carnets-AMC*, 261 (September 21, 1965).
188. *Carnets-AMC*, 261 (September, 21, 1965).

true religion," a traditional thesis in both ecclesiology and apologetics. The very words *de vera religione* had resonated throughout generations of theology manuals and would have shored up the bishops' sense that material continuity with the prior tradition would not be ignored in the emended schema.

In fact, when the new draft (*textus recognitus*) was presented to the bishops for voting in late October 1965, Paul VI had submitted changes to the text. His most significant alteration was in the preamble, concerning the one true religion.[189] The October schema reads, "We believe that this one true religion subsists in the Catholic and Apostolic Church, to which the Lord Jesus committed the task of spreading among all men throughout the world" (§1). With this addition the pope remained faithful to the promise that the schema would be perfected with reference to *de vera religione*, thereby overcoming any suggestion that religious freedom would inexorably lead to religious indifference (a common papal theme heretofore). Paul VI realized that if he wanted to achieve virtually unanimous support for the declaration, then the minority's deepest fear—that the material identity of Christian teaching had not been preserved in *De libertate*—had to be assuaged. Christian and Catholic uniqueness needed to be directly stated.[190]

A little later in the same preamble one reads, "In acknowledging this right of religious freedom, this Sacred Synod intends to develop the doctrine of the popes on the inviolable rights of human persons" (§1). This sentence, accenting the intention "to develop [*evolvere*] the doctrine of the popes," again served to calm the fears of the minority. Paul VI introduced it in an attempt to underline the continuity of papal teaching over time.[191] *De libertate* was homogeneously developing the magisterium of prior popes on the inviolable dignity of human beings—and this teaching was applicable to religious freedom as well.

The voting on this schema took place on October 26-27, 1965. The various parts of the schema were overwhelmingly approved, although with a solid core of some 250 *non placet* votes and a large number of *modi* or amendments. Minor changes were made to the text.[192] Ever sensitive to the issue of homogeneous development, the final text added a word, claiming that *De libertate* is developing the teaching of *recent* popes. The intention was

189. Grootaers, "Le crayon rouge," 323-24.

190. Grootaers notes that the Secretariat for Christian Unity "had a critical attitude towards the pope's initiative, but was unable to block it." "Le crayon rouge," 324.

191. Grootaers, "Le crayon rouge," 324.

192. *AS* IV/6, 703-18. The final schema is known as the *textus denuo recognitus*.

to show that Vatican II's teaching on the dignity of the human person was in strict continuity with the magisterium of Pius XII and John XXIII. To drive home this point, De Smedt, in his *relatio* accompanying the final schema, emphasized that the most recent popes insisted on the state's acknowledgment of the dignity of all human beings in religious matters.[193]

The final vote was taken on November 19, 1965, with still 249 against. The opposition to the declaration, although small, remained united almost to the end.[194]

Discontinuity

Why was *De libertate* such a contentious document? And why did it inspire (and still inspires) such passionate opponents? We have already alluded to the comment of the young Joseph Ratzinger that when *Dignitatis humanae* was formally promulgated, there was a palpable sense in St. Peter's Basilica that this was the end of the Middle Ages, even the end of the Constantinian era.[195] Ratzinger's remark clearly displays the discontinuity of *De libertate* with the prior tradition. Christianity was no longer to be tethered to the civil state. Also, the declaration was insisting on the objective right to worship God in accordance with one's conscience. But these affirmations represented a break with prior magisterial teaching—and it is precisely this break that Ruffini, Siri, and Lefebvre were challenging.

Where, concretely, was this discontinuity? In the following sections, I cite a few statements of the magisterium that go to the heart of our discussion.[196]

Encyclical *Mirari vos* (1832) of Gregory XVI

In this encyclical Gregory XVI rails against religious liberty for fear that it propagates error and endangers souls. With other nineteenth-century popes, he expresses concern over the separation of church and state:

193. *AS* IV/6, 718–23, at 719.

194. In the customary vote taken just before solemn promulgation, on December 7, 1965, the totals were 2,308 positive and 70 negative.

195. Ratzinger, *Theological Highlights of Vatican II*, 144.

196. For an examination of the documents noted below, see Bernard Lucien, *Grégoire XVI, Pie IX et Vatican II* (Tours: Éditions Forts dans la Foi, 1990).

This shameful font of indifferentism gives rise to that absurd and erroneous proposition which claims that liberty of conscience must be maintained for everyone. It spreads ruin in sacred and civil affairs, though some repeat over and over again with the greatest impudence that some advantage accrues to religion from it. (§14)

Nor can We predict happier times for religion and government from the plans of those who desire vehemently to separate the Church from the state, and to break the mutual concord between temporal authority and the priesthood. It is certain that that concord which always was favorable and beneficial for the sacred and the civil order is feared by the shameless lovers of liberty. (§20)

Encyclical *Quanta cura* (1864) of Pius IX

This document condemned the view that society should be governed without the distinction between true and false religion:

> For you well know . . . that at this time men are found who . . . dare to teach that "the best constitution of public society and civil progress require that human society be conducted and governed without regard being had to religion any more than if it did not exist; or, at least, without any distinction being made between the true religion and false ones."

> They [proponents of liberalism] do not hesitate to assert "that it is the best condition of civil society, in which no duty is recognized, as attached to the civil power, of restraining by enacted penalties, offenders against the Catholic religion, except so far as public peace may require." . . . [T]hey do not fear to foster that erroneous opinion . . . that "liberty of conscience and worship is each man's personal right, which ought to be legally proclaimed and asserted in every rightly constituted society." (§3, citing Gregory XVI, *Mirari vos* [1832])

Syllabus of Errors (1864) of Pius IX

The *Syllabus* was not part of the encyclical *Quanta cura* but was an appendix to it; the document is a dossier of errors that had been condemned by past magisterial statements. Both Newman and Francis A. Sullivan make clear that the doctrinal authority of the *Syllabus* is limited, precisely because the weight of the documents cited varies greatly.[197] Although the *Syllabus* cannot be read apart from its historical context, it represents well the attitude of nineteenth-century popes toward freedom of religion. One condemned proposition reads:

> Every man is free to embrace and profess that religion which, guided by the light of reason, he shall consider true. (§15)

Another condemned position holds:

> In the present day it is no longer expedient that the Catholic religion should be held as the only religion of the State, to the exclusion of all other forms of worship. (§77)

Encyclical *Immortale Dei* (1885) of Leo XIII

In this letter Leo XIII holds that it is not lawful for the state to hold in equal favor different kinds of religion. The pope condemns, therefore, the idea that all religions should be treated equally by civil authorities:

> Moreover, it [the State] believes that it is not obliged to make public profession of any religion; or to inquire which of the very many religions is the only true one; or to prefer one religion to all the rest; or to show to any form of religion special favor; but, on the contrary, is bound to grant equal rights to every creed, so that public order may not be disturbed by any particular form of religious belief. (§25)

Encyclical *Libertas* (1888) of Leo XIII

Once again, Leo thinks that religious freedom is injurious to the life of the state precisely because it fosters error:

> Justice therefore forbids, and reason itself forbids, the State . . . to treat the various religions (as they call them) alike, and to bestow upon them

197. See Francis A. Sullivan, *Creative Fidelity* (New York: Paulist Press, 1996), 142–44.

promiscuously equal rights and privileges. Since, then, the profession of one religion is necessary in the State, that religion must be professed which alone is true, and which can be recognized without difficulty, especially in Catholic States, because the marks of truth are, as it were, engraved upon it. This religion, therefore, the rulers of the State must preserve and protect. (§21)

Encyclical *Vehementer nos* (1906) of Pius X

Here the pope expresses grave reservations about the separation of church and state (particularly in France), calling it a "dangerous error":

That the State must be separated from the Church is a thesis absolutely false, a most pernicious error. Based, as it is, on the principle that the State must not recognize any religious cult, it is in the first place guilty of a great injustice to God; for the Creator of man is also the Founder of human societies, and preserves their existence as He preserves our own. We owe Him, therefore, not only a private cult, but a public and social worship to honor Him. (§3)

* * *

This short list by no means exhausts the documents pertinent to our subject.[198] However, these excerpts make clear that several popes taught that religious freedom—precisely because it leads to error and so to the ruination of souls—cannot be countenanced. It is unsurprising, then, that Martin Rhonheimer has stated, "The conclusion is unavoidable: precisely this teaching of the Second Vatican Council [on Religious Freedom] is what Pius IX condemned in his encyclical *Quanta Cura*."[199]

It is similarly unsurprising—indeed, it is entirely understandable—that certain bishops at Vatican II invoked the above-named documents to oppose

198. For example, in his encyclical *Longinqua* of Leo XIII, written to the American bishops in 1895, the pope makes clear that the American idea of "separation of church and state" is *not* ideal. While the church in the United States has been fruitful, "she would bring forth more abundant fruits if, in addition to liberty, she enjoyed the favor of the laws and the patronage of the public authority" (§6).

199. Martin Rhonheimer, "Benedict XVI's 'Hermeneutic of Reform' and Religious Freedom," *Nova et Vetera* 9 (2011): 1029–54, at 1032.

De libertate. When Siri, Ruffini, and Lefebvre cited the prior magisterial tradition against the schema, they were thinking of passages such as those found in these papal statements. Indeed, these documents guided official Catholic thinking right up to the eve of Vatican II. Precisely because of this, De Smedt, in all of his *relationes* (explanations) on the various drafts of *De libertate*—including his speech prior to the final vote on the document on November 19, 1965—repeatedly responded to the claim that the schema is opposed to prior church teaching.[200] Was *De libertate* a major rupture with the church's prior life and thought?

Continuity

While acknowledging that the church adopted the principle of the modern state at Vatican II, Benedict XVI simultaneously stated, when speaking directly about religious freedom, "Indeed, a discontinuity had been revealed but in which, after the various distinctions between concrete historical situations and their requirements had been made, the continuity of principles proved not to have been abandoned. It is easy to miss this fact at a first glance."[201] But where is this "continuity of principles," this homogeneous, organic development?[202] Several points may be singled out.

In the first place, Christian and Catholic exceptionalism is fully confirmed by *De libertate.* If earlier popes had argued that religious freedom would inexorably lead to indifferentism—to the claim that the true religion is unknowable—then Vatican II surmounts this difficulty by affirming *both* religious freedom *and* the truth of Catholic Christianity. The declaration asserts the right to religious freedom (§2) while simultaneously insisting that the church of Christ subsists in the Catholic Church (§1).

Second, there truly *is* organic development in magisterial teaching on the inviolable dignity of the human being, a point increasingly emphasized in papal teaching from Leo XIII onward. As the declaration affirms, "The

200. See *AS* IV/6, 719.
201. "Address of His Holiness Benedict XVI to the Roman Curia Offering Them His Christmas Greetings," December 22, 2005, http://w2.vatican.va/content/benedict-xvi/en/speeches/2005/december/documents/hf_ben_xvi_spe_20051222_roman-curia.html.
202. For an exhaustive (and perhaps overstated) defense of the congruency of *Dignitatis humanae* with the prior tradition, see Basile Valuet, *La liberté religieuse et la Tradition catholique: Un cas de développement doctrinal homogène dans le magistère authentique,* 6 vols., 3rd ed. (Paris: Le Barroux, 2011).

council intends to develop the doctrine of recent popes on the inviolable rights of the human person and the constitutional order of society" (§1). With this addition, Paul VI wished to make clear that certain elements of the declaration *were* architectonic developments of the prior tradition. What was new in the schema was that the "inviolable rights" of the person now extended to religious freedom as well. This marked accent on "development" was intended to respond directly to those bishops who thought the declaration was sanctioning not doctrinal growth but doctrinal reversal.

Third, *De libertate* fully expected that the state would maintain the natural law and the objective moral order, an insistence in clear continuity with antecedent Catholic teaching. Thus, the declaration asserts, "Its [the state's] action is to be controlled by juridical norms which are *in conformity with the objective moral order*. These norms arise out of the need for the effective safeguard of the rights of all citizens . . . which comes about when men live together in good order and in true justice, and finally out of the need for a proper guardianship of public morality" (§7; emphasis added).

Finally, the declaration speaks of the duties of the state toward the true religion, a hallmark of nineteenth- and early twentieth-century papal teaching: "Therefore it [the teaching on religious freedom] leaves untouched traditional Catholic doctrine on the moral duty of men and societies toward the true religion and toward the one Church of Christ" (§1). However, given that *De libertate*'s accent was on the freedom of religion as essential to human dignity, it would be very difficult to ask the state to bestow unique privileges on the Catholic faith—or to recognize the public, societal kingship of Jesus Christ.[203] In fact, as De Smedt said in his *relatio* of 1964, the state did not even have the capacity to recognize the true religion.[204]

More importantly from a theological standpoint, the council had emphasized the *analogical similarity* of other churches—and of other religions (Judaism uniquely)—to Catholicism. Would it now be logical to ask for the maintenance of the confessional state? The idea of the "duties of the state toward the true religion" could not be sustained—at least not in the sense envisioned by Pius IX and Leo XIII—given the other affirmations in *De libertate* and in Vatican II at large. As the declaration itself makes clear, "The *freedom of the Church* is the fundamental principle in what concerns the relations between the Church and governments and the whole civil order"

---

203. See, for example, the 1925 encyclical of Pius XI, *Quas primas*, on the societal kingship of the Lord Jesus.

204. See note 170 above.

(§13; emphasis added). The church was asking, fundamentally, for freedom to preach the gospel, not for societal privileges.[205] Understandably, then, Benedict XVI, in his famous 2005 speech, makes no mention whatsoever of duties of the civil state toward Catholicism, while insisting on the *responsibility* of the state to allow freedom of religion: "It was necessary [for the council] to give a new definition to the relationship between the Church and the modern State that would make room impartially for citizens of various religions and ideologies, merely assuming responsibility for an orderly and tolerant coexistence among them and for the freedom to practice their own religion."[206] Benedict's emphasis here is on the conciliar admonition that the modern state must allow citizens of various beliefs the space for tolerant coexistence and freedom of worship.[207] Rhonheimer accurately sums this up: "Thus, the conception of the tasks and duties of the state toward the true religion, which had been taken as authoritative by Pius IX, was tacitly shelved by the act of solemn magisterium of an ecumenical council."[208]

Theological Implications of Discontinuity

In his landmark 2005 speech on Vatican II, Benedict XVI candidly admitted that Vatican II "corrected" certain historical decisions—corrections that indicate "apparent discontinuity": "The Second Vatican Council, with its new definition of the relationship between the faith of the Church and certain essential elements of modern thought, *has reviewed or even corrected certain historical decisions*, but in this apparent discontinuity it has actually preserved and deepened her inmost nature and true identity."[209] I do not think there can be any question but that *De libertate* was, in some sense, discontinuous with prior magisterial teaching. And that, of course, has important

---

205. John Courtney Murray notes that Paul VI, in one of his addresses soon after the council ended, emphasized that the church asks of the state "nothing but freedom" to preach the gospel, as *Dignitatis humanae* itself taught. See Murray, "Religious Freedom," 693n53.

206. Benedict XVI, "Christmas Greetings," 2005.

207. At the same time, Benedict is well aware that the civil state has failed to maintain the objective moral order. This is precisely the critique that he leveled at the modern state in his extraordinary addresses at Westminster Hall in London (2010) and the Bundestag in Berlin (2011). For an analysis, see Thomas G. Guarino, "Nature and Grace: Seeking the Delicate Balance," *Josephinum Journal of Theology* 18 (2011): 150–62.

208. Rhonheimer, "Religious Freedom," 1047.

209. Benedict XVI, "Christmas Greetings," 2005; emphasis added.

implications for the questions central to this volume: If the declaration did not teach in accordance with the prior tradition, did it then court a *permutatio fidei*, the distortive corruption of fundamental doctrinal landmarks? If not, how is this theologically explained?

As we have seen, many conciliar bishops argued that *De libertate* betrayed the teaching of earlier popes, from Gregory XVI to Pius XII. Again and again, they adverted to this discontinuity, a discontinuity so obvious that it has caused one theologian to remark, "Vatican II's acceptance of the doctrine of religious liberty for other religions and for all persons . . . is another striking case of extraordinary change regarding an important doctrinal question. The magnitude of the change is clear from the strong opposition mounted against acceptance during the council."[210] Can one legitimately respond to this "strong opposition" by stating that *De libertate* represented a "development of doctrine"? "Development," as we have seen, refers to organic, harmonious growth over time. Such homogeneous growth was sanctioned by Vincent of Lérins, the first theologian to treat of doctrinal development *ex professo*. It is unsurprising, then, that John Courtney Murray, one of the principal architects of *De libertate*, did not hesitate to cite Vincent: "The legitimate conclusion is that between Leo XIII and Vatican II there has been an authentic development of doctrine in the sense of Vincent of Lérins, 'an authentic progress not a change of the faith.'"[211]

But is this citation of the Lerinian justifiable? Did *De libertate* truly represent an organic development, as Murray claims? A positive answer can be given, but only in part. As earlier noted, the uniqueness of Catholic Christianity was unhesitatingly affirmed by the declaration. And, as Murray rightly argued, there had been an increasing accent—over the course of several pontificates—on the church's esteem for the inviolable dignity of the human person. In this sense, *De libertate* represented continuity with, and organic growth of, the prior tradition.

As the same time, there were decidedly new accents in the declara-

210. Walter Principe, "When 'Authentic' Teachings Change," *Ecumenist* 25 (July/August 1987): 70–73. Also discussing the significant volte-face represented by *De libertate* is J. Robert Dionne, *The Papacy and the Church* (New York: Philosophical Library, 1987), 147–94.

211. John Courtney Murray, "Vers une intelligence du développement de la doctrine de l'Église sur la liberté religieuse," in *La Liberté Religieuse*, ed. J. Hamer and Y. Congar (Paris: Cerf, 1967), 111–47, at 138. Murray was fond of citing Vincent when discussing religious freedom. For other instances, see Murray, "Contemporary Orientations of Catholic Thought on Church and State," *Theological Studies* 10 (1949): 177–234; Murray, "The Problem of Religious Freedom," *Theological Studies* 25 (December 1964): 503–75.

tion—on the relationship between church and state and on the objective right of religious freedom for all people—that were not developments but *reversals* of the immediately prior tradition. It was precisely these reversals that gave rise to "vigorous and sustained opposition" to the declaration, a passionate defiance that would last almost until the end of the council.[212] As Avery Dulles rightly observes, when compared to earlier Catholic teaching, *De libertate* "represents an undeniable, even a dramatic, shift."[213]

To what extent do the reversals found in this document constitute a significant theological problem? This is undoubtedly the most crucial question that *De libertate* raises for Catholic thought. As Murray stated, *Dignitatis humanae* was the "most controversial document" of the entire council precisely because it raised the issue of development and reversal with unavoidable urgency. The minority bishops were understandably worried that *De libertate* constituted a *permutatio fidei*. After all, on several points the schema blatantly contradicted prior magisterial teaching. Would not such reversals weaken the council's own authority? And isn't this especially the case when we remember that Vincent explicitly warned against heretics who cry, "Condemn what you used to hold and hold what you used to condemn." Even more forcefully, Vincent had cautioned against novelties of any kind: "[Novelties], were they accepted, would necessarily defile the faith of the blessed fathers. . . . If they were accepted, then it must be stated that the faithful of all ages, all the saints, all the chaste, continent virgins, all the clerical levites and priests, so many thousands of confessors, so great an army of martyrs . . . almost the entire world incorporated in Christ the Head through the catholic faith for so many centuries, would have erred, would have blasphemed, would not have known what to believe" (*Comm.* 24.5).

Despite Vincent's warnings (and the minority's concerns), this reversal of field on religious freedom was not regarded as a major theological problem for two reasons. In the first place, Protestant Christianity, and other religions (particularly Judaism), were now evaluated *positively* by the council according to the standard of analogical similarity. Protestant churches were understood as participating formally and substantially—even if limitedly— in the one church of Jesus Christ. Rather than state that other belief systems are "false," Vatican II affirms that they are partially true—secondary analogates profoundly related to the prime analogue, Catholicism. This reevalu-

212. O'Malley, *What Happened*, 40.
213. Avery Dulles, *Church and Society* (New York: Fordham University Press, 2008), 349.

ation of Protestant churches—and a fortiori of other religions—inexorably led the council toward an affirmation of religious freedom.

Second, as we have seen throughout this volume, the reversal of ordinary magisterial teaching is theologically possible within Catholicism. The fact that Gérard Philips—often the principal voice on the *De Fide*—never seriously adverted to the objection that *De libertate* constituted a theological volte-face is revelatory. Deeply aware of Catholic principles, Philips would not let the reversal of ordinary teaching constitute an insurmountable obstacle to conciliar affirmations. As the primary author of *Lumen gentium*, Philips was well aware that the council had overturned prior papal teaching (e.g., on the link between episcopal jurisdiction and consecration)—believing, in fact, that this affirmation was the most important theological advance of the entire council.

Catholic theology has never considered all Christian doctrine, even positions that have been taught over a considerable period of time, to be irreformable. Earlier authentic teaching can legitimately be called into question. However, such reversals must be clearly distinguished from the annulment of fundamental dogmatic landmarks.[214] Both the conciliar minority and the majority understood the legitimacy of homogeneous doctrinal progress over time. The entire history of the church witnessed to such growth. But the majority (and Paul VI) were willing, on occasion, to reverse antecedent magisterial teaching—especially if this allowed the church to recover an earlier tradition that had become obscured over time.

In the reversals that took place in *De libertate*, one sees the influence of *ressourcement* reasoning, which, in this case, occasioned not simply the supplementing but also the supplanting of prior ordinary teaching. There was a recovery of early Christian thinkers such as Lactantius and Augustine, both of whom insisted on religious freedom.[215] Similarly important was the witness of the early church, which asked of the Roman Empire only the freedom to preach the gospel, not for any special privileges from the state itself. Benedict XVI took note of this ancient tradition:

---

214. Some have argued that the church's teaching on religious freedom prior to Vatican II *was* an infallible "landmark." I have discussed why this is not the case in Thomas G. Guarino, *Revelation and Truth* (Scranton, PA: University of Scranton Press, 1993), 158–60.

215. However, the phrase "compel them to come in" (Luke 14:23) was used by Augustine against the Donatists; see Letter 93 (*To Vincentius*). See also John M. Rist, *Augustine: Ancient Thought Baptized* (Cambridge: Cambridge University Press, 1994), 274. Similarly Aquinas: "The acceptance of the faith is a matter of freedom, but one is obligated to preserve the faith once it has been embraced." *Summa Theologica* II-II, q. 10, a. 8, ad 3.

The Second Vatican Council, recognizing and making its own an essential principle of the modern State with the Decree on Religious Freedom, *has recovered the deepest patrimony of the Church.* By so doing she can be conscious of being in full harmony with the teaching of Jesus himself (cf. Mt 22: 21), as well as with the Church of the martyrs of all time. . . . The martyrs of the early Church died for their faith in that God who was revealed in Jesus Christ, and *for this very reason they also died for freedom of conscience and the freedom to profess one's own faith*—a profession that no State can impose but which, instead, can only be claimed with God's grace in freedom of conscience.[216]

Benedict's accent on the role of the early church in the formation of *De libertate* is also visible in an essay he penned on the fiftieth anniversary of Vatican II:

At stake [in *De libertate*] was the freedom to choose and practice religion and the freedom to change it, as fundamental human rights and freedoms. . . . Such a concept could not be foreign to the Christian faith, which had come into being claiming that the State could neither decide on the truth nor prescribe any kind of worship. The Christian faith demanded freedom of religious belief and freedom of religious practice in worship, without thereby violating the law of the State in its internal ordering. . . . To this extent, it can be said that Christianity, at its birth, brought the principle of religious freedom into the world.[217]

But it was not only the principle of *ressourcement* that gave substance to *Dignitatis humanae.* One sees as well the theme of *aggiornamento* or updating. As Paul VI pointed out in a speech on November 18, 1965, an *improper* understanding of *aggiornamento* entails a "relativizing" of Christian faith and truth—of the church's dogmas, structures, and traditions. But a proper understanding of "updating," as the entire theological tradition bears witness, is to take "spoils from Egypt," assimilating every form of thought that is congruent with the gospel. In *De libertate* the church looked to the modern state's understanding of religious freedom and saw that it was deeply congru-

---

216. Benedict XVI, "Christmas Greetings," 2005; emphasis added.

217. For the text of Benedict's article "Fu una giornata splendida" in *L'Osservatore Romano* on the eve of the fiftieth anniversary of Vatican II (October 11, 2012), see http://www.vatican.va/special/annus_fidei/documents/annus-fidei_bxvi_inedito-50-concilio_en.html.

ent with its own earlier history. This is why Benedict, in a 2006 speech, could say, "One must welcome the *true conquests of the Enlightenment, human rights and especially the freedom of faith and its practice,* and recognize these also as being essential elements for the authenticity of religion."[218] In other words, any even-handed evaluation of the Enlightenment must acknowledge not only its problems but also those legitimate advances congruent with the gospel.

De libertate would have risen to the level of a Vincentian *permutatio fidei*—a distortive corruption of the faith—*if* the council had taught that its affirmation of religious freedom entailed the notion that the "true religion" was unknowable (this would have been Lessing's "Ring Parable" updated for the twentieth century), or *if* Vatican II had taught that Christianity was simply one among many equally valid religions, a position the council never remotely approached. Indeed, *De libertate* (with the entire council) strongly defends the unique truth of the Catholic, Christian faith while simultaneously insisting that all men and women have a right in conscience to worship God other than in the way God himself had revealed—in the history of Israel and in Jesus Christ. Men and women must be free to follow "the judgments of conscience," even if such judgments should prove erroneous.

Concluding Reflections on *De libertate*

Let us conclude this discussion of *De libertate* by reflecting on the issues at the heart of this volume. Was Vatican II's teaching on religious freedom in material continuity with the prior doctrinal tradition? Was it a matter of development *in eodem sensu eademque sententia*—the kind of harmonious, organic growth sanctioned by Vincent of Lérins and John Henry Newman? Vincent insisted that change is characteristic of life itself, including the life of Christ's church. But proper change must be a *profectus*, a linear advance, like a child becoming an adult and a seed becoming a plant. Changes that are reversals of landmark teachings constitute *permutationes fidei*, distortive corruptions.

More than other conciliar documents, the Declaration on Religious

---

218. "Address of His Holiness Benedict XVI to the Members of the Roman Curia at the Traditional Exchange of Christmas Greetings," December 22, 2006, https://w2.vatican.va /content/benedict-xvi/en/speeches/2006/december/documents/hf_ben_xvi_spe_20061222 _curia-romana.html; emphasis added.

Freedom attests to the "continuity and discontinuity at different levels" of which Benedict XVI spoke. Of the text's partial continuity with the prior doctrinal tradition there is no doubt. While affirming the right to religious freedom, the declaration also unhesitatingly affirms the unique truth of Catholic Christianity. To see in the declaration a melting of Christian exceptionalism into a general agnosticism about the truth of religion would be illusory. Christian uniqueness is never in doubt, even while religious freedom for all is fully affirmed. Further, in the council's marked emphasis on the inviolable dignity of human beings, one sees a homogeneous development of prior teaching from Leo XIII forward. Of course, the recognition of this dignity is now expanded to include unfettered religious freedom, which had not been the case heretofore.

At the same time, there are significant moments of discontinuity in *De libertate*. And it is precisely this discontinuity that led to "vigorous and sustained opposition" to the schema until the very end of the council. The teaching authority of the Catholic Church had not always seen religious freedom as a necessary implication of human dignity. On the contrary, such "freedom" was seen as a concession to error, a concession that inexorably endangered human souls since it relentlessly exposed them to falsehoods of every kind. Ironically, homogeneous growth in one area (human dignity) entailed the simultaneous overturning of certain firmly rooted positions (that religious freedom served only the promiscuous spread of error, and that the state was bound to offer unique privileges to the true religion). But if religious freedom—and its consequent diversity—were to be fully supported, then the church could hardly expect a confessional state that acknowledged the societal kingship of Jesus Christ and provided unique protections for Catholicism. Indeed, the end of the confessional state was a foreseeable by-product of the council's affirmation of religious freedom.[219]

Given these conclusions, I do not think that one can say, without qualification, that *Dignitatis humanae* represents a "development of doctrine"—at least as that phrase has been understood by theorists of development such as Vincent and Newman. In some areas the declaration is clearly in material continuity with the prior doctrinal tradition. In other areas there is a significant reversal of antecedent teaching. Such reversals, we may say, con-

---

219. Of course, *Dignitatis humanae* states that its teaching "leaves untouched traditional Catholic doctrine on the moral duty of men and societies toward the true religion and toward the one Church of Christ" (§1). But, as noted above, this duty is ultimately compressed into the church's complete freedom to preach the gospel.

stitute part of the *process* of development as the Catholic Church gradually rethought and adjusted its relationship to the modern, secular state.

Despite the discontinuities that exist in *De libertate*, these reversals do not rise to the level of Vincentian *permutationes fidei*. The declaration defends the Christian and Catholic faith in its uniqueness even while recognizing that the dignity of humanity demands religious freedom—even if such freedom can be exercised in a manner that is, at least to some extent, erroneous. The reversals in *De libertate*, while real, are never of doctrinal landmarks, much less of defined Catholic dogmas. The reversals are of the authentic, ordinary teaching of the magisterium. One may legitimately conclude, therefore, that *Dignitatis humanae* represents a Vincentian *profectus non permutatio*.

Conclusion

We started this volume by asking certain questions: Is Vatican II a legitimate development and extension of the Catholic doctrinal tradition? Or did the council, in its ambitious attempt to come to terms with the Reformation, the Enlightenment, and the contemporary world generally, betray prior Christian teaching? Does Vatican II represent a "rupture" with preconciliar Catholicism? Or is rupture, left unexplained, a word that fails to capture this extraordinary event?

To answer these questions, we examined several crucial topics that remain in dispute more than a half century after the council's conclusion. To aid in our examination, we enlisted the help of Vincent of Lérins, a fifth-century theologian who was deeply concerned with the issue of continuity and change over time. In Vincent's day, the church was embroiled in several major controversies: Christ's divinity and humanity remained under debate; Arianism was still a vibrant movement; Nestorianism was thriving although recently condemned; and Vincent's own monastery was involved in a heated controversy over the relationship between grace and free will. On all of these issues, Vincent was concerned with protecting the church's fidelity to and continuity with the biblical and apostolic witness.

In the midst of these debates, Vincent wondered: How does the church ensure that any changes that occur in Christian doctrine are proper, authentic, and legitimate? *That* change occurs is indisputable. Indeed, Vincent readily acknowledged that Christ's church undergoes significant change over time. After all, the church was now using words like *homoousios* and *Theotokos* that were not found in the Sacred Scriptures. However, he presciently distinguishes between two *kinds* of change: a *profectus* or advance, which means homogeneous, organic, linear development, and a *permutatio* or corruption, referring to some modification that alters the fundamental meaning of the Christian faith. Invoking biological examples, Vincent argues that any alteration in church teaching must be similar to the changes that occur when a child becomes an adult and a seed becomes a plant. In both cases there is transformation, but it is a matter of harmonious, organic growth—with the fundamental proportions and structure remaining intact. This is why Vincent insists that *authentic* development must always be growth that is *in eodem sensu eademque sententia* with that which preceded it; that is, the same meaning (*idem sensu*) of prior ecclesial "landmarks" must be preserved, not betrayed. In fact, the stable meaning of these landmarks constitutes the indispensable baseline for future doctrinal progress. Failure to safeguard these foundational teachings—as occurred with various imperial attempts to overturn the central affirmations of the Nicene Creed—led Vincent to react strongly against distortive corruptions of Christian truth.

Change that results not in harmonious growth but in naked reversal is not "development" but alteration *in alieno sensu* (with a foreign meaning). So, for example, theological reflection on Christ's person and natures should continue. But such reflection must always preserve the foundational teachings established by the councils of Nicaea and Ephesus. Their affirmations can be enhanced, extended, and developed, but they cannot be contravened. For Vincent, then, proper change results in a harmonious *profectus fidei*, while improper and illegitimate alterations inexorably result in a *permutatio fidei*, a pernicious betrayal of Christian doctrine.

Using Vincent's teaching, along with several other principles central to Catholic theology, I have argued that Vatican II—even in its most disputed topics—was in continuity with the prior doctrinal landmarks of the Catholic Church. Undoubtedly, there was supplementation and enhancement—true *development* in the Vincentian sense of the word. A good example is the council's teaching on the priesthood of the baptized, which enriched and enhanced prior Catholic teaching on the ministerial priesthood even while leaving this earlier teaching intact (and harmoniously developed).

At the same time, some conciliar affirmations supplanted or reversed earlier authentic teaching. For example, Vatican II taught that the three *munera* (powers or functions) of teaching, governing, and sanctifying are bestowed on bishops with episcopal consecration. This affirmation reversed Pius XII's 1943 encyclical *Mystici corporis*, which held that bishops receive the power of jurisdiction "directly from the same Supreme Pontiff" (§42).

An authentic teaching of the ordinary papal magisterium was thereby discarded in order to restore an older and more traditional position. These kinds of reversals have caused consternation among some Catholics. But, as I have argued, the reversal of ordinary teaching is certainly possible in Catholic theology. If such reversals were not feasible, then every teaching of the Roman magisterium would have to be regarded as per se irreformable and irreversible—an indefensible position that has never been held by any theologian. As evident in our discussions, the Theological Commission of Vatican II was fully cognizant of the reversals that took place in the conciliar documents. Such volte-faces, while not properly called "developments," are part of the *process* of development, a process that requires moments of reform and even the reversal of lower-level teachings.

One must acknowledge, then, as Benedict XVI himself did, that Vatican II reformed earlier positions, thereby countenancing discontinuities with prior magisterial teaching. However—and this is a crucial point—the reversal of ordinary teaching must be distinguished from the reversal of fundamental doctrinal landmarks. Dogmatic landmarks cannot be contravened—or regarded as merely contingent and provisional. Indeed, it was just such contingency that Vincent ardently rejected in his defense of Nicaea and Ephesus—a point with which Vatican II is in full accord. As I have argued, the volte-faces engaged in by the council do not rise to the level of *permutationes fidei*. In fact, as regards foundational dogmatic teaching, Vatican II is in clear continuity with the antecedent tradition, even while developing it *in eodem sensu*.

The argument has also been made in this volume, and at some length, that Thomist ideas are more decidedly present at Vatican II than is usually assumed. At several junctures I adduced the following statement of Yves Congar, one of the principal conciliar theologians: "It could be shown . . . that St. Thomas, the *Doctor communis*, furnished the writers of the dogmatic texts of Vatican II with the bases and structure [*les assises et la structure*] of their thought. We do not doubt that they themselves would make this confession."[1] At first glance, this is a surprising assertion since scholastic and Thomist language cannot be found on the surface of the documents. In truth, the council left behind the conceptual arsenal of the thirteenth century, in

1. Yves Congar, "La théologie au Concile: Le 'théologiser' du Concile," in *Situation et tâches présentes de la théologie* (Paris: Cerf, 1967), 53. Given that virtually all the theologians at the council received their theological education under the aegis of Leo XIII's 1879 encyclical *Aeterni Patris*—which sanctioned scholasticism as the best method for teaching theology—it is hardly surprising that St. Thomas's thought was influential at the council.

accordance with the wishes of John XXIII that Vatican II present the deposit of faith in a way that was invigorating to contemporary men and women and that encouraged ecumenical dialogue.

Nonetheless, as I have argued, while Thomist *language* was absent at Vatican II, Thomist *ideas* were in plain sight.[2] In particular, the council used the notions of participation and analogy as structuring principles in order to enhance, enrich, and explain several of its teachings: the universal priesthood, Mary as *mediatrix*, *subsistit in*, ecumenism, and so on. In fact, this use of analogical reasoning is so pervasive in certain documents that I have called it *the philosophical style beneath the rhetorical style* of Vatican II.

Some of the continuing uneasiness connected with the council is traceable to this turn to analogy: formerly, Catholicism invoked the language of difference and dissimilarity when speaking of other Christian churches, other religions, and the world itself; at the council, it now invoked the language of analogical affinity. Other entities were not defined according to their perceived errors and flaws; rather, in a dramatic shift, the council put its accent on the congruency of Catholicism with other churches, with other religions (particularly Judaism), and with the contemporary world. These bodies participate in, respectively, faith in Christ, in the one God, and in the desire for truth and justice. Thus, they are partially similar to the Catholic faith and analogically related to it. In all cases, Catholicism is presented as the prime analogue possessing—by God's grace—the fullness of divine revelation. Others are presented as secondary analogates, participating with various degrees of intensity in the attributes and "perfections" with which Catholicism is endowed. But this significant change in perspective—from dialectical dissimilarity to analogical affinity—induced vertigo in some sectors of the Catholic world. Even though Vatican II preserved the foundational doctrinal teachings of the Catholic tradition, Catholics, to invoke the phrase of Thomas Kuhn, woke up "in a different world."[3]

The use of participation and analogy was particularly helpful for a council that—convoked in the shadow of a world traumatized by World

2. As Matthew Levering rightly says, "The contrast between *ressourcement* and Thomistic modes of thought [at the council] has been exaggerated, to the detriment of both." See *An Introduction to Vatican II as an Ongoing Theological Event* (Washington, DC: Catholic University of America Press, 2017), 19n37. I cannot pursue the idea here, but one wonders if the Neoplatonic notion of participation—central to both St. Thomas and many of the Greek and Latin fathers—provides the link connecting *la nouvelle théologie*, *ressourcement*, and Thomism.

3. Thomas S. Kuhn, *The Structure of Scientific Revolutions*, 4th ed. (Chicago: University of Chicago Press, 2012), 121.

War II, the Holocaust, nuclear weapons, and the Cold War—sought to forge strong links among men and women. As Cardinal Suenens had argued in December of 1962, it was time for the church to open a dialogue with several sectors of contemporary society. In participatory and analogical reasoning, the council fathers found the philosophical tools that allowed them to accent the "commonality" existing among peoples, their profound similarity one to another. These tools gave birth to, and undergirded, the council's deeply irenic rhetorical style. There is certainly no devaluing of Catholic exceptionalism in the conciliar texts—no dissolution of thick Christian faith into the search for a better world. But neither is there an affirmation that Catholicism alone purveys the truth. Many others possess some share of it.

This shift to analogical reasoning changed the optic through which other entities were viewed and understood. Protestantism was perceived not as an abject heresy but as a deeply Christian reality, strikingly proximate to Catholicism. The Jewish faith was regarded no longer as an annulled religion but as the *fons et origo* of Christianity and itself the exemplar of a living covenant. Nonreligious seekers after truth were viewed not as condemnable atheists and Marxists but as partners in building a better world, a society where justice reigns. Given these intentions, one should not expect from Vatican II a kind of fiery "Barmen Declaration"—that was not the purpose of the council's work. At the same time, Catholicism did not change its traditional self-understanding at Vatican II—in fact, that self-understanding is repeatedly announced—but it did insist on the profound relationship of the Catholic Church to all others. In this way, John XXIII's hope for a council that would engage the separated Christian brethren, as well as foster relations of trust and friendship with adherents of other religions and with the contemporary world, was realized.[4]

I hope this book has explained how both the continuities and the discontinuities of Vatican II can be integrated into an intelligible and fully Catholic theological synthesis. One need not accent continuity to the ex-

---

4. Of course, there are dangers in any approach that is deeply analogical in nature. By stressing the similarity between Catholicism and all seekers after truth, did the council fail to distinguish adequately the Christian faith from other worldviews? Did it fail to prepare Catholics to be "countercultural" at the very time when a rabid secularism was appearing on the horizon? And did the analogical vision become so dominant in the Catholic Church that when the declaration *Dominus Iesus* was issued in 2000—with its strong accent on the uniqueness of Christianity and Catholicism—it was regarded by some commentators as an affront to the council? These questions, though they cannot be discussed here, point to potential weaknesses in any analogical perspective.

clusion of the reforms and fissures that occurred at the council. Nor should one so emphasize discontinuity as if the material continuity and identity of the Catholic dogmatic tradition were not preserved by Vatican II. Through their artful combination of development, reform, and reversal, the conciliar theologians and bishops deftly advanced the doctrinal teaching of the Catholic Church *in eodem sensu eademque sententia*. Foundational Catholic landmarks were clearly defended and maintained. And they were maintained in such a way that Vincent of Lérins—that early artisan of doctrinal development—would recognize Vatican II not only as an extraordinary council but also as a *profectus non permutatio fidei*.

Select Bibliography

Abbott, Walter M., and Joseph Gallagher, eds. *The Documents of Vatican II.* New York: America Press, 1977.

Acta synodalia sacrosancti concilii oecumenici Vaticani II. Rome: Typis Polyglottis Vaticanis, 1970.

Alberigo, Giuseppe. *Fede, tradizione, profezia: Studi su Giovanni XXIII e sul Vaticano II.* Brescia: Paideia, 1984.

Alberigo, Giuseppe, and Joseph A. Komonchak, eds. *History of Vatican II.* 5 vols. Maryknoll, NY: Orbis Books, 1996-2006.

Alberigo, Giuseppe, and Franca Magistretti, eds. *Constitutionis Dogmaticae Lumen Gentium, Synopsis Historica.* Bologna: Istituto per le Scienze Religiose, 1975.

Aparicio, Carmen. "Contributo di Lukas Vischer alla *Gaudium et spes.*" In *Sapere teologico e unità della fede: Studi in onore del Prof. Jared Wicks,* 3-19. Rome: Editrice Pontificia Università Gregoriana, 2004.

Balthasar, Hans Urs von. "On the Tasks of Catholic Philosophy in Our Time." *Communio* 20 (1993): 147-89. Originally published 1946.

Becker, Karl. "The Church and Vatican II's *Subsistit In* Terminology." *Origins* 35 (January 9, 2006): 514-22.

Benedict XVI. "Christmas Address to the Roman Curia." *Acta Apostolicae Sedis* 98 (January 6, 2006): 40-53

Berkouwer, Gerrit Cornelis. *The Second Vatican Council and the New Catholicism.* Translated by Lewis Smedes. Grand Rapids: Eerdmans, 1965.

Betti, Umberto. *Diario del Concilio.* Bologna: Dehoniane, 2003.

——, ed. *Commento alla costituzione dogmatica sulla divina rivelazione.* Milan: Massimo, 1966.

Bossuet, Jacques-Bénigne. *Histoire des variations des Églises Protestantes.* Paris: Desprez, 1760.

Bouillard, Henri. *Conversion et grâce chez S. Thomas d'Aquin: Étude historique.* Paris: Aubier, 1944.

Bulman, Raymond F., and Frederick J. Parrella, eds. *From Trent to Vatican II: Historical and Theological Investigations.* New York: Oxford University Press, 2006.

Burigana, Riccardo. *La Bibbia nel concilio.* Bologna: Il Mulino, 1998.

Select Bibliography

Caprile, Giovanni. "Aspetti positivi della terza sessione del concilio." *La Civiltà Cattolica* 116 (February 20, 1965): 317–41.

————. *Il Concilio Vaticano II.* Vol. 4, *Terzo periodo, 1964–1965.* Rome: La Civiltà Cattolica, 1966.

Charue, André-Marie. *Carnets conciliaires de l'évêque de Namur A.-M. Charue.* Edited by L. Declerck and Cl. Soetens. Louvain-la-Neuve: Faculté de Théologie, 2000.

Colombo, Carlo. "Paolo VI: Il Papa non può essere il semplice notaio del concilio." In *Inchiesta sul Concilio,* edited by Gian Franco Svidercoschi. Rome: Città Nuova, 1985.

Congar, Yves. *A History of Theology.* Translated by Hunter Guthrie. Garden City, NY: Doubleday, 1968.

————. *Le Concile de Vatican II: Son Église, Peuple de Dieu et Corps du Christ.* Paris: Beauchesne, 1984.

————. *My Journal of the Council.* Translated by Mary John Ronayne and Mary Cecily Boulding. Collegeville, MN: Liturgical Press, 2012.

————. *Situation et tâches présentes de la théologie.* Paris: Cerf, 1967.

————. *Tradition and Traditions.* Translated by Michael Naseby and Thomas Rainborough. New York: Macmillan, 1967.

————. *True and False Reform in the Church.* Translated by Paul Philibert. Collegeville, MN: Liturgical Press, 2011.

Cullmann, Oscar. "Comments on the Decree on Ecumenism." *Ecumenical Review* 17 (April 1965): 93–112.

D'Costa, Gavin. *Vatican II: Catholic Doctrines on Jews and Muslims.* Oxford: Oxford University Press, 2014.

Declerck, L., and M. Lamberigts. "Le rôle de l'épiscopat belge dans l'élection des commissions conciliaires en octobre 1962." In *La Raison par Quatre Chemins,* edited by Jean Leclercq, 279–306. Leuven: Peeters, 2007.

de Lubac, Henri. *A Brief Catechesis on Nature and Grace.* Translated by Richard Arnandez. San Francisco: Ignatius, 1984.

————. *The Drama of Atheist Humanism.* Translated by E. Riley. London: Sheed and Ward, 1949.

————. "A propos de la formule: diversi sed non adversi." *Recherches de science religieuse* 40 (1952): 27–40.

————. *Vatican Council Notebooks.* Vol. 1. Translated by Andrew Stefanelli and Anne Englund Nash. San Francisco: Ignatius, 2007.

de Mattei, Roberto. *Il Concilio Vaticano II: Una storia mai scritta.* Turin: Lindau, 2010.

Dionne, J. Robert. *The Papacy and the Church.* New York: Philosophical Library, 1987.

Donnelly, D., J. Famerée, M. Lamberigts, and K. Schelkens, eds. *The Belgian Contribution to the Second Vatican Council.* Leuven: Peeters, 2008.

Doorly, Moyra, and Aidan Nichols. *The Council in Question.* Charlotte, NC: Tan, 2011.

Dulles, Avery. *Church and Society.* New York: Fordham University Press, 2008.

Duprey, Pierre. "Paul VI et le Décret sur L'Oecuménisme." In *Paolo VI e I Problemi Ecclesiologici al Concilio,* 225–48. Brescia: Istituto Paolo VI, 1989.

Echeverria, Eduardo. *Berkouwer and Catholicism.* Leiden: Brill, 2013.

Empie, Paul C., Thomas Austin Murphy, and Joseph A. Burgess. *Teaching Authority and Infallibility in the Church.* Minneapolis: Augsburg, 1980.

George, Timothy, and Thomas G. Guarino, eds. *Evangelicals and Catholics Together at Twenty: Vital Statements on Contested Topics.* Grand Rapids: Brazos, 2015.

Gherardini, Brunero. *The Ecumenical Vatican Council II: A Much Needed Discussion.* Translated by Franciscans of the Immaculate. Frigento: Casa Mariana, 2009.

Grootaers, Jan. *Ecclesia a Spiritu Sancto edocta: Mélanges théologiques, hommage à Gérard Philips.* Gembloux: Duculot, 1970.

———. "Le crayon rouge de Paul VI." In *Les Commissions Conciliaires à Vatican II*, edited by M. Lamberigts, Cl. Soetens, and J. Grootaers, 317–52. Leuven: Bibliotheek van de Faculteit Godgeleerdheid, 1996.

———, ed. *Primauté et collégialité: Le dossier de Gérard Philips sur la Nota explicativa praevia.* Leuven: Leuven University Press, 1986.

Guarino, Thomas G. "Analogy and Vatican II." *Josephinum Journal of Theology* 22 (2015): 44–58.

———. "Catholic Reflections on the Truth of Sacred Scripture." In *Your Word Is Truth*, edited by Charles Colson and Richard John Neuhaus, 79–101. Grand Rapids: Eerdmans, 2002.

———. "'Essentia et non gradu tantum differant': A Note on the Priesthood and Analogical Predication." *Thomist* 77 (October 2013): 559–76.

———. "Fides et Ratio: Theology and Contemporary Pluralism." *Theological Studies* 62 (2001): 675–700.

———. *Foundations of Systematic Theology.* New York: T&T Clark, 2005.

———. "Nature and Grace: Seeking the Delicate Balance." *Josephinum Journal of Theology* 18 (March 2011): 150–62

———. "Philosophia Obscurans? Six Theses on the Proper Relationship between Theology and Philosophy." *Nova et Vetera* 12 (Spring 2014): 349–94.

———. "The Priesthood and Analogy: A Note on the Formation and Redaction of *Lumen Gentium*, no. 10." *Angelicum* 67 (1990): 309–28.

———. *Revelation and Truth: Unity and Plurality in Contemporary Theology.* Scranton, PA: University of Scranton Press, 1993.

———. "Tradition and Doctrinal Development: Can Vincent of Lérins Still Teach the Church?" *Theological Studies* 67 (2006): 34–72.

———. *Vincent of Lérins and the Development of Christian Doctrine.* Grand Rapids: Baker Academic, 2013.

Heuschen, J. M. "*Gaudium et Spes*: Les Modi Pontificaux." In *Les Commissions Conciliaires à Vatican II*, edited by M. Lamberigts, Cl. Soetens, and J. Grootaers, 353–58. Leuven: Bibliotheek van de Faculteit Godgeleerdheid, 1996.

Komonchak, Joseph A. "Augustine, Aquinas or the Gospel *sine glossa*? Divisions over *Gaudium et spes*." In *Unfinished Journey: The Church 40 Years after Vatican II*, edited by Austen Ivereigh, 102–18. New York: Continuum, 2003.

———. "Thomism and the Second Vatican Council." In *Continuity and Plurality in Catholic Theology*, edited by Anthony J. Cernera, 53–73. Fairfield, CT: Sacred Heart University Press, 1998.

Kuhn, Thomas S. *The Structure of Scientific Revolutions.* 4th ed. Chicago: University of Chicago Press, 2012.

Küng, Hans. *Theology for the Third Millennium.* New York: Doubleday, 1988.

Lamdan, Neville, and Alberto Melloni. *Nostra Aetate: Origins, Promulgation, Impact on Jewish-Catholic Relations.* Berlin: LIT, 2007.

Lefebvre, Marcel. *Open Letter to Confused Catholics.* Translated by Society of St. Pius X. Kansas City, MO: Angelus Press, 1986.

Levering, Matthew. *An Introduction to Vatican II as an Ongoing Theological Event.* Washington, DC: Catholic University of America Press, 2017.

Malloy, Christopher J. "*Subsistit In*: Nonexclusive Identity or Full Identity?" *Thomist* 72 (2008): 1–44.

Murray, John Courtney. "The Problem of Religious Freedom." *Theological Studies* 25 (December 1964): 503–75.

———. "Vers une intelligence du développement de la doctrine de l'Église sur la liberté religieuse." In *La Liberté Religieuse*, edited by J. Hamer and Y. Congar, 111–47. Paris: Cerf, 1967.

Newman, John Henry. *Apologia pro vita sua*. London: Longmans, Green, 1895.

———. *An Essay on the Development of Christian Doctrine*. London: Longmans, Green, 1894.

———. *Tracts for the Times*. Vol. 2, *Records of the Church*. 1839. Facsimile reprint, New York: AMS Press, 1969.

———. *The Via Media of the Anglican Church*. London: Longmans, Green, 1901.

O'Collins, Gerald. *The Second Vatican Council on Other Religions*. Oxford: Oxford University Press, 2013.

O'Malley, John W. "Erasmus and Vatican II: Interpreting the Council." In *Cristianesimo nella storia: Saggi in onore di G. Alberigo*, edited by A. Melloni, D. Menozzi, G. Ruggieri, and M. Toschi, 195–211. Bologna: Il Mulino, 1996.

———. "Vatican II: Did Anything Happen?" In *Vatican II: Did Anything Happen?*, edited by David G. Shultenover, 52–91. New York: Continuum, 2007.

———. *What Happened at Vatican II*. Cambridge, MA: Belknap Press of Harvard University Press, 2006.

Örsy, Ladislas M. *The Church: Learning and Teaching*. Wilmington, DE: Michael Glazier, 1987.

Pawley, Bernard C. *Observing Vatican II: The Confidential Reports of the Archbishop of Canterbury's Representative, Bernard Pawley, 1961–1964*. Edited by Andrew Chandler and Charlotte Hansen. Cambridge: Cambridge University Press, 2013.

Philips, Gérard. *Carnets conciliaires de Mgr Gérard Philips, secrétaire adjoint de la commission doctrinale: Texte néerlandais avec traduction française et commentaires*. Edited by K. Schelkens. Leuven: Peeters, 2006.

———. "Deux tendances dans la théologie contemporaine." *Nouvelle revue théologique* 85 (March 1963): 225–38.

———. "La Constitution 'Lumen Gentium' au Concile Vatican II." In *Primauté et collégialité: Le dossier de Gérard Philips sur la Nota Explicativa Praevia*, edited by Jan Grootaers, 189–97. Leuven: Leuven University Press, 1986.

———. *L'Église et son mystère au IIe Concile du Vatican: Histoire, texte et commentaire de la Constitution "Lumen Gentium."* 2 vols. Paris: Desclée, 1967–68.

Prignon, A. "Évêques et Théologiens de Belgique au Concile Vatican II." In *Vatican II et la Belgique*, edited by Claude Soetens, 141–84. Louvain-la-Neuve: Collection Sillages, 1996.

Rahner, Karl. *Theological Investigations*. Vol. 1. Translated by Cornelius Ernst. Baltimore: Helicon, 1965

———. *Theological Investigations*. Vol. 4. Translated by Kevin Smyth. Baltimore: Helicon, 1966.

———. *Theological Investigations*. Vol. 18. Translated by Edward Quinn. New York: Crossroad, 1983.

Ratzinger, Joseph. *Principles of Catholic Theology*. Translated by Mary Frances McCarthy. San Francisco: Ignatius, 1987.

———. *Theological Highlights of Vatican II*. Translated by Henry Traub, Gerard C. Thormann, and Werner Barzel. New York: Paulist Press, 2009. Originally published 1966.

Rhonheimer, Martin. "Benedict XVI's 'Hermeneutic of Reform' and Religious Freedom." *Nova et Vetera* 9 (2011): 1029–54.

Schillebeeckx, Edward. *The Council Notes of Edward Schillebeeckx, 1962–1963*. Edited by K. Schelkens. Leuven: Maurits Sabbebibliotheek Faculteit Godgeleerdheid, 2011.

Stransky, Thomas. "The Genesis of *Nostra Aetate*: An Insider's Story." In *Nostra Aetate: Origins, Promulgation, Impact on Jewish-Catholic Relations*, edited by Neville Lamdan and Alberto Melloni, 29–53. Berlin: LIT, 2007.

Suenens, Léon-Josef. "Aux origines du Concile Vatican II." *Nouvelle revue théologique* 107 (1985): 3–21.

Sullivan, Francis A. *The Church We Believe In*. New York: Paulist Press, 1988.

———. *Creative Fidelity: Weighing and Interpreting Documents of the Magisterium*. New York: Paulist Press, 1996.

———. *Magisterium*. New York: Paulist Press, 1983.

———. "A Response to Karl Becker on the Meaning of *Subsistit In*." *Theological Studies* 67 (2006): 395–409.

Tanner, Norman P., and Giuseppe Alberigo. *Decrees of the Ecumenical Councils*. London: Sheed and Ward, 1990.

Teuffenbach, Alexandra von. *Die Bedeutung des 'subsistit in' (LG 8): Zum Selbstverständnis der Katholischen Kirche*. Munich: Herbert Utz, 2002.

Thurian, Max. "Paul VI et les Observateurs au Concile Vatican II." In *Paolo VI e I Problemi Ecclesiologici al Concilio*, 249–58. Brescia: Istituto Paolo VI, 1989.

Todd, John M. *Problems of Authority*. London: Darton, Longman & Todd, 1961.

Troisfontaines, Claude. "À propos de quelques interventions de Paul VI dans l'élaboration de 'Lumen gentium.'" In *Paolo VI e I Problemi Ecclesiologici al Concilio*, 97–143. Brescia: Istituto Paolo VI, 1989.

Turbanti, G. *Un Concilio per il mondo moderno: La redazione della costituzione pastorale "Gaudium et spes" del Vaticano II*. Bologna: Il Mulino, 2000.

Vincent of Lérins. *Commonitorium*. Corpus Christianorum: Series Latina 64, edited by Roland Demeulenaere. Turnhout: Brepols, 1985.

Vorgrimler, Herbert, ed. *Commentary on the Documents of Vatican II*. 6 vols. New York: Herder and Herder, 1967.

Wainwright, Geoffrey. *Is the Reformation Over?* Milwaukee: Marquette University Press, 2000.

Wicks, Jared. "Augustin Cardinal Bea, SJ." In *The Legacy of Vatican II*, edited by M. Faggioli and A. Vicini, 185–202. New York: Paulist Press, 2015.

———. *Investigating Vatican II: Its Theologians, Ecumenical Turn, and Biblical Commitment*. Washington, DC: Catholic University of America Press, 2018.

———. "Vatican II's Turn in 1963." *Josephinum Journal of Theology* 19 (2012): 194–206.

Index

Printed in Great Britain
by Amazon

17340033R00130